Serious Youth in Sierra Leone

Serious Youth in Sierra Leone

·····························

An Ethnography of Performance and Global Connection

CATHERINE E. BOLTEN

UNIVERSITY OF NOTRE DAME

New York   Oxford
OXFORD UNIVERSITY PRESS

Oxford University Press is a department of the University of Oxford.
It furthers the University's objective of excellence in research, scholarship,
and education by publishing worldwide. Oxford is a registered trade mark of
Oxford University Press in the UK and certain other countries.

Published in the United States of America by Oxford University Press 198
Madison Avenue, New York, NY 10016, United States of America.

For titles covered by Section 112 of the US Higher Education
Opportunity Act, please visit www.oup.com/us/he for the latest
information about pricing and alternate formats.

Library of Congress Cataloging-in-Publication Data
Names: Bolten, Catherine E. (Catherine Elizabeth), 1976- author.
Title: Serious youth in Sierra Leone : an ethnography of performance and global connection /
    Catherine E. Bolten.
Description: New York : Oxford University Press, 2020. | Includes bibliographical references. |
    Summary: "This is an ethnography for undergraduate courses in Peoples & Cultures of Africa,
    African development, globalization, gender, and Introduction to Cultural Anthropology. This is
    for all levels of undergraduate anthropology"—Provided by publisher.
Identifiers: LCCN 2019017359 (print) | LCCN 2019980085 (ebook) | ISBN 9780190886684
    (paperback) | ISBN 9780190886691 (ebook)
Subjects: LCSH: Youth—Sierra Leone—Social conditions. | Young adults—Sierra Leone—
    Social conditions. | Youth—Sierra Leone—Attitudes. | Young adults—Sierra Leone—
    Attitudes. | Sierra Leone—Social conditions—21st century. | Sierra Leone—History—
    Civil War, 1991-2002—Participation, Juvenile
Classification: LCC HQ799.S37 B65 2020 (print) | LCC HQ799.S37 (ebook) |
    DDC 305.23509664—dc23
LC record available at https://lccn.loc.gov/2019017359
LC ebook record available at https://lccn.loc.gov/2019980085

Printing number: 9 8 7 6 5 4 3 2 1
Printed by LSC Communications, Inc., United States of America

For Mac,
For every reason

CONTENTS

ACKNOWLEDGMENTS

A n ethnography is a strange entity. It appears to be a finished product containing a completed thought process. Of course, anyone who has been through the process of writing one knows that this is far from the case. An ethnography is a material manifestation of relationships, years, emotions, wrong turns and dead ends, and the efforts and encouragement of many, many people and organizations.

I would like to start by acknowledging the organizations that put their trust in me and funded this research, from its origins in 2003 when I was in graduate school, to 2014 when some of the final conversations that animate these pages took place. The initial research in 2003 was funded by the African Studies Initiative and the Regents Fellowship of the School of Literature, Science, and Arts at the University of Michigan. From 2004 to 2005 the research was funded by an IIE Fulbright and a David Boren Fellowship. From 2005 to 2006 it was funded by a United States Institute of Peace Jennings Randolph Fellowship and a University of Michigan Rackham Humanities Fellowship. At the University of Notre Dame, research funding was provided by the Joan B. Kroc Institute for International Peace Studies, the Kellogg Institute for International Studies, the Institute for Scholarship in the Liberal Arts, the Department of Anthropology, and the Office of Research. Funding for a four-month sabbatical in which I was able to dive into the writing process was provided by the Notre Dame Institute for Advanced Studies in Spring 2017. The Institute for Scholarship in the Liberal Arts also provided funding for the index.

None of this work would have been possible without the generous assistance of numerous friends and colleagues in Sierra Leone. First and foremost are Martin and Emma Bamin, whose patient good humor in hosting and helping me in Freetown enabled the work for this book and all other research that I have conducted in Sierra Leone. In Makeni, the continued goodwill of the University of Makeni has been instrumental in my ability to thrive. I would like to thank Father Joe Turay, Father Leonard Bangura, Father Henry Magbity, and Father Daniel Samura for years of support, friendship, and the eternal willingness to host my research and encourage my teaching and work with the students. Since 2004 I have owed more than I can express to my close friends, confidants, and research assistants. Thank you to Mohamed Kallon, Abubakkar Nat Taylor-Kamara, Foday and Alimamy Mansaray, Dobson Kanu, Kelvin and Matthew Kamara, and Idriss Conteh. To my fellow researchers, professors, and friends at the University of Makeni, I owe my unending gratitude, especially Zoe Pellatt, Adam Goguen, Carmen del Valle, and the late Victor Kassim. To Victor especially, your passion and enthusiasm will live on.

The University of Notre Dame has been unfailingly supportive with my research and writing, and I have had the good fortune of working with several amazing undergraduate research assistants. Many thanks to Catherine Reidy, Evelyn Bauman, and Timothy Machasio. I have also been surrounded by fantastic colleagues who have patiently offered advice and support as I conducted the research and wrote the manuscript. First among these is Paul Ocobock, my fellow student of African youth, who patiently read through the entire manuscript and encouraged me to push ahead with the most provocative ideas. Thanks also to Susan Blum, Darren Davis, and Chris Ball, who offered feedback at crucial moments in the long arc of the project. Key contributions are due to the input of Jaimie Bleck, Jaime Pensado, and Dan Lapsley. I must also thank my colleagues at The Notre Dame Institute for Advanced Study for their warm encouragement day in and day out in early 2017: director Brad Gregory and deputy director Don Stelluto, and institute fellows John Sitter, Stephen Osadetz, David Hart, Evan Claudeanos, Haruko Momma, Leslie Lockett, John Betz, Cassandra Painter, and Mariusz Tabaczek. Special thanks to Koritha Mitchell for a key theoretical intervention, and to Carolyn Sherman and Grant Osborn for patient daily support. I also owe thanks to Agustin Fuentes for connecting me with Oxford University Press, and to Mark Schurr for encouragement at critical moments. The index was done by my dear friend Anne Just, who has briefly come out of retirement twice now to index my books.

The theoretical orientation is due first to the key intervention of my friend and colleague Christian Davenport, who introduced me to Cynthia Enloe and her work. A very large debt of thanks goes to Cynthia herself, for squeezing in time to read the manuscript and offer her support. I must also thank an anonymous reviewer at *American Anthropologist* who, in reviewing a completely unrelated article, suggested that I look into Karen Barad's work. How strange and wonderful that Barad's theory was even more fundamental to framing this project. I also owe an incredible debt to Sherith Pankratz and Meredith Keffer at Oxford University Press for believing in this project, to Olivia Clark for following through with it, and to the following reviewers who also thought it worthy of pursuing: Anthony Balzano, Sussex County Community College; Cati Coe, Rutgers University; Jennifer Fillion, C.S. Mott Community College; Joel D. Gunn, the University of North Carolina at Greensboro; Doug Henry, University of North Texas; Danny Hoffman, University of Washington; Donna O. Kerner, Wheaton College; Mary H. Moran, Colgate University; William P. Murphy, Northwestern University; Rachel R. Reynolds, Drexel University; Susan Shepler, American University; and Matthew Thomann, the University of Memphis. I owe a special debt of gratitude to Rachel Reynolds, who first saw this manuscript as an anonymous reviewer, and has since provided immeasurable support and feedback as I finished it.

The marvelous cover art is a product of the prodigious talent of my dear friend Juliet Seignious. Juliet insisted on reading the full manuscript before she began this beautiful work in order to do justice to the experiences of those contained within. I am continually moved by her ability to see the truth of the world and to generate it anew in her studio.

I am lucky to have so many fantastic friends, who in ways large and small, and probably more than they ever know, are responsible for me being able to complete this project. I must first thank Jane Kovach, for workouts, cocktails, dinners, dog walks, and conversation, without which I would have been untethered and lost with frightening frequency. To John and Karen Deak, I could not have done this without you. To my fellow friends in Sunday workouts and tacos—Juan Albarracin Dierolf, Santiago Quintero, Maggie Shum, Jason Ruiz, Lucia Tiscornia, and Mike Talbot—thank you. A big thank you to Rachel Feit and Andrea Christensen for weightlifting and cocktails. To everyone in the anthropology department at Notre Dame—I love you all. And finally, a huge thank you to Patrick Griffin for his unwavering belief in me.

It is quite a luxury to have family to thank, from so many years of work among young people who are separated from or have lost their families, to have been with them as they strained due to the distance from their loved ones, or from the loss of treasured members. I have two amazing stepdaughters, Molly and Rosie, who understood even in our precious and limited time together that I occasionally had to sneak away to work. My parents, Dori and Joe, have always believed in my dreams, and my sister Laura and her beautiful family gave me the time to really enjoy the life that nurtures those dreams. To Archie, who even as a puppy was a calming and patient presence in my study, and to whom I owe the knowledge of the necessity of time outside and a good romp. And most importantly, to Neil MacDonald. He has been my best friend and partner for many, many years, and I cannot even begin to think of where to start thanking him. For everything, thank you sweetheart.

Serious Youth in Sierra Leone

Serious Youth in Sierra Leone

The sign at the entrance said "Oxford House." The building itself was unspectacular, an open concrete structure topped by a tin roof, furnished only with a few tables and benches. An old poster of professional soccer player Lionel Messi graced one wall; a tattered photo of the country's president, Ernest Bai Koroma, was taped to another. Young men sat around the tables, some playing cards and others chatting quietly, most of them drinking the strong green tea known locally as *ataya*. It was a cold, rainy afternoon in 2012 in the city of Makeni, in the northern province of Sierra Leone. The little gathering spot, known as an *ataya base*, was beginning to fill up with regulars. I sat down on a bench and struck up a conversation with Ousman, a slender man in his early twenties who was warming his hands around his cup of tea. Ousman introduced himself as a student, explaining that he wanted to finish his degree in agronomy at the local polytechnic university, but had dropped out when the fees rose.

"Why is this place called Oxford House?" I asked the question out of sheer curiosity. Ousman's explanation was much longer than I had anticipated: "Well, the original membership decided on the name because they were all students, and intellectuals, and they wanted to make it clear that this is a place for people who are very serious about the world. But that is not the name anymore, that sign is old."

"What is the new name?"

"It is called 'Future Image Ataya Base.' As the membership grew, and the old chairman and secretary had done their time, the guys we nominated to replace them decided they wanted a fresh start. They want the world to know that we are not just very serious people here, we also have an image of the future, and we the youth are able to lead in that image. But we do not have the new sign finished yet, the artist is still working on it."

Membership. Chairman. Secretary. Commissioned sign. This little building with every appearance of an informal hangout was emerging instead as a formal organization. Ousman pointed to a hand-drawn chart under the old sign. It contained lines of printed names, scrawled signatures, and noted which memberships were paid and which were delinquent. There was a joining fee and monthly dues levied on members, which, though not exorbitant (about $1 a month), were designed to ensure that individuals were "serious" about being members. Another young man, Saidu, saw me studying the sign, and joined the conversation. He pointed to his own name on the list and explained that Oxford House had been the name when the ataya base was located in a more marginal place, a "corner spot," and could boast only thatch and tarp construction. In his words, "We used the old name to announce our presence." Now the base occupied a permanent building on a main road where everyone could see their activities, appreciate their vision, and enjoin them to build the country together. "We just want our slice of the cake," said Ousman. "The country is here for us all to succeed."

I asked about their regular activities, and Saidu went through a list of everything the members were *not* doing: not drinking alcohol, not taking drugs or smoking marijuana, and not engaging in theft or other nefarious activities. "Look at us," he said, waving his arm around the small establishment. "We are here, very visible, where passers-by can see that these are not just idle hands and idle minds, that this is not the Devil's Workshop. This is a place where we can counsel our brothers not to do bad things, we can connect socially and try to lift each other up." He spoke of Sierra Leone's civil war, a decade of bloodshed that had ended in 2002, as the source for much of the extant fear surrounding young people. This was because the bulk of combatants comprising the Revolutionary United Front (RUF), which was largely responsible for the kidnappings, amputations, and use of child soldiers that so dominated news emerging from the country in the 1990s, were under the age of twenty-five (Abdullah and Rashid 2004). When I began conducting research in Sierra Leone in 2003, the phrase "idle hands are the devil's workshop" circulated constantly. The phrase was at the center of a fearful narrative asserting that young people who were not working or studying were criminally inclined and could potentially return the country to war. It drove humanitarian interventions to promote literacy and skills training for "war-affected youth," animated policy designed to turn "marginal" youth into "mainstream" youth by encouraging them to enroll in school, and fed into popular anxiety over and avoidance of young ex-combatants (Bolten 2012c). A decade later, it was young people themselves who exerted most of their energy attempting to convince their elders that they were "serious-minded": trustworthy and hardworking individuals who should be encouraged, mentored, and employed.

As our discussion continued, a new SUV with tinted windows turned onto the road. A perceptible hush came over the ataya base, and all eyes followed the vehicle's slow progress down the muddy, potholed street. I gave Ousman a questioning look, and he explained: "This is the car of one of our city council members, who is running for Parliament. You can see the car is new, and the windows are dark on purpose. He can always see us, and we can never see him, but we know he is in there."

"How do you know he is in there?"

Ousman shrugged. "The roads are bad, yes, but the car does not have to move that slowly, it is new and strong. Why would he move so slowly unless he wanted to see us?" The vehicle turned a corner, and casual conversation continued. The encounter was complete: on one side were the base members, dedicating their meager resources to put themselves on display as serious, talented individuals for perusal and hoped-for sponsorship by their elders. On the other, the politician, the pinnacle of their aspiration, concealing himself in the backseat of a luxury car, observing, judging, and revealing nothing.

Future Image was, as it emerged, part of a widespread phenomenon in Makeni in 2012. The city had dozens of ataya bases, where youth flocked in the afternoon to relax and chat with their fellows while performing their desire to be engaged positively by their elders. Saidu emphasized that these were hangouts where nothing bad ever happened. In spite of the high unemployment rate in the city, with unofficial estimates among the under-thirty-five bracket at 70 percent un- or underemployed, these clubs were proof that the youth were not going to be driven to crime or violence by their poverty. In fact, members were redoubling their efforts, spending money to guarantee a public profile that was undeniably attractive to potential employers and financial sponsors, and ensuring that there was no possibility that anyone could accuse them of joining the Devil's workshop; in essence, that they were serious. They performed their seriousness, day after day, in spite of receiving little positive feedback from adults. The negative responses young people received—from adults berating unemployed young people for their laziness, to canceling the results of university elections because of a fear of the popularity of student politicians—revealed that neither passivity nor aspiration were entirely acceptable. What sense can be made of these young people, their practices, and their relationships with their elders, and how can Sierra Leonean youth generate insights that do more than add another case study to the literature on poor young people in the developing world?

Feminist Theory and Differences that Matter

The literature on youth in the social sciences is characterized by three approaches: youth as a demographic category (see Urdal 2006), youth as a linguistic category (see Durham 2000), and youth as a stage of the life course (see Singerman 2013); however, the lives of the young men of Future Image Ataya Base did not resonate clearly with any of these approaches. These young men forced me to find new ways to conceptualize what was happening when they devoted their resources to purposefully moving their activities into public view, performing their seriousness to others, and how they endured being demonized, surveilled, and repressed. I argue that "youth" is not a person or set of people; instead, it operates more like a verb: "youth" is what happens to an individual when they undertake risky, materially mediated performances in an effort to be treated as a person of consequence in an encounter with another individual, who in turn undermines or forcibly denies the weight of their actions, and prevents them being "adult."

To make this case, I draw on the work of two feminist theorists: Karen Barad (2007), a quantum physicist/philosopher, and Cynthia Enloe (2013), a political scientist. Both are concerned with the relationship between identity, performance, and gender, an approach they share with Judith Butler (2007). However, there are crucial differences. What sets Barad's work apart from Butler is her insistence that gender—or any category—is not just linguistic, and it does not just come into social use, and thus "reality," through repeated performance. Categories are *materially mediated* and come into being through exclusionary practices. She gives prenatal ultrasounds as an example. Butler argues that the ultrasound "girls" the fetus, and thus starts it on its journey to becoming a social "girl." Barad points out that for millions of fetuses, an ultrasound revealing a girl can result in a sex-selective abortion (2007:194). This is not just a linguistic-social idea that becomes real through repeated performance; it is a devastating, concrete outcome—an exclusionary practice—that is a direct result of the encounter between the fetus and the parents through the material apparatus of the ultrasound. With Butler's theory, youth are young people who come into being through being told repeatedly that they are not adults, and by performing their "not-adultness." By using Barad, on the other hand, the initial indeterminacy of one's identity is profoundly affected by the material apparatuses through which they encounter others in the world (Kleinman 2012:80). For example, a young person with a degree and a high-paying job is patently and concretely different from a person of the same age without these material performances, because they are systematically treated differently. Using Barad, we can see where things like wealth and education intersect with age to create the possible contours of youth, while thinking in terms of age alone does not have that power.

As a physicist/philosopher, Barad is concerned with how entities—whether they are particles of light or slime molds—encounter each other. To see youth, it is important to understand that these encounters in the social-material world are not neutral; young people's preparations for them reveal their sense of relative powerlessness in these encounters. Young people understand the consequences of exclusion—many of them have suffered repeated exclusion—which is where seriousness and the work of Cynthia Enloe become important. People who can predict their own exclusion approach encounters through performances of seriousness, but in order to be included, they have to be treated as individuals of consequence by those who are already deemed consequential (2013:3). Enloe's primary example is women's suffrage. It was not enough that suffragettes marched, petitioned, wrote, and spoke out in order to vote. They took massive risks: they were violated, beaten, jailed, and some were killed as a result of their struggle. A "woman" was not just a linguistic and social category but had real, material consequences for those who challenged its boundaries. Even with public performances of seriousness, women still had to be granted suffrage by men—they had to be thought of and treated as people of consequence, whose actions could not be ignored. When suffrage was granted it generated new boundaries for womanhood, even as gender is not "settled" (see Riles 2006:74). The current political battles over transgender rights reveal this clearly. New boundaries are emerging constantly as a result of new encounters.

Enloe articulates that males possess the power to take others seriously; I use her framework to study males on the receiving end of this judgment. Much of the existing work on youth is found in studies of masculinity-as-performance (for example Jeffrey 2010; Liu 2011; Mains 2012; Newell 2013; Reich 2010; Utas 2003; Weiss 2009), without expressly theorizing how these performances emerge from differences that matter in the social world—namely, that not all males are people of consequence. We need to ask why some males must routinely perform mainstream masculinity while others do not. For example, why can a professional wrestler be publicly lauded for being an affectionate father (see Moniuszko 2018), while a working-class mechanic is taunted by his workmates for doing so (see Willis 1977)? Theorizing how inequality is produced is the work of feminist theory. In combining these theoretical approaches, I argue that feminism is good for young men—it helps us see that risky material performances, exclusion, and the reinforcement of inequality happen everywhere in the social world.

My use of feminist theory to frame youth stems from its conspicuous absence in existing work; for some reason youth was never grappled with in the same way as gender. There is a large literature on youth as a category that reflects the discourses of changing social worlds (see Bucholtz 2002:526–27; Christiansen et al. 2006; Durham 2000), as well as one on demographic concerns such as the "youth bulge" (Mitton 2013; Roche 2016; Singerman 2013; Sommers 2012, 2015; Urdal 2006) and the real problems emergent in developing countries with overwhelmingly young populations. However, just as females have vastly divergent experiences of being women around the globe, so do young people. In Sierra Leone, a thirty-year-old attorney who supports his family is youth, according the African Youth Charter's definition of anyone between the ages of fifteen and thirty-five (African Union 2006), but it is not clear how it matters that he fits the category. Trying to bound youth through age renders it more of a question than an answer. Almost everyone in Sierra Leone "has someone in front of him," meaning that every person is subordinate to someone else: adults, children, *everyone*. That one's subordinate status is not necessarily linked to age means that youth as a demographic category lacks analytical and explanatory power.

Treating youth as a stage in the life course—a person not yet fulfilling the criteria that qualify one as an adult—can be powerful for seeing how inequality and poverty stymie individuals and nations, as was illustrated when a forty-year-old man who had neither land nor a family stood up in a community meeting and proclaimed, "I am a youth!" However, this framework also has limitations (see Bucholz 2002). The frustrated forty-something may not have succeeded in fulfilling his modest dreams, but this is true for countless people around the world whose experiences fall short of their expectations. That millions of people are disappointed with their lives does not motivate anxiety-based legislation and humanitarian interventions predicated on fears of political or social instability, and that matters in important ways. Youth as I describe them here generate touchstones for observation and interpretation—fear, hope, questions about the future—and this is how we can locate the concept as a material reality, and not just a demographic or linguistic category, or a social phase.

In formulating her philosophy, Karen Barad acknowledges her debt to Donna Haraway's "diffractive methodology" (Haraway 1992:300). Diffraction is what occurs when light passes through a crystal, separating invisible white light into colors. To diffract one's methodology means looking at the social world through a crystal rather than a window, focusing on differences that matter, rather than what can be gleaned from the whole. Through a crystal the social world appears from different angles, and the colors that make up that light emerge. We must do this because if youth is a category that can be toggled with to suit any purpose, there would be no reason for the worldwide preoccupation with youth-as-a-crisis, from American millennials (Berman 2016; Pope-Chappell 2016; Twenge 2014; Tulgan 2016) to Italian *bamboccioni* (big babies), to British "boomerang kids" (Buchmann and Kriesi 2011; Carrà et al. 2014:239). The concern with the youth bulge in Asia and Africa (Sommers 2012, 2015; Roche 2016; Urdal 2006) highlights where an incomplete demographic transition has resulted in millions of people approaching childbearing and supposed peak economic productivity without any possibility of achieving these goals in socially acceptable ways. In Sierra Leone, 62 percent of the population was under the age of twenty-four in 2015 (CIA 2015). Youth—people who have been identified as socially problematic and potentially dangerous—is a global phenomenon, and their existence maps onto processes of globalization itself. These things matter for social, political, and intellectual reasons.

Barad calls her theory of difference, language, materials, encounters, and exclusion *agential realism*. She articulates that discourses, categories, and representations are entangled with the material world (2007:228); and we can think of the material world as a congealing of agency—for example, a suit on a young man is the congealing of his hard work, savings, and will to impress others. This "stuff," this congealed agency, takes on a socially meaningful existence through *agential cuts*. Individuals create themselves and others as *different* through an observation that "cuts," or makes that difference, and also makes it real: the young man's suit may be something to laugh at rather than admire if it is old and torn, and thus a smartly dressed young man becomes a pathetic figure when enough people scoff at his suit. The agential cut is *the form of observation* that delineates between individuals entangled in an encounter, because it is the actors themselves who determine that a difference is there, and the form that difference takes, using themselves as the apparatus of that differentiation (Barad in Nyberg 2009:1185).

In essence, the agential cut creates the actors in the encounter as material beings because observations have concrete consequences. Barad is clear that cuts are exclusionary practices, differentiating between "you" and "me" and enacting a boundary through that observation, like the politician refusing to lower his window to let the ataya base members see him. Some clear examples of agential cuts occur in job interviews and courtrooms—places where individuals gain determinate identities, if only temporarily, through a materially mediated encounter in which clear differences are enacted. This means that identities can be formed anew in different encounters if they are observed as different by both parties, even as and precisely because those identities are informed by previous encounters. Examples are useful: if a professor and student bump into each other at the grocery store and both of them are buying beer, it changes who each of them is to each other, if only slightly. The beer encounter is generative of new agential cuts, with a student potentially "irresponsible" or "typical" to the professor while the professor might become "cool" to the student, even if as far as the store cashier is concerned, there is just a lot of beer being sold. Young men hanging out in ataya bases become youth when an SUV drives by. Young people comport themselves accordingly, and the man inside observes them and judges them. It is precisely in the moments of encounter where "youth" and "elder" come into being as "phenomena," rather than categories (Barad 2007:33). That encounter generates a difference that matters in the social world; in the case of my example, only the student might be embarrassed when their professor sees beer in the cart, but perhaps only the professor would be discomfited if they were the one wearing sweatpants. A young man becomes youth when agential cuts enact boundaries around him after judgments are made on his bodily and material performances. When he is not taken seriously, is derided, or is called an "upstart," or when fear, legislation, pronouncements, and interventions affect him (see also Hashemi 2015), an agential cut turns a young man into youth. The dejection, frustration, and hopelessness young people feel when they are denied jobs, harassed by the police on spurious pretenses, are labeled "project beneficiaries," are held up as models for development, or used as political pawns are real and consequential, and they are part of the boundary-making that generates youth.

Feminist Theory Without Centering Women

I use feminist theory in this book to talk specifically about young men. The irony of my focus on males, especially when utilizing theories generated specifically to speak back to default modes of male-centric theoretical positions and research orientations, is certainly not lost on me. This was not an explicit choice I made about my subject—nowhere do I argue that only males can be youth. However, the focus that emerged on public performance and risk-taking behaviors gives some insight into why males figure so prominently—and often to the relative exclusion of females—from this particular argument about youth. My theoretical framework and argument is readily applicable to females of all ages around the world; indeed it would be strange if I could not talk about women through feminist theory. However, I think feminist theory gains particular power when it is so obviously resonant in the absence of the people around whose perspectives it was generated. I focus on young men partly because the applicability of feminist theory to them is powerful, even though it is initially unexpected.

Every day of their lives, girls are subject to boundary-making practices—what they can and cannot do, what is expected of them to become women, what in their conduct threatens that sense of social order—and in Sierra Leone nothing illustrates this more clearly than the phenomenon of "the pregnant student." In 2007, Sierra Leone's new gender laws banned marriage for girls under the age of eighteen, bringing the country in line with international human rights standards (GoSL 2007), which was met with general approval by citizens. However, a legislative decree in 2015 banning pregnant girls from public schools was justified by the minister of education as responding to a need to prevent their "bad influence" spreading (Starecheski 2015), as though seeing a pregnant friend would induce others girls to have sex. I asked everyone in Makeni with whom I raised the subject, "When does a girl become a woman?" The answer was always a variation of, "When she has her first child." To become a woman was automatic for a girl, but to do so too soon was a difference that mattered—a diffraction pattern—that caused particular exclusionary boundaries to be drawn around them.

The ban was articulated partly as a response to the fact that many teenage pregnancies occur in advance of a girl undergoing initiation into the female secret society. Initiation involves a period of seclusion in the sacred bush, learning the secrets and lessons of womanhood from society elders, and clitoridectomy, which are considered vital elements of a girl's eventual marriageability and her social connections to other women (Ferme 2001:62). For an uninitiated girl to become pregnant raised questions about the effectiveness of social reproductive practices themselves. These practices have been in flux since the end of the war, as international pressure to ban female genital cutting increases and the practice of bringing communities together in celebration are weighed against the needs and desires of the girls (Coulter 2005). Boys also undergo extensive processes of initiation (see Ferme 2001; Murphy 1980), but this is the beginning and not the primary point of their transition to adulthood. It is understood that initiation is but one performance of the male body bound up in its status. For a woman, that is not so clear-cut. The fact that most students became pregnant by their male teachers was not brought up in the legislation, nor were those teachers dismissed—illuminating that part of exclusionary boundary-making is predicated upon who has the power to decide what boundaries look like. To ban girls was easy, to confront the problem of ethically compromised professional men exercising power over their students much more difficult. These boundaries are evident, and they are the substance of many political battles. The exclusionary practices that boys suffer, and the boundaries drawn around them, are not as obvious, though they are insidious, and thus my decision to focus on them here.

Youth Is a Phenomenon of Embodied Globalization

Because it is an entanglement of materials and discourses, youth is a phenomenon of globalization (Cole and Durham 2008:3; Greenberg 2014:29). The popular and scholarly characterizations of generations in the twentieth century—from baby boomers, to mods and rockers in 1960s Britain (Cohen 1980), to Generation X in the United States (Arnett 2000)—emerged as entanglements of global materials with global discourses in particular historical moments. In short, the way scholars characterize generations emerges from the narratives and representations circulating in those historical moments, combined with the physical "stuff" that shapes those moments. Baby boomers are characterized by the work, status, and consumption expectations of a world emerging from a second global war into mass Fordist production and fears of Communism (Gibson et al. 2009). It is impossible to understand the apparent cynicism and self-reliance of Generation X without the latent fears of the Cold War, corporate downsizing, and the rise of electronic consumer culture spurred by Japan's meteoric rise. The young people of every period in history are molded and understood through the events and discourses of the moment and the global flows of stuff produced in and of that moment. This is especially true for African youth, who embody colonial pasts and uncertain postcolonial presents, and are "dangerous" because of the transnational flows they represent (Diouf 2005; see also Bucholtz 2002:529).

That the phenomenon of youth is contoured by globalization means it is just as patchwork and varied as globalization itself. The Future Image Ataya Base had illiterate members and members with advanced degrees, members who were fourteen and members who were forty, some who were employed and others who were not. This is one reason it has been so difficult in scholarship and practice to conceptualize youth. A phenomenon can be seen and known in social encounters, but its boundaries do not sit still. They are generated, challenged, and reconfigured in every encounter, with no supposition that one is a youth already before an encounter with others (Barad 2007:197). This is why a youth can also be a parent, or a student, or a politician. Embracing the instability of youth allows a shift away from demographics, social categories, and life-course transitions. Instead, we focus on where differences are enacted, and the effects of those differences in the social world.

The effects of youth in Sierra Leone are most apparent in fear and panic around crime and unemployment, but also around blue jeans and sunglasses, student politicians and motorbike riders, and fears that young people who grew up during the civil war are socially "lost" (Bolten 2012c). Encounters that spark hand-wringing about social etiquette and reproduction, tradition, respect for authority, the perils of globalization, and an uncertain future are where youth are visible (Cole 2008:101). These reactions became especially salient during the war, where images of young children invoking *Rambo*, wielding Chinese-made AK-47s, and joking about taking lives forged an indelible connection between being young, embracing globalization, and being dangerous (Richards 1996). Sierra Leonean youth are a phenomenon produced in every moment of globalization, from the international slave trade and British colonialism to Western education, and, more recently, declining child death rates due to biomedicine (Alie 1991; Bledsoe 1990; Shaw 2002; Singerman 2013). They encountered a globalized war characterized by conflict diamonds, war movies, and urban fashion (Richards 1996; Peters 2011), followed by massive influxes of bilateral aid (Bolten 2013), which were followed by foreign investment, new flows of capital and goods, and Sierra Leone's binding commitments to international treaties and conventions (TRC 2003). Everyone in Sierra Leone embodies their own particular history with globalization, but the difference that matters is that for youth, global influence is considered noteworthy, and a cause for concern and intervention.

Youth Is a Phenomenon Characterized By Risk

In agential realism, beings lack a determinate identity outside of their relationship with others, and what renders a being relatable is that it undertakes a performance of self (Barad 2007:361). Everyone performs their "best selves" as part of social life (Goffman 1959), but what sets youth apart is that their best self involves an element of *risk* that is less marked in others (Cole and Durham 2008:10). Unemployed young men and professionals may both own suits, but the former and not the latter is a youth through the risks undertaken to enact that performance (Diouf 1996, 2003:4, 2005:33; Guyer and Salami 2013; Simone 2004, 2008, 2011). Lawyers wear suits as part of their professional presentation. A young man courting attention by wearing a suit likely skipped meals to afford it, with no guarantee of a job. This risk becomes embodied in young people's performances—creating youth at this juncture—because the current demographic profile in the developing world, with populations that are overwhelmingly young (Population Pyramid 2017), have disturbed older forms of social reproduction. There were once sufficient resources for the old to invest in the young, and a known place for everyone in the social world, however unequal that world. The current world is characterized by "endemic uncertainty" (Beck 1999:12), where instead of waiting one's turn—which may never happen—individuals will "make a move, make it big, and wait and see what happens" (Simone 2011:266).

Subservience is characteristic of Sierra Leonean social worlds, but risk is not always present, and it is this difference that sets youth apart. The phrase *yu boboh deh* illustrates myriad ways of understanding age and subservience within social webs. Young men I spoke with translated the phrase variously as "Your boy is around" to "Anything for me to do here?" to "Don't forget to consider me." Anyone can deploy the phrase to claim subservient social status, doing things for and asking to receive support from a social superior (see also Ferguson 2015). However, this phrase does not help us understand youth—in fact it echoes youth as a category that shifts according to its use (Bucholtz 2002:527; Durham 2000). The phrase is invoked by people who are explicitly drawing on obligations between the powerful and powerless within social networks. This subservience is socially sanctioned and a necessary part of individuals acquiring "wealth in people" (Bolten 2012a; Ferme 2001; Guyer and Salami 2013; Miers and Kopytoff 1977; Nyerges 1992). Part of how we understand youth is that they *lack* these networks, or they cannot leverage their networks in any meaningful way. This is in part because of their numbers: many of them migrate from rural villages and to relative social isolation in urban areas (Sommers 2015; Enria 2015 Lahai 2012), and their urban life is an experience of navigating dislocation and daily uncertainty (Diouf 2003, 2005; Enria 2015; Simone 2004, 2011; Vigh 2006). For other young people, urban migration frees them from exploitative networks and is a risk worth taking to throw off the yoke of powerful elders (Millar 2015 Murphy 1980; Peters 2011; Tom 2014). In both cases their networks are fragmented, and are neither durable nor powerful, and this difference matters because it produces risk-taking behaviors.

Emphasizing risk frees us from the limitations inherent in mapping youth onto an inability to complete a life course transition to adulthood. The experiences of social dislocation and an incapacity to become socially sanctioned adults has led to a wealth of scholarship on youth experiences of marginalization (Boersch-Supan 2012; Jeffrey et al. 2008; Jeffrey 2010; Mains 2012; Newell 2013), with a consensus building around the idea that youth are "stuck" (Cole 2008:102; Sommers 2012) and "waiting" to become adults (Honwana 2012; Singerman 2013), with waiting an active process of self-fashioning designed to manifest adulthood-by-trying (Hashemi 2015). However, thinking in terms of positions as marginal or bodies as waiting precludes fully exploring the analytically productive space of how youth emerge as contentious actors at the heart of the social world (Durham 2008:166). Youth do not live in shadows. The fact that Sierra Leone experienced a coup at the hands of twenty-somethings, and a war that was fought largely by children and adolescents makes that clear. Marginalization is an experience that is fundamental to social worlds (Diouf 2005:37; Weiss 2009:32) and is publicly visible, where risks are often enacted because they require an audience. Almost all the research for this book took place in public locations, where young people performed seriousness for others, and hoped the observations of their performances defied exclusion as youth.

Why Focus on Serious Youth?
Why Not All Young People?

I sat in a university cafeteria one afternoon sipping soft drinks with a group of students. The discussion ranged from the national secondary school exam, to the high urban unemployment rate, to politicians ignoring young people. The conversation centered on the struggles of young men especially, and how mistrust because of the war, and older men's perspective on the difficulties of the next generation forced an attitude of seriousness, as young men believed themselves to be scrutinized constantly. One student recalled an encounter in his village, explaining how common it was: "Most of the time, if the youth come to one of these guys with open appeals for their future, the man will say, 'Eh, don't disturb me.' He will berate the young guy saying that the youth are all drunkards and they spend their time smoking *dagga* [marijuana]. The old man will say the youth are useless in society, they are people who do not want to work, that they are definitely not serious. And that will end the discussion. So you always think to yourself: if these men are watching me, I must be very serious-minded. I can't play around. At all." To be serious was the starting point for social life; not to be serious was to be labeled a social deviant (see Durham 2008:156; Van 'T Wout 2016).

"Seriousness" emerged consistently in discussions about what was required to be treated as someone of consequence. Its relevance to understanding the dynamics of the social world cannot be overstated, because it is never enough for someone to assess the social cues that denote seriousness and undertake those actions. Cynthia Enloe writes that seriousness is in the eye of the beholder. It is a quality that those in power can bestow on others or withhold from them (2013:7). Individuals, Enloe argues, have little control over who takes them seriously, or if they are taken seriously at all. To be deemed serious is a reward, denoting individuals whose actions cannot be ignored (2013:8; Greenberg 2014:79). The two negative reactions to a display of seriousness are the exclusionary configurations I examine here. They are *know-your-place aggression* and *moral panic*. A systematic refusal to respond to people's collective actions to be taken seriously or active punishment of their success—whether this is women's suffrage, or African American civil rights, or young people's desires for adulthood—is an exclusionary practice of "know-your-place" aggression (Mitchell 2013, 2015). Being referred to as "uppity," or "impudent," or "disrespectful" are hallmarks of know-your-place aggression. The phenomena of suffragettes and Black Lives Matter are requests to be taken seriously, emerging from repeated encounters where the opposite occurred, where performances of personhood were configured as overstepping one's status as an inferior.

The elder man's tirade against youthful sins, from alcohol abuse to joblessness, was a statement aligning the young man with the worst possible qualities a Sierra Leonean could imagine. It reminded the young man that he was the source of the nation's ills, a cause for moral panic— the inverse and companion to know-your-place aggression. A moral panic occurs when a social group is perceived as a threat to social values, causing elites to "man the moral barricades" of society and point fingers at those they see threatening it (Cohen 1980:1). It is a quintessential boundary enactment. Calling a youth "lazy" meant he lacked the will to be "useful," a core tenet of sound personhood in Sierra Leone (Bolten 2008). This was often voiced as the difference between civilians and ex-combatants after the war, with the latter, mostly young men who struggled with social dislocation and unemployment, being dubbed "useless" (Bolten 2012b, 2012c). In an urban area with estimated 70 percent unemployment for those under thirty-five, youth became an easy target for moral outrage. If the youth are not useful, if their personhood is defined by joblessness and assumptions about their idleness, they become a problem and generate panic (see Durham 2008:157). If they strive too hard, overtaking adults in education, or style, or communication ability, they are upstarts and impudent, and generate aggression.[1]

Focusing on seriousness was a choice I made deliberately to shift away from categories of people and toward performances. I do not want to differentiate between serious and unserious people, but serious and unserious *performances*, being taken seriously or being put in one's place. As is clear from the ataya base, a young person can perform seriousness when they enter their base, but their next encounter may configure them as "half-baked" if they appear to be idle, and their clothing betrays their student status or their lack of employment. Young people shift between encounters that configure them variously as "not adult" even if in one moment they may encounter know-your-place aggression, and in the next generate moral panic. These encounters are mediated by the material world, which means there is no possibility of simply singling out individuals for categorization of one or the other based on arbitrary criteria. The only criterion is whether or not they are acting serious.

Young people approached their encounters with adults through "stuff," and the commonness of that stuff created paradoxes in their encounters—generating exclusion where they imagined inclusion was possible, creating agential cuts that they did not predict. The stuff in this book is what Bowker and Starr refer to as "boundary objects" (1999), seen simultaneously as serious and adult by the young people who adopt them, and as evidence of anything but serious and adult by older people. Young people were serious through their structures, clothes, paperwork, and politics—tenets of globalization old and new. The fact that so many young people engaged in serious performances is where I posit the boundary of *in/visibility* and *in/distinction*. That young people were believed to be war-affected generated problems of *il/legitimacy* around their use of global inputs. The slash separating the prefix from the root word reveals that performances lack predictable or determinate boundaries; they are, paradoxically, both the thing and its opposite. This is where, throughout the book, you will consistently see agential cuts: the slash denotes a literal "cut"—it is possible for one person to observe and react to something as legitimate, or distinct, or visible; it is possible in a different moment under different circumstances they will see it as illegitimate, indistinct, or invisible; and also possible for another person to make completely different determinations on the same observation.

As young people pursue similar strategies to be taken seriously, their public performances blur together. They are judged as a group, resulting in youth who are indistinct or invisible. Young people believed to be war-affected have their efforts to be legitimate rendered illegitimate. As they act collectively or similarly, efforts to stand out result in more blending in. Dozens of suit-wearing young men cannot stand out from all the others, hence in/distinction. Young people struggling to render their commercial motorbike business legitimate by tracking their police bribes court il/legitimacy. Ataya base members who hope that hanging out make them visible instead produce in/visibility, as none is seen apart from each other or their hangout. These terms highlight that a young person's hoped for impression often produces the opposite effect, but young people double down on those efforts because there are so few alternatives to these material practices and their boundary objects. If young people are successful, they do not necessarily defy the phenomenon of youth so much as they are no longer subject to those boundary-making practices themselves; they are adults. Nor would they necessarily want that boundary to disappear if they are not subjected to it. Serious young people do not want revolution; they are inherently conservative, reproducing the norms of their social world, desiring only to be included (see Diouf 2005:37; Durham on Mead 2008:165).

Youth as Performance

That young bodies engage in performances has been stated many times thus far, and it is a theory with a long history in anthropology. Bodies are enculturated within and exist through performance (Turner 1987). What agential realism brings to this discussion is that performance does not grant some categorical reality to a body that is otherwise a tabula rasa. Rather, the way Barad articulates bodily performance in agential realism is that "bodies are not situated *in* the world, they are part *of* the world" (2007:376). That people comport themselves in a particular way, wear certain clothes, converse in a language, and display items on their bodies are intricate parts of how the world continually comes into being. Youth have no existence without the things of their material performances by which they are part of the world, just as I, a professor, have no existence that matters without my office, university, students, the classes I teach, the research I conduct, and the writing I publish. We are *of* the world through our performative entanglements with things.

Performance in this book is limited to the stuff through which youth act serious. As Erving Goffman states, "The individual act[s] so that he intentionally or unintentionally *expresses* himself, and the others will in turn have to be *impressed* in some way by him" (1959:2). Goffman defines performance as the communications offered by an individual that comprises speaking (the impression he gives) and bodily comportment (the impression he gives off) (1959:2), which make it a material-discursive practice. Speech and bodily comportment generate observations and reactions that have real impacts *on* the world. Age can be performed, within certain boundaries, and that performance can be accepted, or invite questions. When do we comment that young people are "acting like adults"? Why is this pronouncement made? This is where the form of observation—and the observer's entanglement with the observed—create a phenomenon. What happens when a child talks back to its parent? When is this acceptable? To return to diffraction patterns, we can know youth as a phenomenon of their entanglement with adults—a phenomenon produced in their encounters.

This became a concern in Sierra Leone after a war characterized by young militant groups who upended social norms as a war tactic (Richards 1996; Shepler 2014), a subject I will explore fully in the next chapter. Young rebels forced their civilian counterparts to perform domestic chores to generate power imbalances between age mates (Bolten 2012c). Armed children looted villages, committed rape and murder, and called themselves commanders. The international community and Sierra Leone's government moved rapidly after the war to reassert the prewar social world, "reintegrating" children into families and putting them in school in an effort to strip them of the very adult qualities personified in their participation in violence (Shepler 2014). The reintegration of youth was fraught, for what is a twenty-year-old who has lived without parental guidance for a decade, is illiterate and unskilled, has children from a wartime relationship, and has a dozen people under his command? The struggle to define a social place for young people after the war, and the fears surrounding them, were ongoing for a decade when I visited the ataya base at the beginning of this chapter.

The civil war illustrated that the social world was fragile, with the positionalities of old and young the most difficult questions in the aftermath. Discerning differences between people takes place on the level of performance and observation, as Goffman reminds us: "We live by inference" (1959:3). There was no foolproof method for determining on the spot whether a young person was a rebel, whether they had good or bad character, and whether they were capable of harm. People discerned these qualities from dress, speech, mannerisms, and other bodily performances. Just after the war, older men in Makeni habitually pointed out alleged rebels to me that they saw walking down the street, inferring ex-combatant status from a young man's dress (jeans, high-top shoes, and sunglasses), manner (a swagger in the walk), and the cigarette he smoked. In essence, if it looked like a rebel, walked like a rebel, and smoked like a rebel, it must be a rebel. Performances of seriousness as a counter to the "all youth are rebels" fear began around this time.

Organization of the Book

The chapters are organized around the global stuff entangled in the encounters that produce youth. In most chapters this stuff is physical material—paper, concrete, textiles; in one it is how all of this stuff agglomerates around the most visible of public performances, political campaigning. Organizing the book around the stuff of daily practice allows me to focus on the practices in which all youth engage, the variations on a theme that characterize how they signal their seriousness to adults, and how agential cuts created the opposite effect young people hoped for with those performances. It also keeps the focus on the tangible entanglements that generate youth rather than categories of representation or checking off boxes in the life course. Also critical is "language materiality" (Shankar and Cavanaugh 2012). This refers to how the material world exists in language: in essence, how young people articulate their use and manipulation of things in their self-presentation. This creates new meanings in the material world, such as the value of a college degree or the importance of speaking English, that influences encounters. It also refers to the material dimensions of language, and how language becomes manifest in the material world—that to announce the formation of a political party, for example, is to create a real "thing." The synergy between materials and words is a sum greater than its parts (Shankar and Cavanaugh 2012:358), and youth generate reality through language constantly. For example, a shabby hangout is nothing to take notice of; that it is an ataya base, one of dozens around a city defined by this unifying idea, gives each material weight and becomes an index for encounters with adults. A group of young people hanging out and talking politics has no particular social and political value, but when they register themselves with the government as a youth political party, they come into material existence and can engage in novel encounters.

The first chapter, "Ethnography and Entanglement in Makeni," describes the history of the town and its young people during the war. The rebel occupation, the pressure on young men to join the rebels, and the difficulty in rebuilding in the aftermath colored the particular boundary-making practices around youth in the last decade, and molded my own experiences as a young ethnographer in that place. Karen Barad articulates that the phenomenon observed cannot be separated from the apparatus of observation (2007:148), which, though she generated her framework from experiments in quantum physics, is particularly apt for ethnography. The ethnographer is part of the phenomena she observes, and in this case my position as a young student and empathetic ear enabled many of the encounters that I describe, as did the fact that I shared with my interlocutors the lack of a determinate social identity.

The second chapter is "Cinderblocks and Plaster." This encompasses the structures that youth build, display, and inhabit to showcase their ability to invest in being permanent "somebodies." The chapter begins with young entrepreneurs, many of whom start as itinerant traders who then invest their profits into stationary "boxes," while craving small structures in which they can sit. It moves next to the ataya bases, their physical existence and the relationship between the businesses and youth associations that inhabit them. It then considers the ataya base owners, and the fact that youth idolize them as icons despite them never being youth in the way that today's young people are. Next is the history of the Motorbike Riders Association (MBRA) headquarters. The association formed after the war to transform a maligned ex-combatant motorcycle taxi service into a legitimate business. The association performs seriousness on their headquarters, painting elaborate murals of nonexistent street signs they have seen on the Internet on the walls and collecting objects—a broken computer, empty ledgers—to arrange around their officers in official photographs. The chapter finishes with a young man who performed his loyalty to the president by commissioning a statue. He tried to raise it in the main square, and was blocked by politicians who feared he would overshadow their own displays of loyalty.

The third chapter is "Papers," which investigates young people's obsession with acquiring and displaying documents, in the hope that it will translate into being taken seriously. Though the obsession with certificates stems from a century of status acquired through formal Western schooling, the importance of papers does not stop with degrees. Account ledgers, tax receipts, and dues tickets also contribute to a paper trail of youth aspirations for social and legal visibility and legitimacy. The chapter begins with the importance to youth of carrying paperwork during the war, and their rapid adoption of humanitarian language and practices in the aftermath, where young people suffered adult resentment because their literacy was an advantage in the globalized job market. Adults criticize the substitution of "big English" and "papers" for "real wisdom," even as they rely on youth's facility with English and paperwork to render their own businesses official. The chapter then returns to the MBRA and their struggle for legitimacy through documentation, with elaborate paper trails validating their existence as a "real" organization. Simultaneously, the members cannot afford driving licenses and bike registration, so they struggle with the police over their so-called illegal activities—which reinforces the idea that motorbike riding is itself a criminal activity, as it illustrates the risks youth take to live every day.

The fourth chapter is "Cloth," which focuses on the "social skin" (Turner 2012) that youth don. Clothing is where the element of risk and youth-as-globalization emerges clearly. The chapter begins with a boutique that thrived in Makeni at the end of the war, where young people purchased expensive fashion to forget their troubles and attract fortune to themselves, even as it rarely resulted in success and germinated adult disapproval. A decade later, apprentice tailors sewed, wore, and peddled European high-fashion knock-offs and patchwork fashion to other young people, countering older tailors' persistence in creating traditional clothes. In direct contrast are poorly paid student teachers who spend their income on traditional suits so that senior teachers—and students—will treat them with respect, even as they go hungry. Last is a phenomenon I call the "Arsenal effect," where youth's fanatic devotion to the British Premier League soccer team Arsenal generates the team's jersey as a boundary object. Red, Arsenal's color, also represents the All People's Congress (APC), the party of erstwhile president Koroma, whose home is in Makeni. Arsenal's ardent supporters seek out secondhand and knock-off jerseys to profess team and party loyalty. This has created a clothing arms race with APC party elders, who counter the sea of red jerseys with elaborate bespoke costumes and accessories.

"Politics," the fifth chapter, examines young people's exuberant political participation as they create and join political parties to achieve a larger slice of the national cake. Boundary-making encounters are common and brutally exercised here, as the country has a long history of suspicion of student politics, especially as it materializes in parties with leaders who seem to challenge elder authority. The chapter begins with early youth politics in the country, and how the first truly progressive political party under colonialism defined "youth" for a generation. It then turns to "the children's coup" during the war that produced Maada Bio, the country's current president and a former member of the coup, revealing that the boundaries around youth refuse to sit still. The chapter then examines student government at the private and public universities in Makeni, with one stripping student politicians of power as the other quashed a "revolution" they saw in the election of a popular student politician, while the young people who want "real training" as politicians go to Freetown. It moves through the conservative politics of ataya bases, and how clubs established ostensibly to assist unemployed youth endorsed and replicated the inequalities of the social world. Their visibility led to their incorporation into the electoral college of the APC, creating the illusion of inclusion and participation. The chapter finishes with an examination of a short-lived youth party called the United Democratic Movement (UDM). The rise and fall of the UDM encapsulates the entanglement of materials and discourses in boundary-making encounters around youth that became commonplace after the war. From a sordid history of visible corruption of leader Mohamed Bangura, to the party's rental of an empty building that they painted purple, to their youth membership, their origin story, symbol, and the flyers that the young candidates produced, the UDM reveals the material-discursive dimensions of youthful struggles to be taken seriously, and how their elders systematically abuse and exclude them.

This book is about the creative, colorful, connected global entanglements that are embodied in young people and are generative of youth, but it also serves as a warning. Self-conscious performances by the young and the consistent erection of hostile boundaries around them by the old are products of the current global juncture, where Sierra Leone's colonial history and globally inflected war meet postwar global trends in a landscape of constrained natural and economic resources and population pressure. It is a landscape of perpetual uncertainty, and unpredictability emerges from so many factors colliding. Agential realism was generated from quantum physics as a way of processing the stochasticity—the chaos—of atomic and subatomic-level encounters, where the apparatus of experimentation determines the form of observation, whose interpretation determines the next experiment and thus the form that discovery can take. We move through the world by discerning, determining, and acting, with real consequences for ourselves, others, and the universe at every step.

In writing this book, I could not shake a concern that existing theoretical orientations, based on social reproduction, life course transitions, and development discourses, lacked the explanatory power to engage the messy, intimate, and unpredictable entanglements of the present day. I use agential realism specifically as a counter to the "youthmasculinityviolence" coupling, even when violence is a result of the kind of exclusionary practices I tackle here. This does not mean, however, that violence will never occur again. The young people I know have hope, they work hard, and they are transparent in their pleas for respect and assistance (Lahai 2012). This is not all young people, but they are in the majority, and if respect and empathy emerge from their encounters, more young people may be inspired to seriousness. Young people are a demographic majority and their percentage of the whole continues to grow, which serves as a constant reminder to adults that their own numbers are dwindling, and their power will wane if not defended. If adults cannot find ways to mentor, engage, and trust their children, it is the adults themselves who bear responsibility for problems that may follow.

Notes

1. The boundary practices of moral panics and know-your-place aggression are not meant to infer that intergenerational conflict is universal and unrelenting in Sierra Leone (let alone the rest of the world), nor that it goes indubitably with globalization. Gable (2000), Sharp (1995), and Rasmussen (2000) reveal that generation is not necessarily a clear-cut battle line around Africa, while Ferme (2001) reveals that conflict in Sierra Leone is not inevitable.

CHAPTER 1

·······················

Ethnography and Entanglement
in Makeni

W riting about youth and Makeni means writing about the civil war that gripped the nation between 1991 and 2002. Writing about the war and its aftermath means talking about how this research project unfolded. My positionality as a researcher became entangled with the ethnographic methods I employed *because* I began work in the immediate postwar period. This connection between researcher and method did not loosen over the ten years of research engagement. Rather, the ways I changed, the ways my interlocutors changed, and the shifting social context in which we worked and lived highlighted the texture of those connections, the negotiability of our relationships, and the experiences that precipitated the understanding of youth articulated here. Agential realism, in addition to being the theoretical framework that I apply to seriousness and performance, is also applicable for understanding ethnographic method, my primary methodological framework. Agential realism speaks not only to how youth come to be, but how the ethnographer comes to be, and thus how this project came to be.

This chapter combines a history of the war and the occupation of Makeni with an explanation of my position as an ethnographic researcher, the methods I used, and how a theoretical apparatus drawn from feminist philosophy brought it together. This all began in 2003, when I first visited Makeni to answer a particular question: Why were hundreds of ex-combatants who disarmed in Makeni but were not local residents staying put after the war rather than returning home to their families? Many of these ex-combatants were young—at twenty-six, I was a contemporary to the bulk of my interlocutors—and discussions about their postwar lives often dovetailed with much larger existential worries of how they would make their way in a world that was suspicious of their motives and their apparent lack of good social training. Their ex-combatant status cast doubt on their essential humanity (Bolten 2012c), which dovetailed with questions about the future of war-affected youth (Shepler 2014).

The town's population boomed over the next ten years, and important infrastructure improvements occurred: paved roads, electricity, public buildings. The young people I worked with also changed, with many completing high school and others college, with some nurturing long-term relationships and having children, and yet they struggled to overcome being treated as youth by adults. I also changed, as did my relationship with local adults. I completed my PhD, got married, and went from being a student to being employed as a visiting lecturer at a local university. These shifts manifested interpersonally when people I had known for a decade initiated more formality between us, calling me "Doctor" instead of "sister." When I questioned several of my closest friends on this matter, they explained that it would be rude not to honor my accomplishments, that people are not serious for no benefit at the end. To agentially cut this small distance between us was an acknowledgment that I had, in fact, succeeded.

These changes forced me to confront deeper questions about the material and social entanglements of youth, and the nature of boundaries configured in encounters between people. I pondered the field notes I had collected from years of participant observation, the interviews and focus groups we conducted, and the role positionality plays in determining the data an ethnographer gathers (see Colic-Piesker 2004; Cook 2010; Hautzinger 2007; Sultana 2007). By the end of this chapter, our careful journey through context, positionality, and methods will make it clear why feminist theory is an appropriate tool for talking about young men, for talking about ethnographic research, and for talking about me, a white woman conducting ethnographic research with young African men.

Global War, Global Youth

The history of Sierra Leone's war has been, from the first moments scholars grappled with writing about it, a messy, complicated, dense affair, with the greatest clarity existing in its global orientation, and the least clarity around the primary reason it began, and then raged for a decade. The war started when a rebel group calling itself the Revolutionary United Front (RUF) came over Sierra Leone's southern border from Liberia in 1991. Some scholars have posited that Foday Sankoh, leader of the RUF, exploited southern Sierra Leone's history of resource exploitation and marginalization to gain coverts to his revolution (Alao 1999; Gberie 2005). Others see the war as a revolt of rusticated elites who had been marginalized under Siaka Stevens's government and used rural poverty to stir up discontent (Abdullah 2004; Rashid 2004), others still as a modern slave revolt of the exploited young against their cruel elders (Peters 2011; Richards 1996). It was experienced in Makeni, as I wrote about in previous publications (Bolten 2012a; 2014a), as a maelstrom of competing factions of fighters that formed, dissolved, realigned, looted, raped, and killed, and generally wreaked havoc in the town. More was *unknown* about who was fighting and why than was known about them. The war was conducted mainly through and by its young people, and in Makeni that meant young men hiding from other young men who threatened to variously recruit them, enslave them, beat them, kill them, or some combination thereof. Others chose to jump rather than be pushed, hoping they could better control their fate if they had some hand in managing it. Because the balance of power shifted within the town and in the country frequently, navigating this uncertain terrain became the primary activity of young men (see Vigh 2006). The war ended after a coup, a palace coup, a democratic election, another coup, three failed peace accords, an invasion of Freetown by combined RUF and mutinous military forces, a battle for the capital, and a massive deployment of regional, British, and United Nations troops. Peace finally emerged in 2002.

The war's complicated timeline is covered in a myriad of other publications (Gberie 2005; Peters 2011; Bolten 2012a), and I will not devote as much space to it as I will to how the war was specifically and explicitly fought on and through young men, how scholars talked about them, and how the war emerged as a product of a long history of globalization. The young people who lived through the war embodied an entanglement of global materials and global trends (see Hoffman 2011b; Richards 1996). Makeni was the official headquarters of the RUF from December 1998 to the end of the war in May 2002, and when I arrived in 2003 it was a landscape of prewar, wartime, and postwar globalism. The movie theater, which for decades screened movies from Hollywood and Europe, had been destroyed by a rocket-propelled grenade made in China. The grenade blast also took out the Barclay's Bank next door, but untouched was the National Lottery Building, which still had "RUF Headquarters" painted carefully in red over the door. In a town that was historically populated by the Themne ethnic group, languages from around the country were spoken by ex-combatants, refugees, and aid workers assigned far from home. They mingled with the French, Dutch, and English spoken by foreign aid workers, and the Nigerian pidgin and Bengali of United Nations peacekeepers, all who frequented a bar called the Reconcile. The bar occupied the site of the old public library—also burned during the war—and acquired its odd name when it hosted the Truth and Reconciliation Commission (TRC), which was based on South Africa's TRC (Shaw 2010). This was the only bar where one could relax over a cold Heineken or Coke. In 2003, aside from aid workers, it was mostly the ex-combatants with United Nations-supplied transition allowances who could afford such luxuries.

The war itself was an equally patchwork agglomeration of global influences. There is no agreement on the single most important *reason* the war occurred, though scholars have articulated an array of responsible factors. There is agreement on when and how it began, which was in March of 1991when former army corporal Foday Sankoh led a small band of rebels into southern Sierra Leone from Liberia. For a year the war was confined to skirmishes in the south and east. Grim tales of terror occasionally trickled back to Freetown, of rebels high on "brown-brown" (a mixture of crack cocaine and gunpowder) armed with machetes looting and burning villages, engaging in terror tactics to make up for their lack of advanced weaponry (Nordstrom 1997; Richards 1996), and seizing supplies and uniforms from ambushed military convoys (Bolten 2012a). The poorly resourced and poorly paid Sierra Leone Army (SLA) was left to fight the war without help from the APC government. A group of young army officers, supported by student radicals in Freetown, stormed the capital and toppled President Joseph Momoh in a coup in 1992 (Bolten 2009b). They called themselves the National Provisional Ruling Council (NPRC), and for the next four years the country was run by a young army captain called Valentine Strasser, who, upon assuming power at the age of twenty-six, became the youngest national leader in the world.

By that time the RUF had grown into a much larger force, bolstering the numbers of volunteers through kidnapping and forced recruitment (Bolten 2012a; Richards 1996; Peters and Richards 1998). Rumors abounded that the still underfunded SLA soldiers fighting the war had turned into *sobels*: soldiers by day and rebels by night, ostensibly fighting the RUF while also looting villages themselves (Bolten 2014b). Pressure mounted on the NPRC to initiate democratic elections, but Strasser dragged his feet, not wanting to give up power. He was ousted in a bloodless palace coup in January 1996 (Bolten 2009b). The new leader, Maada Bio, promised democratic elections that year, which in turn initiated a shift in tactics from the RUF. A campaign of mass amputations unfolded in the countryside, with the RUF chopping off hands to scare people away from the polls. Rebels told the civilians they mutilated to ask Tejan Kabbah—the presidential frontrunner—to give them new hands (Gberie 2005:95). The elections went ahead despite this, and Kabbah became president in a peaceful transfer of power in May 1996.

The war entered a different register at this point, as Kabbah announced that he was disbanding the SLA, which he accused of aiding the RUF and engaging in guerilla tactics. He transformed the civil defense forces—informal militias that emerged from local village hunting societies—into the country's main fighting force, naming their leader Hinga Norman as Minister of Defense. He used these changes to force the RUF to the negotiating table. The first peace agreement, the Abidjan Accords, was signed in November of 1996, but did not hold. By May 1997, enraged soldiers and officers from the sidelined SLA joined with the RUF to invade Freetown and overthrow Kabbah's government, installing the Armed Forces Revolutionary Council (AFRC) coup. For eight months the AFRC terrorized Freetown as Kabbah worked from exile to regain control of the country. Utilizing help from foreign mercenaries and the Nigerian Army, Kabbah ejected the AFRC from Freetown in February 1998. The AFRC was not crushed, instead it regrouped in the bush outside of Makeni. Nigerian troops working for Kabbah deployed around the country, but a revitalized AFRC/RUF faction invaded Makeni in December 1998, with another faction marching back to Freetown. The Nigerian troops fled from Makeni, and the RUF initiated what became a three-and-a-half-year occupation of the town. The rest of the AFRC/RUF invaded Freetown on January 6, 1999, killing thousands of people in a bloody campaign to retake the city. The combined forces of the Nigerian Army and a few reformed battalions of Sierra Leonean troops beat them back, and civilian democratic order was once again restored to Freetown.

This initiated yet another phase of the war, with Tejan Kabbah's government fighting the RUF/AFRC around the country while laying the groundwork to bring Foday Sankoh to new peace talks. A time Makeni residents call "the infights" unfolded, with rebel factions battling for control of the town, which Sankoh had declared the RUF's headquarters (Bolten 2012a). Kabbah, Sankoh, and other leaders met in Lomé, Togo, in July 1999, and signed a peace agreement that gave the RUF amnesty, offered Foday Sankoh the vice presidency of the country, and created the United Nations Assistance Mission to Sierra Leone (UNAMSIL). Everything appeared to be on track until May 2000, when, feeling that Foday Sankoh had sold them out, a group of rebels attacked a UNAMSIL disarmament center in Makeni, killing fifty Kenyan peacekeepers. A furious Tejan Kabbah announced that he would destroy the town because Makeni was home only to "rebels and rebel collaborators" (Bolten 2012a). For the next four months the government's gunship bombed Makeni regularly, sparking a mass exodus from the town, which calmed only with the signing of another ceasefire in Abuja, Nigeria, in November.

Though the war gradually drew to a close after this ceasefire, with new disarmament centers set up in Makeni six months after the second Abuja Accords, the period of rebel occupation in Makeni was a critical time in generating local ideas about youth: how to identify them and how they behaved. Occupation by a rebel force commanded by a thirty-year-old, Issa Sesay, whose minions included children from the "Small Boys Unit" armed with AK-47s, imprinted in residents' minds that young men had unbridled potential for violence. Young male civilians were particularly vulnerable to RUF harassment, beatings, and torture during the occupation. Some endured regular beatings for resisting rebel commanders' drive to recruit them, submitting themselves to degrading domestic labor for rebel commanders to avoid injury and death. Many "joined" the rebels, a euphemism for going through the motions of being an RUF member outside of Makeni, even while refusing to engage in violence among one's friends and neighbors where one could be seen—and judged—in town. The young people I interviewed for my first book almost universally articulated the bind of trying to survive and also look after their families—which often required collusion with RUF rebels who had access to food and supplies—while being hyper-aware of how these activities appeared to other civilians who might accuse them of being rebels. Being called a rebel could have lasting consequences once the war ended (Bolten 2012a). Survival required food, shelter, and safety, but it also required that one maintain one's reputation as a good person, or rekindling relationships with friends and family would be impossible once the war was over.

Much of the scholarship on Sierra Leone's civil war has focused on young people, and how the habits of the young in the 1980s and 1990s reflected trends occurring in small wars around the world. Some focused on the war as an example of how youth bulges propagate violent crises because of the unemployment and disaffection suffered by the young (Kaplan 2000; Urdal 2006), and that it is resource scarcity combined with high population growth and poverty that will nurture violent conflicts around the developing world in the future. Others maintain that the war was in fact a crisis perpetuated *on* the youth. Instead of anarchy, it was corruption that drove rebel recruitment. Instead of scarcity the war was driven by resource wealth, specifically the quest for diamonds and the abuse of the young men forced to mine them. Instead of warring African nations being "backward" they are incorporated, in extremely marginal ways, into world systems, with the youth getting the last and least scraps of "development" (Richards 1996, 2001; Peters 2011; Utas 2003). These scholars entered a debate with Sierra Leonean historians and political scientists who published an edited volume that focused instead on the internal trends in youth politics in Sierra Leone, and how it was important to hold young fighters accountable for the destruction of the country. They emphasized that in spite of corruption and poverty, most youth had *not* joined the RUF (Abdullah 2004; Rashid 2004; Gberie 2004). These latter scholars proposed that the war emerged from the development of a large underclass of "lumpen" youth who pushed radical answers to a corrupt regime without a true emancipatory program. Lacking maturity and leadership, they led an ideology-free movement and used terror tactics against their own communities. This collection, which was published by a West African press and circulated within Sierra Leone, supported the fear and mistrust at official levels that followed young people—and molded the policies meant to address them—in the aftermath of the war. It comprised one of the earlier postwar configurations of what Sierra Leone youth became locally for the next decade.

Young people were and continue to be embodiments of the global influences that molded prewar Sierra Leone, shaped strategy and fighting, and colored how it was rebuilt in the aftermath. Between a colonial system of indirect rule that precipitated oppression of the young, to the tremendous economic and social disparities that emerged as a result of the elitism in the education system, to the global demand for diamonds, to the influence of Hollywood movies on young rebels, the civil war was the culmination of global influences that generated a symbolic, material, and social framework—a boundary—erected around young people. This was reflected in the work of scholars who posited that youth are subject to conflicting and contrasting local and global social forces. They highlighted that the discourse about the war being a crisis perpetuated *on* youth reflected international legal norms and humanitarian programming that aimed to treat anyone below the age of eighteen as a victim (Rosen 2007; Shepler 2005, 2014), even as those young people may have seen violence as a productive form of work (Hoffman 2007, 2011a, 2011b). Young people's actions during war and their treatment afterward reflected the entanglement of the local and the global, as child soldiers who had been officially "reintegrated" through a "discourse of abdicated responsibility" (which framed anyone under eighteen as a child [Shepler 2005]) clashed with communities determined to hold them responsible for their actions (see Shaw 2010). The government spoke about "war-affected youth", a nebulous term referring to young people who were not "mainstream" and needed to be put back under adult control. Once these young people encountered international NGO programs, they began referring to themselves as "stakeholders" and "target beneficiaries," and repeatedly performed their social exclusion by generating proposals and programs rather than humbling themselves and requesting adult sponsorship (Bolten 2008, 2014c). The young people who emerged from this era in Sierra Leone's history in urban areas perform these contradictory configurations, enacting performances designed to appeal to the people they encounter—foreign or local, older or younger, urban or rural. They had no determinate identity that could be easily mapped onto their culture, ethnicity, or location, instead, the way they participated in and were affected by the war instead revealed them as embodied products of Sierra Leone's long history with global inputs.

The Long Historic Reach of Globalization

Though Sierra Leone's connections beyond Africa began in the 1600s with the arrival of Portuguese traders and slavers (Shaw 2002), the influences most evident in the current articulation of young people began more recently and recognizably with colonialism. The British government established Freetown, the capital, as a colony for freed slaves in the early 1800s, extending their reach beyond the colony to set the boundaries of modern-day Sierra Leone with the Sierra Leone Protectorate in 1895 (see Figure 1.1). The protectorate was governed by the British colonial standard of indirect rule. Rather than station British administrators in every chiefdom, indirect rule required finding local individuals who were willing to govern in Britain's name and according to their dictates. Administrators divided the protectorate into chiefdoms, each with a British-appointed "Paramount Chief" (Alie 1990:134). Because the British were intent on stopping internal warfare and slaving—two primary sources of income and power in the protectorate—the chiefs "ate their chiefdoms," imposing taxes, labor levies, and court fines on their people to replace the wealth they would have accrued through war and slaving (Shaw 2002:237). In creating paramount chiefs, the British

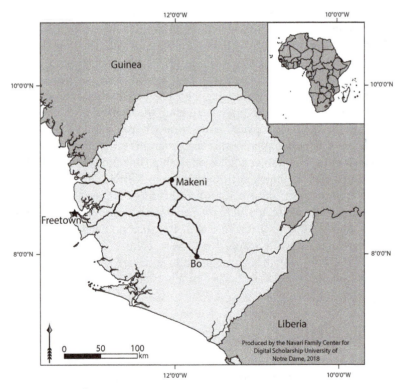

FIGURE 1.1 **Map of Sierra Leone.**

also drew new lines around chiefdoms and banned people moving between them, which prevented people escaping from particularly predatory chiefs. The burden of taxation, exclusion, and forced labor persisted for decades and fell especially heavily on young people. Young men who were forced to work on their elders' farms had no access to education or land, were unable to marry because their elders limited their access to women, and were fined for sleeping with women outside of marriage (Tom 2014:4). This mass disaffection and exclusion, which resulted in some willing recruits to the RUF who were "tired of the rotten system" (5) was not a result of them being detached from global systems; indeed, it originated from their incorporation through colonialism.

Connected to the chiefly abuses was the British education system that also arrived with colonial rule. From the first school established in the protectorate—the Bo School for Boys in 1906—formal education in Sierra Leone was not about self-rule or equality (Corby 1990). British administrators believed schooling performed two functions: educating the local elite as colonial handmaidens who would do their bidding in the "native" areas, and teaching local people "useful tasks" that would help them "to accept their place" in a racist social order (CO 267/630/6 Kegiwin 1928). Western education, though not widespread in the protectorate, was quickly recognized by Sierra Leoneans as having the potential to transform one's social, economic, and political prospects. It became a place where local understandings about elite status and political power unfolded (Bledsoe 1990), even as the British tried initially to ensure that most people received only "vernacular" education in agriculture and domestic hygiene (CO 267/630/6 Kegiwin 1928). Without access to formal education, a child was guaranteed an impoverished life in the countryside. This remained the case for most rural young people eighty years after the first schools opened. Rather than creating the possibility for equality among socially unequal children (Labaree 1997), Western education became a tool for the already privileged and connected to secure their place in the elite (Bolten 2015). For poor rural children to enter education required migration to urban areas and being fostered by uncaring adults, a burden so great that most children did not succeed (Bledsoe 1992). This persistent inequality, with social exclusion guaranteed through the exclusiveness of the education system, was one factor that aided the RUF. Early recruits were often swayed by the vague ideology of throwing out "the rotten system" that favored urban elites (Peters 2011).

One of the most important global factors driving prewar economic decline and fueling the war was diamonds. Sierra Leone had exported diamonds to Europe since the 1930s, but a boom in demand in the 1950s prompted a mass exodus of young men from farms to the mining areas—a massive shift in economic activity that moved the country from exporting to importing rice, the staple food (Campbell 2002:19). With basic survival now tied to the ability to purchase rice, the loss of agricultural labor, and rice swamps converted to alluvial mines, a formerly robust system of rural agriculture went into steep decline. Large communal farms were replaced by small subsistence farms and a reliance on cash to purchase rice; food insecurity became more prevalent; and, in a vicious cycle, young people flocked to the mines (Bolten 2009a). Though Liberian warlord Charles Taylor's hunger for diamonds has been suggested as a main cause of the war (Gberie 2005), that fact is not as important here as the global dimensions of the diamond industry in the 1990s, and the role it played in further implicating young men in the war. Young men whose prospects for economic mobility were destroyed by colonial chiefdoms, elitist education, and agricultural decline were ripe targets for the RUF. The lack of any international oversight made diamonds a potentially lucrative and "legal" business for anyone who had access to them, including rebel organizations. This is how diamonds became "blood diamonds": the RUF captured mining territory, enslaved the young people working there, and exported the stones (Campbell 2002). Any diamond the RUF found was smuggled easily through Liberia (hence the Charles Taylor connection) and sold in Brussels and New York. The revelation that an engagement ring in the United States was potentially mined by an enslaved child in a warzone in Sierra Leone prompted further global entanglements, generating movies such as *Blood Diamond* (Zwick 2006) and Kanye West's song "Diamonds from Sierra Leone" (2005).

The international desire for diamonds perpetuated the war from which fears of youth were generated, but more recognizable to Sierra Leoneans as global influence "spoiling" their children were the popular media inspirations for many of the young fighters. Paul Richards famously called the war "a crisis of modernity," noting that *Rambo* (Kotcheff 1982) was often shown in RUF camps as a way of inspiring their cadres to defeat "the rotten system" (Richards 1996). Richards interviewed young people about their movie-watching habits, and many described the films as a form of education, teaching them how to tackle problems (Richards 1996:109). Most RUF commanders adopted nicknames that were recognizable because of their derivation from action movies; indeed, two RUF commanders who fought for control of Makeni were nicknamed Rambo and Superman (Bolten 2012a). Similar to their nicknames, music videos also inspired a rebel style, with Tupac Shakur and NWA mentioned by many of my interlocutors as icons emulated by rebels in Makeni (see Utas 2003 for similarities in Liberia).

From the oppressive power relations generated under colonialism, to the inequities bred by Western education, to diamonds and Rambo, the young people I met in the aftermath of the civil war were formed by globalization. It was impossible to understand a young person in 2003 outside of the oppressive social relations in the rural areas, the unequal opportunities produced by elitist education, the global hunger for diamonds that destroyed agriculture and fueled the war, and of the long reach of media. Youth were generated by the postwar government as marginalized and spoiled by violence, and thus as a cause for fear. Much of the scholarship on Sierra Leonean youth after the war stressed the rapid reinstatement of norms designed to establish the authority of elders and chiefs over young people in the war's aftermath (Archibald and Richards 2002; Boersch-Supan 2012; Hanlon 2005; Hoffman 2003; Reno 2008; Shaw 2010; Tom 2014), and emphasized that these were warnings that the war might ignite again because a rejection of patrimony was a primary cause. However, these articles lacked the space to trace patrimony back to its global inception. In essence, the problem lay not with a traditional social system of adult power over young people, but in overlooking the fact that young people embodied a century of global trends that systematically disadvantaged them.

When I attended the swearing-in ceremony of Makeni's first postwar elected town council in 2004, President Tejan Kabbah's opening speech highlighted the country's many development successes since the war's end a year and a half earlier. The speech contained undercurrents of fear for and of the country's young people. For Kabbah, young people fell into two categories: mainstream and marginal (see also Diouf 1996). He saw a Sierra Leone straining under the burden of war-affected youth, whose minds had been dulled by violence, who were discouraged and disaffected, and who had to be mainstreamed to ensure peace. This mainstreaming involved reasserting adult control—in schools, vocational programs, and apprenticeships—to turn their minds "away from the Devil's work" of violence, and to make them believe that "they are the leaders of tomorrow." The speech had sinister tones, insinuating that any young person who was not in school was socially dangerous, and adult authority was the only solution. Though only one speech in years of postwar programming and aid, Kabbah's argument illuminated how the war initiated new ways of seeing young people as potentially violent and needing adult supervision, and informing the kinds of boundaries configured around them, which is where we see the incarnation of youth that unfolds in these pages.

Researcher Positionality in Postwar Makeni

I arrived in Sierra Leone in 2003 to study postwar recovery and sought a location to engage these questions productively. During my initial research in Freetown I was warned against going to Makeni, which was viewed as a lawless rebel stronghold. The main reason cited was the scores of young ex-combatants who had been demobilized in Makeni over the previous year and still resided in town. "They must like it there," was the reason given for this, which supported popular conceptions at the time that Makeni still "belonged" to the RUF (Bolten 2012a). These reactions kindled my interest in working there, as the idea of master narratives that excluded a regional capital town to punish it for being occupied was puzzling and intriguing.

When I moved to Makeni I discovered that in spite of the notion that aid organizations were largely absent, there were enough white aid workers present to force me to perform a student identity. Aid workers traveled in SUVs, so I walked everywhere. As a consequence, I met a lot of young people who were also making their way around town on foot. Many of them were curious about why a white woman was not driving, and this prompted conversations about my position as a student and anthropologist, and as someone interested in how people were emerging from the war. A student was a known social status as someone who was educated but not wealthy or powerful. The war had brought the country's already under-resourced education system to its knees, which meant most of my contemporaries (I was twenty-six when I moved to Makeni) were trying to finish high school. Nongovernmental organizations (NGOs) were the town's primary employer, and young people knew they needed office skills to obtain work. Most of our early conversations focused on education, and how young people were scrimping and saving to finish high school, which would allow them to secure a job and participate in the temporary boom of the postwar economy. Our conversations became a form of snowball sampling—meeting students through their friends and developing a network of (primarily) young men whose goal was to graduate and enroll in college.

A good example of how agential cuts fashion determinate identities is the fact that after a time I became a "social male" (DeWalt and DeWalt 2011:100), which had profound consequences for my social networks and how I came to understand youth. That I was educated meant I had more in common with other educated people than I did with uneducated people, and most of the educated twenty-somethings in Makeni were males. I had several close female friends, but they were all professionals—teachers, town councilors, nurses, police officers—who were also older than me. Young women found me intimidating, even though I spoke *Krio*, Sierra Leone's lingua franca, and spent many hours hanging out with them. Most of our conversations involved them apologizing for not being as interesting as boys because they were not educated, and for not being wise because they lacked the life experience of their mothers. Though this constrained access and heavily filtered information affected my research profoundly—there was no possibility of achieving gender balance in my field notes or interviews, no possibility of equal representation of how genders perform seriousness (see Sommers 2012, 2015)—it shed light on how the ethnographer's positionality is deeply entrenched in her project.

As time passed, I changed, my interlocutors changed, the town of Makeni changed, and the relationships we had originally built were renegotiated. Reconfiguration—of the relationships between people and between people and places—is a fact of time. I finished my PhD in 2008, and at that moment I stopped being "Kati" to my interlocutors and became "Doctor," even though I still dressed simply and walked everywhere. I went from being a hosted student at a Makeni university to a visiting professor. The university was established as a private unaccredited tertiary school 2005; by 2010 it was fully accredited, had expanded to two campuses, and was conferring advanced degrees. I had a tenure-track job in the United States and had moved from a position of sympathetic but young outsider to an advocate for my friends, negotiating jobs for them. We were still contemporaries, but our relationship had shifted from "sister" and "brother" to "sponsor" and "sponsored." As of this writing in 2019, these bonds are as strong as ever; it is just their texture that has altered—another perfect example of the agential cut: our identities become determinate through how they are perceived and in part enacted through encounters with others. My existence as someone with a PhD in Makeni—as opposed to being a student—had no substance without or outside of how this was enacted between me and my interlocutors. Having participated in and embodied these reconfigurations helped me grasp fully the power of agential realism for describing social worlds.

A Decade of Ethnographic Methods

The research for this book took place between 2004 and 2012, a timespan that began with a focus on the social world of a post-occupation town. The primary method of ethnographic research is participant observation (DeWalt and DeWalt 2011), but it also involves interviews, focus groups, and, in this case, a longitudinal cohort study. The research that generated this book emerged organically. I had no notion when I moved to Makeni, with a focus on ex-combatants, that youth would comprise a fundamental aspect of the inquiry that generated my dissertation and would inform my research for years after that. So many of the conversations that I had with Makeni residents focused on their fears for the future, with youth comprising the keystone of that fear. The young people I met when I started my daily walks in 2004 became primary interlocutors helping me to answer questions about themselves and their fellows in response to these fears, and a dozen of them became the cohort that I followed over the next eight years.

Participant observation is, at its heart, a struggle to both participate and observe well. The possibility of being both a participant and an observer sheds light on why the ethnographer's position is central to the research, rather than being an impediment to collecting good data. When James Clifford's disparagingly described participant observation as "deep hanging out," Clifford Geertz used the idea to suggest that instead of participant observation lacking rigor, it instead highlighted that the researcher herself is the primary tool of inquiry (Geertz 1998). We are all humans moving through a world of humans, with our own bodies and minds our tools of discerning and acting in that world. Participant observation is embodied practice (Cook 2010), which Geertz called playfully "an abuse of the privilege" of the fact that "all the human sciences are promiscuous, inconstant, and ill defined" (1998). Participant observation takes seriously the accusation that it cannot be objective, instead rendering its very subjectivity the primary means of inquiry.

In the years I spent in Makeni working on this project, the act of living and moving through town, encountering others, and weaving our way into and out of each other's lives was fundamental to generating data. I sat in on school classes from first grade to high school, sometimes filling in for an absent or ill teacher, and also taught my own classes in development studies and qualitative methods to university students. I attended events and meetings, from political rallies to student government, from celebrations for returning Muslim hajj pilgrims, to funerals for friends who had passed on. Weddings, card games in ataya bases, meals with friends, dress fittings with local tailors, resting in the shade of a mango tree and watching the world go by—these are all facets of participant observation that reveal diffraction patterns and the differences that matter in the world. As I honed in on young people, I followed them from schools, to events, to street corners and ataya bases. I also worked with the people they described as adults, eating meals, coordinating events, and socializing over drinks and conversation to understand their perspectives. Each of these moments was carefully recorded in my notebook and later transcribed into polished field notes (Emerson et al. 2011), with the writing, reading through, and pondering my primary mode of analysis.

Interviews were a key aspect of the project. My first book utilized life histories as a core method, elucidating how people narrated and interpreted their survival during the war by conforming their stories with local notions of moral personhood (2012a). Life histories also informed this research, as I spent hours hanging out with people, coming to grips with how they thought about the defining details that made them the people they had come to be. Life history interviews often generated snowball sampling, as the individuals my interlocutors cited as critical to their lives were their companions and friends, thus prompting further interviews and elucidating the social webs within which people young and old lived. I also conducted structured and semistructured interviews, following up a life history that I had conducted with an individual with more targeted questions designed to gather their thoughts on issues such as education, employment, politics, fashion, and football.

Many of these interviews took place one-on-one, but just as often they were impromptu focus groups. Though focus groups historically utilized in consumer and sociological research involve the deliberate assembling of people who do not know each other over a preselected topic (Hollander 2004), most of my focus groups were spontaneous gatherings discussing a topic of common and often abiding interest. I sat in the university canteen and talked politics with student government officers, chatted about unemployment in ataya bases, and joined conversations on fashion trends in tailoring cooperatives. In Hollander's experience, a designed focus group will tell you more about the social context of how information circulates in the social world, more than any "real" information (Hollander 2004:603), but in this case these sessions unfolded more as "interest" groups because, as often as not, I was entering a conversation that had begun long before I arrived, and would continue long after I left (Geertz 1973:9).

The bulk of these life histories, interviews, focus groups, and moments of participant observation involved the cohort of young people that I met in 2004. They became my primary interlocutors because they were interested in the questions I was asking and helped build my social web. This cohort emerged from the subjective process of making friends and spending time with them based on our commonalities of being students who enjoyed cold drinks and long conversations. From the dozen young men who comprised my primary interlocutors in 2004 and 2005 emerged a longitudinal study, where I followed the events that marked their lives, the successes and failures, the questions and obstacles, and their interpretations of their struggles. They narrated the problems they encountered with adults and in being taken seriously, the strategies they used, and how poorly, and infrequently, those strategies worked. It was the nature of these struggles that generated the argument framework for this book.

These methods do not and cannot engage a random sample of people, and they are most definitely partial. This is not a weakness of ethnographic method. What appeared to me to be poor fieldwork because of a primary focus on young men was not only normal, but a fundamental aspect of scientific inquiry. The vagaries of ethnographic method and its built-in subjectivity are often highlighted to distinguish socio-cultural anthropology as a "soft" social science, aligned with the humanities. This is based on the idea that interpreting and describing is neither systematic nor conclusive. However, the drive for scientific objectivity, even in "hard" sciences such as physics, is consistently undermined by the fact that science is a human activity (Barad 2007:54). Everything about scientific inquiry, from the questions asked to the apparatus designed to investigate them, are products of subjective human thoughts and actions (232). Though anthropologists have been describing and defending ethnography, as Geertz does, as inherently subjective to illustrate biases in other sciences, Barad's approach, and Cynthia Enloe's perspectives on seriousness, are generative of a convergence. Barad's own path through scientific inquiry also illuminates how it is possible—indeed necessary—to embrace subjectivity, and as a consequence to use feminist theory to think about young men, and to take them seriously. What I aim to argue here is also how feminist approaches can not only help reconfigure the relationship between so-called objective and subjective inquiry; they can also help us think about how identities—of youth and anthropologists—form and become consequential.

Feminist Theory and Young Men

As I described in the previous chapter, Karen Barad articulates that separations and differentiations between people (and people and things) only occur in encounters; that is, no entity is shaped prior to or in the absence of its relationships (Barad in Kleinman 2012:77). Barad discovered this through her own journey in quantum physics. The questions of what is "real" that dogged her research was one that had been taken up by other feminist scholars but had not been resolved to her satisfaction with respect to the "world of matter." She was not satisfied with Judith Butler's assertion that bodies are "a mute substance, a passive blank slate on which history or culture makes the[ir] mark." She argued that to make such an argument "is to deprive matter of its own historicity, to limit the possibilities for agency" (2007:60). Barad needed to reconcile her conviction that the material world *does* matter for its own sake—that the world is not just representations and social categories—with the fact that the material world does not exist in absence of perception, and of talking and thinking about it. Representation *also* matters. How to do this?

Barad's research was inspirational for her philosophy of the world as the entanglement of materials and discourses. She worked on slime molds, which are agglomerations of amoebas that shift themselves to serve differentiated functions of an organism. As she discussed in an interview, there was no way to talk about slime molds as individuals—or to talk about the amoebas that comprised them as individuals—because they were neither and both. Slime molds lack "determinate identities," as they are neither individual nor community in any scientific sense

(Kleinman 2012:80). The wealth of scholarship on youth that struggles to define who youth "are"—whether social or demographic categories (Durham 2000, 2004; Roche 2016; Sommers 2012, 2015; Urdal 2006), or liminal social beings (Bolten 2012c; Christiansen et al. 2006; Honwana 2012; Jeffrey 2010; Mains 2012; Singerman 2013)—has converged on but not stated the fact that youth lack determinate identities. Words such as "liminal," "waiting," and "stuck" are used to discuss their suspension and in-between-ness in space and time, while only circling around what it is that precisely comprises who, or what, a youth "is." It is only one step further to see a lack of predetermined identity as a productive starting point. Indeed, the trouble with gender that Judith Butler describes is the centrality of the performance of one's identity to their bodily status (2007:136). The fact that young people *must* take risks and perform their seriousness publicly is fundamental to their indeterminate natures. Indeed, the defining characteristic of adults in Sierra Leone is their ability to control their worlds by *concealing* their power and intentions (see Ferme 2001)—as did the politician who drove by the ataya base, rather than displaying them as did the people he was observing.

Insisting on a lack of determination of identities is also a productive way of thinking about ethnographers. Before I started this research, I was a cis-gendered white female graduate student. When I arrived in Sierra Leone, how these aspects of myself gained social salience—and in turn informed the identity I carried and through which I was known—were constantly up for interpretation and reconfiguration. I have spoken already about how being a white foreigner configured me as a social male, given access to people, events, meetings, and interviews that would be rare for a Sierra Leonean female student my age. The fact that I was an anthropologist and not an NGO worker was far more important to my social identity than I initially realized. People did not know how to interpret my daily routine, the questions I was asking, and the lack of material output outside of the guise of NGO work. Describing myself as an anthropologist meant that my identity was configured as an intellectual activist, that I was there to serve as Makeni's own social historian and write their history of the war and occupation (see Bolten 2012a). How my role, and thus my identity, unfolded was generated afresh in every relationship, every interview, and every encounter through new agential cuts. After departures and returns, these relationships were renegotiated, especially as my own position in America changed from student to professor. These kinds of negotiations were familiar and comfortable for my interlocutors, who were also engaged in the everyday work of performing their own desired identities and navigating how others saw and engaged those identities. We were all indeterminate in this research, and thus recognizable to each other.

Bringing Cynthia Enloe's discussions of seriousness into this mélange of theory and method is critical for understanding the ethnographer doing ethnography on youth. Enloe writes women back into the story, stating that so much of the time women's stories aren't heard because their bodies, voices, places, and spaces aren't taken seriously as objects of inquiry (2013); in essence, that the boundaries configured around them seem so self-evident and immutable that they are not worthy of study. Youth want to be written into the story, but they face the same problem women do of not being considered actors of consequence. Adults have to incorporate them into the story—to generate determinate identities for young people in encounters with them—but they are not the only ones who can or must take youth seriously. This book is in your hands because I took young people seriously, and because they took me and this project seriously enough to engage with it. As my central aim for this project was to address how the fears surrounding youth are generated almost entirely by the way adults engage condescendingly, dismissively, or violently with them, configuring youth as actors of consequence, as products of a profoundly important global moment, is only a starting point.

CHAPTER 2
....

Cinderblocks and Plaster
In/visibility and Permanence in Public Space

"Without a wall, it is impossible to speak of my dreams."
Musa spoke softly as we sat in the shade of a mango tree in front of his family home. The sun was hot and I was grateful for the Fanta he offered me. He drained his bottle of Coke, then carefully dropped the glass bottle into a crate that was propped against a wall, the same wall that was the subject of our conversation. Five feet high and made of rough concrete cinderblocks, it stuck out awkwardly from his parents' home, clearly unfinished and yet already serving as his place of business. He had painted "Amerikan Boy Relaxation" on the top row of blocks and carefully arranged crates of soda underneath, with a small table arrayed with tea and instant coffee next to it. A wooden bench and a few plastic chairs under the tree completed the scene.

Musa's girlfriend Ramatu strode out of the house, followed by multiple indecipherable but irate female voices. Her face was set in angry lines, and she awkwardly settled her hugely pregnant body in a rickety chair next to Musa. She sighed as Musa rubbed her shoulder, and revealed the substance of the argument, which was with Musa's mother and aunt. "They are saying that the business is taking too long to become profitable, and the money is not enough. Every day they stare at my belly and say that the baby will need the money from the relaxation, but the building will never be finished. So, we cannot get married."

Musa and Ramatu were in their late twenties. They had fallen in love years earlier, and had two children that Ramatu's mother was look-ing after in her home village, forty miles away. Musa had never com-pleted secondary school, as he had apprenticed to his grandfather as a traditional medicine man, selling herbal cures for a range of common ailments. The market for herbal cures had crashed since his childhood, leaving him economically stranded: "The problem is that the cures do not sell now the way they did in our fathers' time. People have access to tablets and they prefer them to our fathers' cures." The remnants of this business were also arrayed under the tree, with small bags of dried bark, leaves, and roots arranged under a sign announcing "Musa Kanu's Medicines." He had diverted money from his faltering medical business to his new "modern" enterprise, selling soft drinks to passersby on the busy road. Before Musa sold his first Coke, he had invested the bulk of his money in cinderblocks. It was enough to build the short wall.

He explained, "There are people who just have crates of drinks and they will set them up anywhere, but if they do not have a structure in which people can relax, they cannot make anything of their business. As I get money, I will put up the second wall, and then a roof. I want to do that before the rains come or the business will be spoiled."

The goal was simple: build the walls and thus the business, make enough money to support the impending baby and stop the family squabbles, and eventually offer Ramatu's parents her bride price, offi-cially sealing the deal on their decade-old relationship. If Musa could never afford to give Ramatu's parents the dozen goats that they required for their daughter's hand in marriage, their children would be continue to be illegitimate. Musa would worry later about the ramifications of building the relaxation on land owned by his mother. He hoped that if he eventually contributed enough to the household to justify her loan of the land, he and *not* his brother would inherit the precious home in the center of Makeni. For Musa, being recognized in encounters with others as a man began with the equivalent of $30, the cost of materials for an unadorned cinderblock wall eight feet long and five feet high.

Cinderblocks in Makeni are as much of a global–local hybrid as the young people who believe building with them will transform their fortunes. For young men, cinderblocks represent permanence and investment, and should be judged by others as belonging to a "serious-minded somebody." The design of cinderblocks originated in England and arrived in Sierra

Leone with colonialism in the late 1800s. The blocks available in Makeni were made by hand by unskilled young men and were dried in the sun as they were in the nineteenth century at a workshop a mile from Musa's house. They were rendered from cement from a German-run company based in Freetown that mined sand directly from Sierra Leone's beaches, and cost Le4,000 ($0.75) each in 2012. Using them represented an expensive move beyond mud bricks, the traditional building material that had to be repaired or replaced regularly. To build with mud indicated poverty and potential impermanence; to build with cement indicated intent and investment (see also Sommers 2012:116). Young people saw cinderblock structures as a declaration of seriousness by which adults could not help but be impressed (see Weiss 2009:100). Musa hoped that both his parents and his potential customers would agree.

Musa wanted the Amerikan Boy Relaxation to attract a certain clientele. The first time we met, he pirouetted for me, asking if he looked "American" in a tattered baseball cap he wore backward and baggy jeans belted with a shiny silver buckle. He explained that bringing his style to his relaxation would build his name recognition and attract people who were interested in American culture. He played rap music and hoped to decorate with American movie posters, attracting other young people who might have some money to spend participating in his vision of global culture (see Weiss 2009:4). Every bit of profit went to his family or his business, reinforcing his identities as devoted father and dutiful son, but only possibly contributing to someone taking him seriously in an encounter.

The way young men in urban Sierra Leone see the importance of structures—building, decorating, and inhabiting them—is based on a long local history of status and recognition derived through permanence in the landscape. When youth spoke of "real" adults, they invoked places associated with those adults—workshops, cinderblock homes, market stalls—that were widely known and admired. Young people often explained that without a building they were "nowhere" socially, because construction was the best way of performing their moral uprightness, as opposed to "wasting" money on transient pleasures (Goffman 1959:13). A young person who saves his money to build a wall, paint a building, or engage in other acts of permanence, no matter how paltry, presents the moral front of someone who is decidedly *not* useless or shiftless. The agential cut made in encounters with this person must necessarily incorporate his permanent imprint on the landscape into one's observations and reactions. Buildings are, in young men's thinking, impossible to ignore, and demanding admiration.

Youth with structures announce their intention to invest in a—literally—concrete future, and counter adult claims that they universally suffered from "a war mentality," even though this often backfires. Many adults in 2012 believed the war created a consumer mentality among the young, with short-term horizons and simple pleasures dominating their desires. Even an incomplete structure conveys a young man's will to become somebody in the community, and to distance himself from the socially problematic short-term thinking decried by elders (see Bourdieu 1992:120). More than merely demonstrating seriousness, a wall is an *honest* performance of his self. Few adults in the postwar period loaned young people money for projects, so a young man may have skipped meals to save money for this structure. He may have gone without new clothes for a year. A structure is a hopeful activity where a young man shows his "*truer* self," in essence, the self he would like to be (Robert Park in Goffman 1959:19), the self he hopes will be observed by adults (Van 'T Wout 2016:17). The risks are that in a patchwork, visually messy town there is no guarantee that a structure, or its builder, will be visibly or morally distinct from his surroundings (Simone 2004:407). The frantic, haphazard construction boom among young men generates youth through in/visibility. The omnipresence of half-built walls and shoddily built sheds renders their builders visible as one in a crowd of thousands, spoiling the landscape with "half-half" construction, according to adults. No hopeful display is viewed as unambiguously positive; no agential cut is predictably predicated on the universal admiration of construction.

In addition, the businessmen typically idolized by youth because they became successful through their structures were never youth in the same sense as their fans because of the vastly different social contexts in which these businessmen made their own fortunes. Young people imagine that their "successful brothers" struggled with being called war-affected, and yet still found investors, thus epitomizing what youth can achieve if they can only finish their own structures. However, the three revered businesses presented in the following sections—Johnny Boy Boutique, Future Image Ataya Base, and the original Makeni Motorbike Riders Association (MBRA)—are owned by individuals who established their credibility and networks before or early in the war. These successful businessmen experienced their own period of youth through encounters with adults when identities were not molded by the war, and who configured young men as apprentices and investment opportunities, and not as lazy, shiftless, and war-affected. The young men who erected and displayed structures after the war were often targets of harassment and censure by adults who interpreted their efforts as foolishness or threats, rather than earnestness and industriousness. This chapter examines the ways young men imagine, inhabit, and build structures as performances of seriousness for adults. It also highlights the subtle and overt ways in which adults configure boundaries around these youth, disparaging their efforts as "unserious" and "lacking in future thinking," or the youth who engage in them as "too young" to know what they are doing. If youth achieve visibility, instead of promoting those efforts adults are aggressive, co-opting, manipulating, and deriding the young as "upstart" and failing to know their place. The "cuts" made on youth exclude them based on an observation of exactly how their actions threaten adult social worlds.

The chapter first examines the historical importance of property in Sierra Leone. It then moves to the struggle over property between civilians and rebels that was a centerpiece of rebel-occupied Makeni, with the destruction of property by young people tainting adults' perception of young men's construction efforts. It then moves to "box traders," the young men whose investments in tiny, impermanent businesses are derided as proof of a war mentality. The chapter then examines young men's admiration of businessmen who achieved their dreams but are impossible to emulate. These business owners represent subtle but important differences between pre- and postwar formations of youth. It then moves to the MBRA headquarters, where motorbike riders attempt to display their legitimacy as professionals. The chapter finishes with a youth who leveraged his business and NGO to commission a statue of the president and hoped for national recognition. Local politicians, alarmed at his boldness and the possibility that he might gain the president's favor, quashed his efforts and left him destitute. Since the end of the war, the way youth build and inhabit structures is characterized by agential cuts of in/visibility. Their mass investment in small permanent structures renders each individual performance unremarkable. Where adults are forced to notice visible youth structures, their alarm translates into know-your-place aggression (Mitchell 2015:229), with MBRA riders labeled ex-combatants, and the young man who commissioned a statue of the president told he was not big enough to succeed.

Property and Status in Sierra Leone

From the capital city of Freetown to the rural villages around the country, owning land and building structures are critical to the boundary around adulthood. Property owners automatically hold higher social prestige than landless people. On a community level, changes in people's fortunes are most strikingly apparent in changes to their home, which serve as announcements of the respect with which one should be treated in encounters. Buildings are also important as sources of income, as real estate has social and political as well as financial implications. People who can rent structures, collecting tenants who depend on them and support them, become wealthier and gain more prestige than those who cannot (Millar 2015:1706). Someone who can employ others to build for him also gains prestige, as the ability to command labor is a signal that one is no longer a dependent, but a patron in his own right (Ferme 2001:82).

The colonial record's description of young people's involvement in building and occupying structures is scant but also fraught. The first official school established outside of Freetown was Bo School in 1906 (Corby 1990), which was designed to educate the sons of chiefs to support colonial rule. The dormitories were the same mud-and-thatch huts that characterized students' own villages (Corby 1990:326), and thus failed to confer elite status on the students. The students refused to maintain their own buildings, and by 1937 the campus was in complete disrepair. The school could not attract good teachers or administrators for the same reasons, and parents began pulling their sons out and sending them elsewhere (CO 267/661/14 1937). Though the school eventually gained cinderblock construction, its original rudimentary, village-like campus meant students and their parents failed to take it seriously. In contrast was Koyeima School, which the British Director of Education, H. S. Keigwin, established not far from Bo School in 1930 to educate pupils in "vernacular education," namely to teach practical skills instead of, in his own words, "creating imitation Englishmen" (CO 267/630/6 1928). The first students built the school themselves under the guise of masonry and carpentry training. This they did "cheerfully" until a contractor began treating them like "common laborers," cursing at them and forcing them to work on weekends (CO 267/630/13 1930). Rather than building their own future, which would have articulated their status and skills, the boys were glorified slaves (see Bolten 2018) and walked out of the school ten weeks into their work. We will return to the Bo and Koyeima Schools in later chapters; needless to say at this juncture, youth build and inhabit structures with a conscious eye toward using structures as performances of prestige and seriousness.

In urban Sierra Leone, homes play an important role in determining the social position of families. Wealth in Freetown is "grounded in the city" with the Krio investing most of their savings in buildings

(Cohen 1981:51). Cohen reported entire streets and neighborhoods in Freetown in the late 1970s being owned by Krio families who made a living renting space to shopkeepers (52). Rural people who moved to Freetown found it difficult to gain a toehold in the city because they could not afford to purchase land; they were literally confined to the impermanence of renting accommodation and shop space. The Krios' dominance of Freetown real estate provides an important parallel in understanding how structures fit into a youth/adult boundary configuration. With limited land available in the city, this small group held the line against newcomers from the countryside by refusing to sell property to them. In Makeni, a town lot cost at least 1.5 million leones (about $300) in 2010. A few important families owned much of the land in Makeni for most of its history, and very few landowners would sell their properties for less than a small fortune. There was little possibility of young people purchasing land, especially if the owner did not want to sell to a young person. During the rebel occupation, young commanders forcibly occupied homes and ejected the owners, and residents did not forget this. The occupation negatively colored the observations that landowners made of the young, further configuring a boundary around youth as "dangerous."

In 2004 I often visited one of the town's elder statesmen, Mr. Kamara, whose imposing home stood on a main road. He had only regained possession of it the year before, after evicting Commander Kill Man No Blood and his entourage of teenagers. Before they left the rebels defaced the walls with graffiti, smashed floor tiles, broke windows, and ripped out the plumbing. They burned the furniture in a backyard bonfire: a coup de grâce to their scorched-earth retreat. "It wasn't enough," said Mr. Kamara, "that they occupy my home and leave my family stranded until we had legal recourse to remove them. They had to spoil everything and force me to accommodate my children in this hell. I could not even remove the insults from these walls with soap and water. I have to wait until I can afford to paint over them" (Bolten 2012c). The image of the destructive young rebel inhabited the minds of Makeni residents as they rebuilt their destroyed homes. In Mr. Kamara's mind, youth had no notion of building for a future, only negating the futures that others had built.

The young people who were civilians in occupied Makeni recognized this and fought these pronouncements through creative construction. At one moment during the infighting, Superman confronted and killed Rambo. Rambo's minions held an elaborate funeral, burying him in a grave in front of the town hall in the center of Makeni. One night soon after, a handful of young men exhumed the body, stripped the corpse, and dumped it in a muddy ditch on the highway. Returning to the gravesite, they destroyed the decorations, filled it with cement, and wrote "Constructed by the Youth" in one corner. Issa Sesay, incensed by this display of hubris and defiance, demanded the culprits be found. The residents closed ranks around their youth, and no one was ever punished for the transgressive construction, which remained visible until the site was repaved in 2006. This act of defiance was important, but as it was specifically a *deconstruction* of rebel power, rather than building anew, it could not endure.

The population of Makeni swelled once the war ended, but the destruction of so many buildings during the occupation created a housing crisis. Refugees poured in from the countryside, returning families reclaimed their property, and ex-combatants squatted in every semi-built structure they could salvage. Young people without families in Makeni often rented rooms at exorbitant prices from landlords determined to make money from the population boom. Large groups moved in together, sleeping three to a mattress and ten to a room to avoid homelessness, and struggled with landlords who demanded a year of rent up-front. Though few people could purchase land, young men's housing insecurity was used to condemn them, as their poverty was seen as proof of their laziness and unwillingness to work. Musa was lucky because his family owned their land and were willing to give him a small plot. However, his ability to be a man was constrained by the fact that Amerikan Boy Relaxation's future hinged on whether he inherited the land from his mother, or whether she would give it to his older brother. Although his structure was potentially temporary, he was in a much better position than most.[1] For every Musa, another young man rented a tiny plot from a landlord, risking his structure being demolished if he fell behind on rent (see Weiss 2009:76).

This pattern of construction resonates elsewhere in postwar West Africa. In Monrovia, Liberia, young ex-combatants inhabit "life in the gap" of parking lots, ruins, dumping grounds, and taxi ranks. Not all landscapes are open to them, and if they build, they do so in temporary ways in transient spaces (Hoffman 2017:54). For the majority of youth, as is clear in this chapter, the best they can do is occupy permanent places owned by others, and hope that the visibility acquired from being associated with established places will confer an air of respectability that contours their encounters with adults (Goffman 1959). For young people in Makeni with no social connections by which they could access land, permanence was both a means and a goal—enacting adulthood through performances that beg to be taken seriously.

Box Trading: Boundaries of War and In/distinction

"It would be easier to make money from stealing mobiles [cell phones] than doing this." Mohamed waved his hand unenthusiastically at his small wooden box, which sat on a low wall. The roughly hewn suitcase-sized container held chewing gum, cigarettes, soap, matches, and other cheap sundries. "But if I make my living from stealing phones and selling them in the market, people will know me facially [visibly] as not a moral somebody. No, it is better to struggle this way, saving a few leones so that I can get a stall." He pointed across the road to a small wooden booth where a woman sat behind a counter, selling similar items (see Figure 2.1). The advantage of having a stall was that successful negotiations with a landlord would mean it could be left there permanently, rather than moved every day. Mohamed saw more dignity in a stall than being perched on a wall, feet dangling, being forced to move if a policeman harassed him for conducting trade without a license.

Mohamed was one of hundreds of box traders in Makeni, itinerant sellers struggling to be known as entrepreneurs, whose small profits might one day be rolled into a permanent business (see Fioratta 2015:296; Utas 2005). Though the profit margins were tiny, Mohamed refused to engage in more lucrative, morally questionable activities because of his determination to be known as a "serious somebody." He was proud that he had, in his words, "moved up" to a box. The year before he had started his business with Le4,000 (about $1.50). He bought two packets of cigarettes and sold them individually. "I was always moving, this side to that side, selling one, two cigarettes here and there, and at the end of the day I was so tired!" It took a year to save enough to fashion the box and furnish it with small goods, but this was an improvement from running around with cigarettes. If an entrepreneur can stay in one place, he can become known to passers-by. Exchanging greetings every day may result in a sale, a repeat sale, a friendship, and perhaps a small investment in the business.

FIGURE 2.1 The aspirational stalls of box traders.

Even as young men see box trading as an important step toward permanence, it is also, because of its visibility and its ubiquity, almost universally disparaged by adults; an agential cut of il/legitimacy. Contrary to youth's own understandings, adults saw boxes as laziness rather than seriousness. I had breakfast one day with three teachers who embraced development projects for youth, but were extremely critical of box traders. According to a one, "The youth get a box and they call it development! But what will ever become of that box of matches except a little money to replace it with?" The others agreed with him, and I asked them why. The answer was that being happy with quickly gained, tiny profits is indicative of moral failing, rather than moral strength. If one was making real profits from a real occupation with long-term inputs and returns, one had the ability and imperative to think big—house, marriage, and children. But because the profit margins from box trading were small, one teacher explained, "you can see that they are pleased to have just a little money now. But after they eat, there is not much left, so they will go and spend it on a night at the bar. Maybe they will get some jeans. The youth who do this trade still have a war mentality. If they were thinking long-term, if they were not lazy, they would engage in activities like farming." This pronouncement on box trading as shiftless frivolity generated "lazy youth" *because* the expectation was that nothing long-term would emerge from it. If the occupation is disparaged, like gambling or crime, the money it generates can only go to unproductive ends like entertainment and petty consumption (see Cole 2005; Zelizer 2017). This is in spite of the fact that youth saw farming, with the uncertainty of weather and crop yields, as much riskier (see Guyer and Salami 2013:215), in addition to farming ensuring that they remained "boys," beholden to whoever owned the land they farmed.

Boxes were a performance of serious intent, interpreted as a moral failing around which a boundary of "unserious youth" was drawn. With the critique that box trading was not real work because of the minimal physical effort involved (Ferguson 2015:17), adults viewed the profits as bad money, therefore making it impossible that they would be used for real expenditures such as a family and future (Cole 2005:898–99). The fact that young people have no capital to begin a real business, or that they might lack the land, connections, or capital to farm, is irrelevant to a discussion of what seriousness actually looks like. The fact that box traders *did* spend some of their profits on clothes and entertainment was seen as proof of their war mentality. The gist of a war mentality is that it is short-term thinking focused on enjoyment and hedonism because of the possibility that there might be no tomorrow.

The youth themselves understood their focus on friends and entertainment not as wasteful consumption, but as nurturing their social networks. According to one trader called Ibrahim, "I want my business to grow, I would like to get a market stall, so I won't *chop* [eat] all of my profits, but I need to spend time with my friends. If I don't take time with them, they will scatter and won't help me." Essentially, one's friends are one's economic infrastructure (see Simone 2004:407). No one begins box trading if they have extensive social networks from which to get start-up capital for a larger business; on the contrary a box is proof that one's social network is extremely poor. They also have no one else to turn to for funds aside from their friends if they are robbed, or if they have an opportunity to purchase goods that they lack the money to invest in alone. By cementing their social networks through communal consumption—eating, going to clubs, or drinking ataya—young box traders maintain a fragile social and economic safety net. From this net, they hope to move to a stall.

I asked every box trader I spoke with in 2010 the same question: "What business in Makeni do you aspire to?" The answer varied from building supply stores, to household goods, to automobile parts, but the most common answer was "Johnny Boy Boutique." Located prominently in the town square, the boutique was the first store in Makeni that sold new imported jeans, button-down shirts, and tennis shoes after the war. The owner was a hero to box traders because of the rumor that he had started with a box and had built a boutique solely through his own efforts. I myself first shopped at Johnny Boy in 2004 on the advice of my neighbor. I was searching for clothes hangers, which, in the immediate postwar period, were difficult to find. Johnny Boy had them, and I gratefully purchased a dozen from the dapperly dressed entrepreneur. I had commented to him that he seemed remarkably young to have an upscale boutique, and he smiled bashfully, stating, "I put so much sweat into this!"

The boutique had transformed by 2012, as Johnny Boy had stopped selling clothes and was now selling electronics. Gone were the racks of jeans, dresses, and shirts, the rows of shoes and wall of accessories. In their place were boom boxes, radios, refrigerators, and lighting fixtures. Considering that Makeni had just been electrified a few months earlier, this was a bold and extraordinarily prescient business move. But for it all, the owner, whom I will call Johnny, had a business story that resonated at first with the box traders who so admired him. His humble start was not a rumor:

> I finished my secondary schooling in 1990, and I was doing business for somebody else, selling clothing for them. By 1994, I had saved enough money to do business for myself. I had only a very small capital of Le70,000. With that money I bought some dresses to sell. At that point I only had a table, not a shop. And I lived in a pretty small village. When the war came I grabbed the clothes and came to Makeni, because I thought it would be safer. I had to leave the table behind and I didn't know anyone here who would help me, so I had the dresses on my head and on my arms, and I sold them like this [he stands like a scarecrow], walking around town.

Johnny's beginnings as a shop assistant who scrimped and saved to start his own table could be the story of any box trader. Forced to flee to Makeni during the war, Johnny lost his table and his regular customers, and spent almost a decade as an itinerant seller, unable to rent a building during the uncertainty of the occupation. Like Mohamed selling individual cigarettes, an entrepreneur with no social or economic connections is limited to small stock and small returns. At the end of the war Johnny used his entire savings to purchase and repair a storefront, leaving him only Le8,000, about $3, to acquire stock. It was enough for bus fare to Freetown, where Johnny sought out business connections:

> My shop was empty, so I went to Freetown. I believe business is about honesty. I went to Freetown and I went to these business tycoons, these big men. And I told them, "You people know that I was once a businessman, and I have renovated my shop, but I don't have anything to sell. Please supply me something to start with, and then I will give you your money back." They gave me the chance of up to fifteen million leones, yes! So I said, "Okay, that is a lot for me, if I go above eight million, I won't be able to pay it." So I paid them bit by bit, reducing the amount, until it was finished, and I had six hundred thousand leones left. So I started going to Conakry [Guinea] to buy new clothes, and did business for myself again. It takes many things to do business, but really it is trust. Trust, which is how I got the loan in Freetown, and then I paid it back.

Johnny's story diverges sharply from the experiences of postwar box traders: he was trusted by business tycoons in Freetown, he had a shop, and he received a *huge* loan, unimaginable to other box traders, that he repaid in installments. Having spent years carving out prominence in a desultory market—Johnny was one of a handful of merchants selling clothes in occupied Makeni—he became respected, which made it possible to secure the loan. He is now an independent businessman, but this would never have happened unless someone "put a hand under him," which is precisely what box traders after the war need, and precisely what the boundary configured around lazy box traders possessing war mentalities forecloses. The problem is that they, *unlike* Johnny during the war, are ubiquitous and undifferentiated, a mass of boys perched on walls with boxes, selling the same stuff, thinking of themselves as serious but subject to cuts that see them as lazy and common. They are in/distinction. They see Johnny as a successful youth, but he is successful because he was always distinct, taking wartime risks that were tied to his business and not his identity as a young man. Johnny was never a youth by the same standards as his admirers, who are precluded from following the same path.

Ataya Bases: Configuring Boundaries through In/visibility and In/action

Box traders frequented Makeni's ataya bases, as they were good places to relax and socialize. Here they mingled with the city's vast population of unemployed youth, who paid their ataya memberships because they preferred the company to sitting alone at home. They enjoyed being supported by friends and being visible, as one youth stated, "If I sit at home, the neighbors think bad things about me, that I am idle. It is better to be seen in public, doing something." This doing something speaks to a general need, expressed by unemployed youth around the world, to impose order on otherwise unstructured time. They hang out publicly according to a schedule (Ferguson 1999:224; Jeffrey 2010:93; Mains 2012:45), because there is simply no good reason why they should stay at home (Simone 2011:266). Chakrabarty describes these places as "perches" (as in birds), temporary spots from which to see and be seen (1999). Ataya bases are settings for public performances, bracketing when and where youth do nothing with purpose (Goffman 1959:22), so that their identity is not fashioned as idle simply because their activities are invisible. What young people viewed as a performance of visibility and action emerged in encounters with adults as invisibility and inaction. Ataya bases encouraged the configuration of lazy youth as strongly as box trading (see Figures 2.2 and 2.3).

Ataya base members saw the organizations as fundamental to their social lives and futures. The appellation of a base is about foundations, and the club names presented their youth as visionary, talented, studious, and future-oriented. According to one member, "This is where the logical thinking of unemployed youth begins in the morning and ends in the evening. The base provides a place where unemployed youth feel they are accompanied, that they have meaningful contributions to make that are just being wasted but everyone here appreciates their capacities. In the base, everyone is equal and the administrators make sure the atmosphere is one of peace and harmony." In direct contrast to a military base, or the possibilities of violence that appear inherent when cities are full of unorganized, unemployed youth who are "waiting for opportunities" (see Hoffman 2007), these bases were the *basis* for everyday hope and mutual support. Rather than being unemployed at home, going to an ataya base was an act of *doing* something (see also Greenberg 2014:48; Mains 2012:56) that affirmed one's social foundation.

FIGURE 2.2 Exterior of an ataya base, with hand-painted sign.

FIGURE 2.3 Card games in an ataya base, under the membership list.

The doing was comprised entirely in the active occupation of public space, rather than actual permanence. The owners of each of the four ataya bases I visited were adults in that their businesses supported their families and brought them respect. The owner of Future Image Ataya Base had a story remarkably similar to Johnny's: his struggle to establish a business began before the war, when the boundary between adults and the young was one of patronage and potential investment rather than fear and approbation, and it was common for adults to "put a hand under" a young person. The owner, whom I call Alusine, grew up in Makeni next to a building owned by a Lebanese shopkeeper. He lost his mother while very young, in the 1980s, and remembers struggling to help his older sister and two younger brothers, as their father was infirm. His neighbor's grown son pitied him and granted him use of a small plot on their property to start a business. He sold tea because his Lebanese benefactors were Muslim, even as selling alcohol might have been more lucrative:

> When I started this business it was so small! I only had one pot to make tea, because it was not popular at the time, but I was able to build it more as people wanted ataya, because they know that it gives you energy! I would have lecturers stop for ataya on their way to school, business people, they said it made them strong for the day! If you drink *poyo* [palm wine] you can become frustrated and violent. So that was where the business started.

Like Johnny, Alusine created a niche for himself by selling a rare good that was visible and prized. The sale of extremely strong, sweet green tea that served as an energy drink for young professionals created a good reputation for him, as it was embraced as an alternative to the region's famous *poyo* in a predominantly Muslim town. His neighbor's son drew up an agreement paper to transfer sole rights of use to Alusine. Soon after, his benefactor died tragically, and the man's brother wanted to seize the shop, "threatening violence if I didn't give it back to him." Alusine took his grievance to the paramount chief, who sided with the landowner, saying that the shop was a loan and remained the Lebanese family's property. Alusine was bereft, but he had generated sufficient admiration from his regular customers that they rescued his business after the war:

> These guys I had known for a long time saw that the brother was just jealous, and that he wanted to take the business because it was successful. It didn't matter anyway, because the old base was spoiled completely during the war, and I had nothing to start with. Several of them

gave me money to start a new place, and I was able to buy this piece of land with the money, but nothing for a building. I was just trying to make tea out in the open, until one day one of the guys who had bought tea from me before the war came back. He had been a politician and when he came back after the war his party was in power, so he was also in power. He found me making tea in the open here and pulled hundreds of dollars from his pocket for me, which allowed me to build the structure that you see today.

Once his ataya base began making good profits, Alusine was able to also purchase land across the street and move his family into new accommodation. The establishment of a membership club in his business brought a steady income, and he was thinking about future construction. Just like Johnny, Alusine benefitted from multiple people "putting a hand under him" because, even though he was once young and needed help to get started, he started working before the war, when pity for an orphaned boy, and not a performance of seriousness, prompted people to invest in him. He was an uneducated young man who was visibly struggling, but this generated an agential cut of sympathy, rather than moral panic about his lack of will to be useful. Multiple times as we chatted he spoke of the people "in front of" him, and that he was still ready to take advice from his benefactors about his business, even as he was ostensibly an adult.

Alusine was forthcoming about the benefits of the base for its membership—that "elevated" youth (those with an education or a job) used their positions to counsel and "pull money" for their unemployed brothers—but he also had rules that prevented members from loafing all day. This was another exercise in seriousness, like membership dues, that prevented the base from becoming just another hangout for idle youth. Alusine wanted youth to "refresh themselves" with tea and conversation for an hour or two, but it was bad for business and bad for the youth if they spent the whole day talking and playing cards. The rules were akin to a two-drink minimum in bars. One cup of ataya had to be purchased for every ten card games, which kept Alusine's income steady and ensured that the youth were, in his words, "motivated" to use the base for "doing things in common" and not just idle talk. The dues were used in part for scholarships for members who impressed the club administrators (all of whom were educated) as particularly motivated, and Alusine advised the administrators on his choices for scholarship recipients. This meant that unemployed youth had to pay into their own scholarship fund while also having to perform seriousness of purpose to the other members and the owner to benefit from it. But what came from impressing the only adult who saw them regularly?

The commonness of ataya bases, their large memberships, and the composition of members across the social and employment spectrum provoked agential cuts from adults that the young people never intended, with *invisibility* and *inaction* observed where youth performed visibility and action (see Jusionyte 2015:241). The membership rules of ataya bases did not exclude youth who were always "half-baked" or "unserious" in their actions from hanging out (see Bolten 2013; Newell 2012), and being seen as an undifferentiated mass of youth could potentially backfire for members who were always serious, as the transgressions of one reflected badly on all (Cohen 1980:56). In addition, the bases were *not* sites of young men's own permanence, because the members, though they named the bases and ran the clubs, were also just customers. The pay to play system meant that the members risked reinforcing adults' perceptions that they were wasting their time and money on consumption rather than long-term goals. The bases, like trading boxes, were sites of *in/action*—an apparently advantageous step forward from sitting idle at home that replicated the same vision of idleness in large public groups. All members paid dues monthly, but only the most serious members benefitted from the scholarships that were awarded from dues, and any success they had was rarely recognized by adults as emerging from the base. In essence, youth were occupying sites they imagined as places of positive self-creation, self-presentation, and social reassurance, where adults saw a short-term consumption ethos, with youth wasting their money on diversions. For adults, ataya bases were trading boxes that were big enough to sit in.

The youth in the ataya bases worked hard to establish the moral basis of their encounters with adults, though their seriousness was not seen by adults, who had the impression of them as just loafing in public. I heard from many young men that the bases gained a bad reputation in 2007 when politicians, eager for the youth vote, arrived with crates of rum and bags of marijuana as gifts—politicians' agential cut that both discerns and generates ataya bases as not serious. As one member explained, "The elders were crying down the youth in 2007, saying that they were running around town with rum and marijuana, but where do you think the youth procured these things? The youth didn't have any money to buy rum and drugs, it was all the fault of the politicians! They thought this was what the youth wanted and then they called us criminals when they saw the youth using drugs!" Configuring youth as dangerous began with adults who imagined that the youth vote would be swayed by alcohol and drugs, creating the "folk devil" of the drug-addled youth that would return the country to a state of war (Cohen 1980:10). The ataya bases learned to guard themselves against politicians bearing gifts, of tempting their poverty with the tools of their moral condemnation. During the 2012 election ataya bases across Makeni banned alcohol and drugs, and politicians who offered these things were barred from entering. In essence, serious youth in the ataya bases continually performed their precarious respectability to adults who threatened it for their own gain, creating and reinforcing youth as a dangerous phenomenon by offering them the tools of their own demise. Youth in an ataya base revealed how performances of seriousness became idleness and danger, fueled through agential cuts made by adults that, by gifting alcohol and drugs, created the very devil they decried.

The Motorbike Riders Association: Boundaries of Il/legitimacy

The Makeni Motorbike Riders Association (MBRA) was the most contentious and visible organization associated with youth in Makeni. Motorcycle taxis emerged widely with the war's end in 2002, as young riders transported passengers and cargo on the country's ruined roads, which four-wheeled vehicles struggled with after years of infrastructure neglect. The popular perception was that motorbike riders were ex-combatants who committed atrocities in their home villages, and, forced to leave their families, rode in urban areas to survive. In Makeni, bike riding became popular during the occupation because people were afraid of walking around at night and private motorcycle owners offered rides for money (Bürge 2011:68). Riding commercially became associated specifically with ex-combatants because the RUF cadres were the only individuals who could leave the town between 1999 and 2001 and had access to gasoline. Residents who wanted to travel to Mile 91, an town that was still controlled by the government, paid combatants for rides. Riders dropped them at the edge of the occupation zone and left them to walk the rest of the way. Riders returned to Makeni once they had passengers who wanted to make the journey.

The practice boomed after the war, as young people saw riding as a way of earning enough money to "stand for themselves," in the words of one rider. They believed their work would be appreciated and lauded, as the majority of Makeni residents depended on the services of *okada* men[2] every day (Bürge 2011:60). The continued association with the war generated agential cuts of illegitimacy around them in everyday encounters with passengers, police, and policymakers, and, knowing this, they courted legitimacy partially through their headquarters. Acquiring, occupying, decorating, and self-consciously presenting themselves in a building were fundamental aspects of the okada men's efforts to gain respect and treatment as a labor association comprised of men, rather than as a rag-tag gang of boys.

In 2010, the organization was an association—it was striving to become a union, but could not call itself such unless it had been recognized by the Ministry of Labor—and was headquartered on a main road, next to a building supply store that was owned by their chairman. The freshly painted storefront was open to the street, with parked bikes spilling out onto the driveway and riders sitting on benches outside. On my first visit the treasurer sat behind a desk near the road, huge ledger open as he marked down the details of a disgruntled looking rider who sat on the bench. This was his typical post, as his main duty was ensuring that every commercial rider paid daily association dues in exchange for a "ticket to ride." A ticket was Le1,000 (about $0.25), and dues comprised the association's operating budget. The youth on the bench could not pay that morning, and his bike was impounded. The collectors who worked for the association rode up occasionally on other impounded bikes, with their riders as passengers, depositing them at the mouth of the headquarters so that they could either wait out the day, or leave on foot and return with the money. The front of the shop was a performance of legitimacy, as any observer could see the orderly execution of the association's rules and the high standards to which it held its riders (see Goffman 1959:35).

As interesting as the storefront itself was its history, and how the chairman, whom I call Pa Sulay, came to head the association and to also own a building supply store. The story is familiar, as it involves Sulay building trust with patrons before the end of the war, which provided him starting capital without undertaking the postwar performance of seriousness that characterizes younger men. This history is common knowledge among his friends but not among young okada men. Young riders imagine that he came by his fortune and respectability through riding, which drives their hopes that the same is possible for them.

Sulay lived adjacent to several RUF commanders in occupied Makeni. They knew him as quiet and honest, and at one point several of the rebels gave him their money every evening so they were not robbed by other rebels while they slept. Several months later, a high-level commander came to him with a request. He wanted to take his platoon on a looting mission to Guinea but had thousands of US dollars that he did not want to take with him, so he gave it to Sulay to keep until he returned. Sulay rolled the money in a tarp and buried it in his backyard. He waited for a year, but the commander never returned to claim the money. Sulay did nothing with the money until an itinerant bike rider reported that the rebels had been ambushed and killed by the Guinean army. Sulay dug up the money, opened a building supply store, and purchased a dozen bikes, which he rented to his friends to ride for him. Sulay eventually parlayed his success into two other building supply stores, opening one in Freetown. He never rode to make a living; he had only ever been a "master," a bike owner. As the chairman and a businessman he extended his legitimacy to the association, housing it in the same prominent building as his own business. It was easy for young men to connect his presence with the possibility for success as an okada man, as they saw it every day. According to Makeni residents who knew the association's history, Sulay's closest confidants—the treasurer, secretary, and vice chairman—were the first people to whom he gave bikes, and they all knew the stroke of luck that initiated his good fortune. The younger riders were unaware of this story, believing that any young man who just worked hard enough at riding would be as successful as Pa Sulay.

The townspeople needed okada men and respected Sulay; however, the legal troubles that riders experienced in 2010 were straining Sulay's legitimacy. In spite of the fact that neither he nor any members of his administration were ex-combatants, the typical agential cut generating "ex-combatant okadaman" meant their activities were interpreted with suspicion and fear by others. Ex-combatants who stayed in Makeni after disarmament often became okada men because they lacked the local connections required to engage in other work. Most riders rented bikes from masters—businessmen who purchased bikes as an investment—who required a daily rental fee, around Le10,000 ($2.50 in 2010), for use of the bike. Considering that the price of a ride within town was Le1,000, the rental cost was exorbitant, and many riders sped recklessly to acquire more fares. Most masters did not register the bikes nor provide licenses to their riders (which I explore in detail in the next chapter), and therefore any legal troubles fell on the riders. Their fear of being caught by the police, who were cracking down heavily on un-licensed riders in 2010, meant that any rider involved in an accident would "bang and go," fleeing the scene of the accident even if they left someone badly injured behind, in order to avoid the police. The public hospital had even created an "okada wing" for injured riders. It was a dumping ground where hospital staff could safely ignore them in favor of more deserving patients. Through the material association between the occupation, legal limnality, and hit-and-run accidents, okada men were configured as a menace and a threat, as dangerous youth rather than working young men trying to make honest livings.

In addition to these everyday troubles, the riders had a terrifying clash with the police and military over their use of public space in 2010. One of President Koroma's pet projects was to finish a clock tower in the central square of Makeni, and the contractor asked that the square be cleared on the day he started work. The square was a prime location for riders to wait for fares, and they refused to move, arguing that they paid taxes, so the government must find them a new parking place. The police refused their request, and the okada men moved dozens of bikes onto the square in protest. My research assistant was buying bread on the square when the police and military converged. A huge fracas resulted in damaged bikes and badly injured riders, and people fled in terror. When I encountered him, shaken, a few hours later, he explained that it was like the infighting of the RUF cadres during the war, when rebel fac-tions fought in the square and killed each other for territory. The refusal of the riders to move was an open plea to the government to recognize their legitimacy as taxpayers. However, the confrontation was so bloody that it reinforced the perception that riders were violent ex-combatants, and their use of public space was as illegitimate as they were, even as there was no legitimate place for them "inside" the social world (Diouf 2005:32). As Mbembe states, "It is precisely the situations of powerless-ness that are the situations of violence par excellence" (2001:133). The confrontation was a phenomenon, with violent youth emerging in that moment. If the police had negotiated with the riders, they would have been configured as taxpayers and citizens, and not ex-combatants.

These events stained Pa Sulay's reputation, and he stepped down as chairman and forced the riders out of his storefront. When I returned in 2012, the association had a new chairman, had relocated to a stand-alone building on southern end of downtown, and was working with the national bike riders union, located in Freetown, to gain union status for themselves. The new building was rented using the dues that riders continued to pay, and revealed new forms of legitimacy-seeking, new application of seriousness. The building's foyer, which was open to the road via large double doors, was covered in a mural. One wall featured British road signs, from stop signs to yield signs to forked roads and road works, even as none of these signs appeared in Makeni. The other featured a motorcycle and the association's new motto (see Figures 2.4 and 2.5).

On my first day hanging out with the new administrators, I asked them why the mural featured road signs that were absent from Sierra Leone. The treasurer was surprised, asking, "Don't you recognize them?" I answered affirmatively, and he continued, "We want people to know that the riders also know these signs, that there are rules and regulations to the road, they are something all riders should know, because they are important. Don't you think they are important?" I agreed that they are important, and rephrased my question: "How is it important

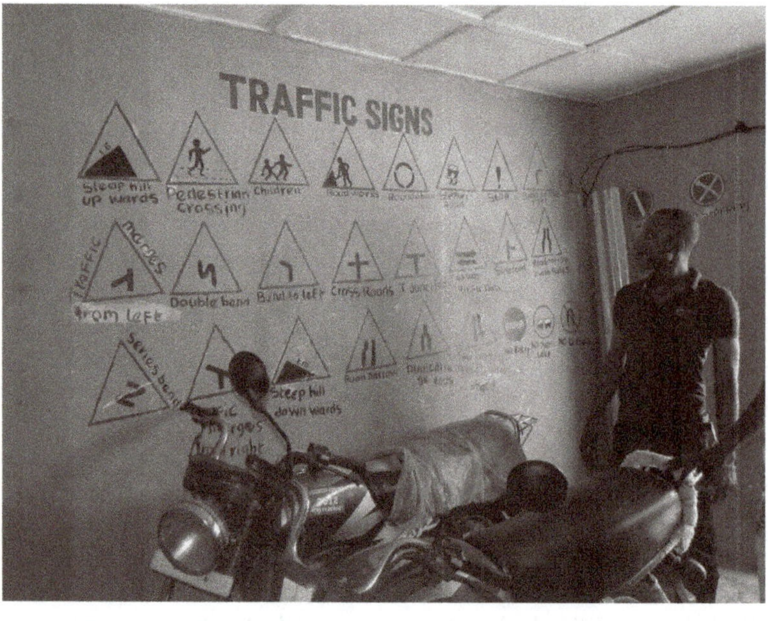

FIGURE 2.4 British Road Signs in Makeni.

FIGURE 2.5 **The MBRA motto.**

in Sierra Leone, when the signs don't exist here?" His answer tied the young riders to a performance of knowledge, and thus a request to be seen as legitimate: "Even though most of our riders do not have their licenses, because of the cost, they can still know all the rules and regulations. The lack of paper does not stop them knowing the rules and regulations, and now everyone can see that." The mural joined the riders in a performance of a global knowledge of road safety that transcended their limitations in Sierra Leone. Most okada men started riding because they were school dropouts, and yet here was a demonstration of the specific, worldly knowledge they possessed, an entreaty to be taken seriously. He explained further that residents relied on and despised okada men. The mural demanded that residents see riding as a profession, a body of knowledge, and a public service; that their value was not delineated by history or legal status. They wanted to be engaged with as service providing men, not reckless youth.

The office revealed the full extent to which the association strove to be taken seriously. My tour began innocently, when I revealed to one administrator, whom I call Saio, that I had met Pa Sulay but did not know the current chairman. His face brightened, and he said, "We have a picture of him!" We moved from the foyer through the middle room, which contained broken bikes in various states of repair, into the dark, dank back room, which had "Main Office" painted above the door-frame. It contained a beaten-up desk and broken chair, and on the desk were the remnants of an ancient computer. The screen was cracked and the keyboard was broken. A stack of ledgers sat beside it. A filing cabinet and table were behind the desk, covered in piles of magazines and on top, completing the scene, a trophy that Saio picked up triumphantly, exclaiming, "We won this three years ago in the city football tournament!" Around the walls were photos of the chairmen.

I studied the line of photos carefully, beginning with candid photos of the early administrators hanging out or standing astride bikes. From the previous two years, since the relocation to the current headquarters, there were four chairman in identically composed photos: sitting behind the desk with one hand on the ledgers and another on the keyboard, staring intently at the blank, cracked computer screen, which faced away from the camera. The magazines were lined up behind the desk, and the trophy sat on the filing cabinet (see Figure 2.6). Each photo used the symbolically significant materials of serious businessmen—computer, ledgers, filing cabinet—to create the impression, indeed, the physical imprint, of an association with a long history of professionalism. The magazines and trophy were incongruent with this scene, their presence a reminder of the unadulterated pride the riders took in their football victory, and also articulating their real differences with the adults they aspired to be. As Goffman states, "We expect coherence between appearance, setting, and manner, and the performance is less convincing when one or more of these is out of step" (1959:25).

This building was rented, and the cost rose every year, making riders ever more conscious of their impermanence in that location. In 2011 the rent was Le2.5 million (about $500), which the landlord raised to Le3 million (about $600) in 2012 despite having no other bids for the building. Even without bids, he simply moved the bar on the association to see if they could cross it. The riders were negotiating national union membership when we spoke in October 2012, and the details of how this change, with new costs and possible rewards, would affect their coffers were still unknown. They spent inordinate amounts of money keeping their temporary site, with the knowledge that at some point the rent

FIGURE 2.6 **Photos of the chairmen.**

might be too much, and they would have to move. They had invested huge amounts of time, money, and effort on performances of legitimacy in the mural and the chairmen's portraits. This reveals their understanding of the importance of articulating a dignified professional history to configuring a determinate identity as a union and as men, whether or not they had a permanent home, or even a working office. If the landowner decided to raise the rent again, it was no trouble to move the staging materials and portraits to a new location. What mattered was the appearance of seriousness that the site could convey through visual materializations of legitimacy. In the end, if they were forced out, the mural would be an imprint of their importance to the residents, at least until it was painted over by a new occupant or faded away with time.

The MBRA headquarters exemplifies what Goffman calls *idealization*. In short, "When an individual presents himself before others, his performance will tend to incorporate and exemplify the officially accredited values of the society, more so, in fact, than does his behavior as a whole" (1959:35). As the established, visible face of the MBRA, the headquarters exterior and the chairman photos reached to the height of respectability for its members, performing seriousness in ways that its members could not do in their everyday activities. Other youth also perform idealization, as is illustrated by the young man in the next section, who imagined that his work to honor the president would be celebrated and prompt him being seen as a man. However, his efforts caused tremendous friction among politicians who pushed him down vehemently, arguing that only real adults should undertake elaborate performances of loyalty.

The President's Statue: A Boundary of Il/legitimacy

I mentioned in the introduction that boundaries do not sit still, and up to this point it appears that anyone who achieves a recognizable imprint in the landscape has at least a small chance of being taken seriously. This is not always the case; as Barad makes clear, boundaries move and are reconfigured in every encounter due to agential cuts (2007). In the following example, a young activist called Dauda who commissioned a statue of the president reveals the configuration of "uppity" when a young person clearly does not know his place. The resistance Dauda encountered when he attempted to erect the statue in Makeni's main square is a quintessential example of how young men who take the risk of declaring themselves adults have boundaries of youth forcibly configured around them, of know-your-place aggression. In a situation of so many young people trying to get noticed, sometimes young men "throw eligibility to the wind" and put themselves in the public eye, risking failure in an attempt to be seen (Simone 2011:267). The risk was taken by a young man—socially ineligible for high status—who pursued the president's attention in a manner no local politician had considered, and so they acted forcefully to render him illegitimate. The single adult ally he had was in a precarious political position himself and was hoping to raise his own fortunes if the youth succeeded with his statue. The youth's opponents overcame his single supporter and the statue remained in storage, a significant reminder of how a performance of distinction and legitimacy can be cut as illegitimate through an aggressive boundary configuration excluding an uppity young person. Having invested all his money and connections in statue, Dauda lost his business and credibility, and as of 2017 was, according to his friends, "subsisting on the margins of life."

I met Dauda and his mother in the building supply store he had inherited from his late father. Though he had a profession that most young men dreamed of, he struggled to be taken seriously by his customers, most of whom mistook Dauda for the shop assistant. "I felt the problems of the youth so keenly; even if we are succeeding a little bit, our elders just don't want to know," he told me. "So I decided to start an organization so that I can make positive changes in the country." He started the Sierra Leone Alliance for Advancement from his storefront, pursuing projects to promote concrete changes in people's circumstances that would influence social change. Throughout our conversation he emphasized this: "The changes must be physical! They must show your work, and not just your talk." His emphasis on physical changes was inspired by the president, who also emphasized physical infrastructure in his development policy:

> Everything the president is doing is development activities. You see it, it is physical: the lights, the streets, so let us try to do something that is physical, let's try to get a token for His Excellency the president. If he happens to succeed in this election for the second term, then what will happen? The gift will motivate him to do more, so that Sierra Leoneans can benefit. If he fails, another person gets there, then what will happen? They will just try to copy his style. And people will still appreciate it. So we thought about what we should give to him, and we thought let's try to get a statue. As a symbol, this can't just be an image, a portrait is not enough. Let it be a physical symbol for Sierra Leoneans so that it can serve as a legacy. So we said, let's fix the statue on its base on inauguration day.

The plan was bold and imaginative. In commissioning a statue of the president, Dauda linked himself to the reasons he saw for the president's popularity, the material changes he had wrought around the country: roads, electricity, sidewalks, and public infrastructure. He also cited statues of famous leaders around the world—most notably the Lincoln Memorial—as a reason to "fix" a legacy of the president, thus also linking him to global histories of great leaders. Dauda wanted the alliance to rise above all other efforts to get the president's attention by linking his work into the president's emphasis on the material. He ushered me next door to his storage room. Between the bags of cement stood the statue, over seven feet high, with the president standing in the official robes of his office painted in red to match the colors of his party, the

APC. Around the base of the statue were the acronyms of every major and minor party. I mentioned how much I liked this touch to Dauda, and he exclaimed, "Yes, because for all of the parties, this is the man who represents you! It was very expensive for us, but we have to do things right." Dauda tried to do everything through the correct channels of local authority, to ensure he had the permission to erect the statue in a public place. His first stop was the president's deputy in the region, the resident minister for the north:

> So I went to talk to the Resident Minister and say that it was a gift for the president. And he said, "Oh, you guys can make it?" We said yes, he said, "Are you sure?" We said yes. He said, "You should make sure that you know the whole situation, because he is the head of state, so you should make sure that you have expert opinion on this." We said we didn't need expert opinion. If we fail to take chances, then we will never do the right thing. He said, "Really? You guys are wasting money, because at the end of the day maybe you will fail."

The implications of Dauda's conversation with the resident minister were clear: you *will* fail. This was not because Dauda and his alliance members lacked ambition or talent, or even that they lacked the money. They would fail socially, because a prestigious elder said so. This is a clear example of youth being configured in an encounter even with no precedent, with the minister's remonstrations generating the boundary between youth and adult. Dauda was unfazed. He raised money from alliance members and covered the rest by selling half of his business stock. The total cost came to 18 million leones ($3,500), a staggering investment from a young man who courted distinction and legitimacy straight from the president. And it was not just for himself that he did this, but for the alliance, as he said, "We could only get things moving nationally if we can get the Ministry of Youth and Sport involved, and so I thought this would be the way to get the president to join us to that ministry."

Dauda returned to the resident minister when the statue was complete, and the elder man was incredulous. He insisted that the alliance get permission from every possibly interested elder in town—the paramount chief, the mayor, the inspector general of police, the Ministry of Works—before he would grant permission to unveil it. All the "stakeholders" visited the statue, and were so impressed and alarmed that they reacted by "youthing" Dauda: "All of them appreciated the job, but they said, 'This job is bigger than you guys, how did you guys get this idea?'

So that was the end." Dauda thought it was the end, except the mayor loved the idea, and told him to raise the statue in the town's public center, at the base of the clock tower in Independence Square. This is the same square on which the okada men brawled with police two years earlier over the clock tower's construction.

The mayor had his own reasons to support the project. The APC party had rejected his bid for renomination, instead supporting a female candidate as a nod to the Truth and Reconciliation Commission's recommendations that 15 percent of political offices be held by women (TRC 2003). If the president loved the statue, he would be able to rise once again in party ranks. He sent his chief engineer to meet secretly with Dauda and help him pour the platform for the statue. Dauda was suspicious, because there were too many people who publicly opposed the project, and indeed one of them strolled by as the concrete was drying. The stakeholder stopped the construction, and that was where Dauda was left four months later: with an open tussle between the resident minister and the outgoing mayor, and no time frame for unveiling the statue. I asked him, "Why do you think they opposed the statue so strongly?" He answered, "Because they did not want us to grow." I persisted: "Why did the mayor support it?" The answer was short: "Because *he* wanted to grow."

Dauda did not resent the mayor's own reasons for supporting the statue, as the local history of patronage requires that sponsors see a return on their investment (see Bledsoe 1990, 1992; Bolten 2012a). The mayor risked nothing in supporting Dauda because his political career was otherwise at an end. For the rest of the politicians, Dauda explained that "jealousy is their policy." From the resident minister to the director of works, no one could believe that a young man had been able to execute such a gesture while they had not. If he had succeeded in erecting the statue it would have rendered him adult immediately, leaving the rest of the local political elite scrambling to distinguish themselves once again. What Dauda did was not revolutionary; it was just too good an idea for a youth to have. For that reason it could never come to fruition, and he was made to know his place. Soon after this failed attempt at recognition, Dauda found himself unable to pay the rent on his storefront and lacking the stock to cover his losses. He closed his business and was no longer a threat to the political establishment.

Structures—wood, concrete, plaster, paint—are physical performances generated from local and global inputs that generate, support, and configure social boundaries. They denote an interior and exterior, a physical imprint, and some kind of permanence—or impermanence—in the landscape. They also embed the individuals who build, decorate, and inhabit them in relationships of difference. As such they are fundamental to the boundaries that are generated between people in encounters. People' identities—the determination of who they are—are fixed in these moments in part through how their linkages with materials are performed and also interpreted. As structures are built, destroyed, moved, and repurposed, so do the concomitant social boundaries around individuals also change. As the design, purpose, and display of structures are deliberately linked to global historical and popular points of inspiration—Oxford University for the ataya base, the Lincoln Memorial for Ernest Koroma's statue, American rap culture for Amerikan Boy—so too are the individuals whose lives are materially mediated by these structures embedded in, and determined by, these global flows.

Notes

1. As Danny Hoffman writes for Liberian ex-combatants who invest in building finished, permanent structures that they know the government will eventually tear down, "The larger and more solid one's footprint, the greater one's claim to citizenship, understood here . . . as the right to compensation for one's work" (2017:54).

2. The word *okada* comes from a low-cost Nigerian airline operating in the 1980s, with Nigerian riders using the name to reference their ability to get passengers to their destinations quickly, but not necessarily comfortably.

CHAPTER 3

....

Papers

Documenting Boundaries of Il/legitimacy and In/distinction

I first met Ibrahim at the headquarters of a small political party, the United Democratic Movement (UDM), for which he served as regional public relations officer. It was a lofty title for a volunteer position. The party had a meeting scheduled, but the torrential rain had delayed most attendees, and so we sat on the porch. As we watched the sheets of water coming down over the roof, we talked about the upcoming elections and Ibrahim's own journey to political activism. It was accidental; as he emphasized, "I am not a political man." Rather, Ibrahim had spoken forcefully in a public forum about the problems youth faced if they lacked educational paperwork. A politician noticed his eloquence and offered Ibrahim this unpaid position. Hoping that it would bring connections that might one day get him a "real job," he accepted.

The impassioned speech stemmed from personal experience, as he explained: "I would not have been in a position to make that argument about education if not for my own sad story." Ibrahim's education ended when his school lost his paperwork for the West African Secondary School Certificate Exam (known by its acronym, WASSCE), which he was required to pass to graduate. "My own paperwork was submitted late, so I was not allowed to take the exam with the rest of the students." Not able to afford to take the exam through a private organization, Ibrahim left school empty-handed, with no prospects of attending college. With tertiary education effectively foreclosed, he tried to "gather papers" another way: "I joined this agricultural organization as a volunteer, because they promised me a job one day. After two years of volunteering, there was still no job. I had to leave, but I had my ID card from them, and certificates saying that I was a field technician. I then volunteered for another organization hoping for a job, but after two years and without my WASSCE, nothing. But they did give me another certificate in reproductive health education." He opened his backpack and handed me a file, dog-eared and worn, that he took with him to meetings, forums, and political gatherings—anywhere he might meet someone interested in his credentials. It was filled with certificates from local and national organizations certifying Ibrahim's aptitude in social organizing, sex education, tractor operation, and "data leader production," the last from an organization ostensibly offering computer literacy training. Ibrahim had paid to have each certificate laminated before adding them to his file. However, none of these informal qualifications had led to a job, because in spite of his performance of competence and perseverance, he could never produce his WASSCE results, which displayed the assessment and approval of that competence by the state (see Bourdieu 1996:376). A dozen certificates conveying ingenuity, flexibility, and drive failed to confer the legitimacy or legibility of a single school exam, as without the paper, he had no student identity that mattered (see Greenberg 2014:91). He sighed, and concluded, "Those in my class who were fortunate to take the WASSCE can get jobs. I can *never* get a job." I asked him what he was doing the next day, and he brightened, explaining, "The Internet café is offering a course in web page design, so I am enrolling tomorrow." In spite of insisting that only the WASSCE mattered, he pursued other paperwork with gusto.

Ibrahim's focus was signing a contract, which epitomized his understanding of "a job." Any position involving paperwork that articulated terms of employment fell into this category. The employment contracts I had seen ran to ten pages and beyond, incorporating dress code, nondisclosure of trade secrets, nonsolicitation, and noncompetition, signed by multiple administrators. One of my early research assistants joyfully e-mailed me a copy of his first contract, commenting that the stationary of the company was quite fine and that it was signed by six people. The longer, more elaborate the contract, the more signatures it contained, the more legible he was as an employee, the more legitimate the employment would appear to others, and it served as proof he was taken seriously. A contract bounded someone as adult.

Ibrahim's belief in the power of a contract was not the single story of young people's experiences with paperwork. On the contrary, illiterate adults saw credentials as a direct threat to their authority—it tested a different boundary of adulthood—and engaged in know-your-place aggression (Mitchell 2013). Uneducated adults de-legitimized the credentials of young men, while educated adults articulated the superiority of their own credentials because they were held by men with wisdom rather than by uppity youth with papers. As young men performed with their paperwork in their encounters, so did adults continually configure a boundary, redefining wisdom and experience around qualities that excluded their younger counterparts, reconfiguring what paperwork represented in order to emphasize their own superior acumen.

I witnessed know-your-place aggression one day as I spoke with two brothers in their fifties who owned a metalwork shop where they trained young men in welding. Family poverty had forced the brothers out of school without credentials, and we spoke in Krio, the local lingua franca, about the importance of skills training for uneducated youth. They pointed to their half-dozen apprentices and repeated several times that although the apprentices had all left school without their WASSCE, they were capable of making beautiful metal doors and gates (see Figure 3.1). The apprentices worked quietly, often averting their eyes when speaking to their bosses, answering questions with, "Yes, sir." As we chatted, a young man entered the workshop and approached the men, a new file folder in his hands. The men initially ignored him, but he refused to leave. One brother, clearly annoyed, turned and asked him in Krio, "*Wetindu yu don kam na ya?* [Why are you here?]"

The young man thrust a file heavily laden with laminated paperwork forward and answered in English, "Please sir, I am looking for work as an accountant. I could do your bookkeeping." The brothers stared at him, incredulous. One pushed away the file, and answered in Krio, "*No yuse yu big English wit mi! Mi na yu elda, yu na smɔl pikin! Yu no fityay mi!* [Don't use your "Big English" with me! I am your elder, you are only a small child! How dare you disrespect me!]." With the men clearly uncomfortable conversing in English, articulating a preference for training uneducated youth who knew their place, this encounter created an upstart youth out of a young man trained in accounting. His crime was not just his use of English but being a "small child" with no right to approach his elders unsolicited. Cut as il/legitimate, he quickly stuffed the file into his bookbag and left, his head bowed.

FIGURE **3.1 Young metal shop apprentices.**

Papers—material performances of knowledge, competence, and recognition—are a principal place where encounters consistently configure boundaries around youth. Papers in Sierra Leone are *fetish objects*: they represent in a condensed, dehumanized form the people who possess them, and they have real social power to determine one's life chances and opportunities (Marx 1906:83). As I mentioned in the introduction, they are also *boundary objects*: simultaneously representations of completely different things to different people (Bowker and Star 1999), in this case, the legitimacy of their holder. Young people acquire, preserve, and display a spectrum of paperwork, from Ibrahim's ID card to the aspiring accountant's WASSCE certificate, in the hopes that documents will convey their seriousness. They hope that impressive documents serve as extensions of themselves, and distinguish them from other serious youth so that their status is not only defined for them by others (see Reed 2006:175). As Ibrahim's experiences revealed, educated adults take advantage of ambitious young men without credentials—his life after secondary school was a string of unpaid positions—but rarely feel compelled to treat them as actors of consequence. On the other hand, uneducated adults openly disparage educated young people, arguing that youth are credentialed young people who fail to know their social place, and brazenly try to jump into adulthood without the necessary life experience. They will only assist young people whose lack of credentials and risk-averse behavior render their performances unthreatening to historical boundaries of adulthood.

Paperwork is an integral substance to boundary configurations around adult and youth, although paperwork boundaries also do not sit still. At one moment paperwork enables a person to be taken seriously, in another it renders one an illegitimate upstart. There is no consensus in the urban areas, where farming and secret society initiation are no longer paramount to understanding productive personhood, as to what counts as knowledge, and therefore how it should generate adulthood in encounters. This chapter starts with the "credential race," the drive to acquire paperwork conveying the superiority of the holder over those who lack documents. The chapter then examines how people use documents to convey legitimacy—betting on the belief that documents are so important (so fetishized) that they force others to take the holder seriously. It then moves into an exploration of the contested history of the written word in Sierra Leone, focusing on the role of literacy in self-representation, as occurred when literacy was proposed as a requirement of Legislative Council representatives in the 1940s.

Paperwork became especially important during the intensely globalized postwar period. With education disrupted during the war, documents took on new significance, as youth traveled with their documents to prove their civilian status. After the war, papers were required for jobs with international organizations, which stoked the fires of resentment of "upstart" youth among uneducated adults. This resentment sparked a "credential race" (Collins 1979:191) between adults and youth, with adults pursuing degrees to defend their social status. The chapter finishes by considering how individuals who lack credentials court legal and economic legitimacy by generating their own paperwork, even as it encourages them to be judged illegitimate. The MBRA logged bribes to police and payments to residents hurt in accidents, which reinforced rather than undid their illegitimacy with authorities and residents.

Documents became a more powerful mediator of boundary generation after the war than they were before it. Before the war schooling was neither universal nor compulsory, and degree holders were a minority.

After the war, the demand for qualifications among international organizations fed the credential frenzy. This massive shift in the education landscape disturbed the fundamental reason Sierra Leoneans in the twentieth century sought education, which was distinction (see Bolten 2015). This creates agential cuts of in/distinction: youth who hold certificates are not seen as particularly serious or worthy because they are just like hundreds of other youth. The association of young people with documents also generate boundaries from il/legitimacy: paperwork is either deemed proof of degenerate status (as with the MBRA) or proof of impudence, as occurs in encounters between young people and uneducated adults.

Paperwork as a Global Fetish

That young people in Makeni habitually carried around their carefully preserved qualifications may seem odd at first; however, the practice sheds light on an older globalized fetish for written documents, and documents as a shorthand for knowing the person who holds them. For the last hundred years, school certificates and degrees offered social mobility to some people while being dead ends for others, depending on the assessed quality of the certificate, and thus of person holding it, and the landscape in which the degrees were acquired. Outside of the realm of education, the success of individuals who wanted their concerns to be taken seriously, whether by state officials, NGOs, or elites, often hinged on them being able to produce written documents to support their claims. An individual's ability to use paperwork was often the node around which their social, economic, and political mobility turned (see Gupta 2012).

The history of education in the United States makes clear that documents are forms of representation that produce differentiation—boundaries. A person with a degree from an Ivy League university is much more likely to rise through an applicant pool than is someone with a degree from a lower-tier university, as the degree is shorthand for their intelligence, motivation, and likeliness of succeeding (Collins 1979:32, Dore 1997:5). On the flip side, school dropouts are seen as morally inferior, lazy, and possibly also stupid (Woronov 2016:2). Because the US system has no branching points—there are no places within the schooling process where students are sorted into different life trajectories—education becomes a form of *contest mobility*, a race to acquire the most, and most highly regarded, credentials (Collins 1979:91). Sierra Leone's school system is similar, as students who do not pass their exams are driven out of school. For those who complete all the levels, their credentials are the same.

Education in the United States and in Sierra Leone is a private rather than a public good (Labaree 1997:2). The goal is *only* distinction: students do not strive to become better citizens or useful workers. They strive to surpass others by getting the best grades, exam results, and university offers, and hopefully attract the attention of potential employers (Bolten 2015). This renders education fundamentally a process of acquiring and performing paperwork, rather than fostering thinking or acquiring knowledge (Dore 1997:11). This drive for distinction creates a global phenomenon that Ronald Dore refers to as "the diploma disease," namely the impulse to acquire more and better credentials to stand out in an increasingly crowded field (1997; Birzle 2017). Education is defined only by the perceived quality of the paperwork. This question is vital in Sierra Leone, as a hallmark of traditional adulthood is that adults possess life wisdom, which people only acquire with experience. Whether paperwork can substitute for wisdom, or supersede it, generates boundaries between youth and adult in their encounters.

There are many examples of the social cost to young people of the credential race. China adopted an exam-based mobility system in the mid-twentieth century, and a national exam in ninth grade determines the entire course of a student's future. Failing the exam means quality secondary education and tertiary education are foreclosed forever (Woronov 2016:6). Those who pass the exam, on the other hand, compete for university placements and high-paying jobs. Those who do not are banished to the lower echelons of society, even as the grading curve means that 50 percent of students fail (Woronov 2016:2). They occupy the "precariat": precarious lives of low-skilled, transient jobs with few benefits, little security, and no future (20).

In India, lower-middle class young men form the glut of the country's millions of educated unemployed. They wait for jobs, a situation generated by their parents' ability to pay for their education, however without the social networks to rise through a fiercely competitive job market (Jeffrey 2010:11). These young men engage in class-based practices of distinction, using speech, clothing, and manners to differentiate themselves from the uneducated masses, even as the masses may be employed (Jeffrey et al. 2008). Unemployed secondary school graduates in Ethiopia replicate these practices, refusing to perform manual labor they consider beneath them (Mains 2012:74). They believe their degrees denote a difference that matters: a boundary between themselves and the uneducated. Sierra Leone is part of a larger global pattern of credentials creating masses of unemployed, struggling students and graduates who use their degrees to perform their desired distinction.

Papers are also key components of self-presentation for uneducated youth and can be *more* important to them than they are to students, because they link young men to socially recognized forms of legitimacy. Uneducated young people recognize that one does not need a degree to be gainfully employed; however, their ability to get a bank loan, navigate bureaucracy, or defend themselves in legal situations hinges on their ability to handle documents. Poor people around the world engage with, or avoid, relationships with the state through the medium of paper. In Pakistan and India, for example, the government exists through its documents, which means that a request or complaint is not real—has no existence that matters—unless it is paperwork (Hull 2012; Gupta 2012:208). The importance of paperwork for the poor cannot be overstated if they are targets of police harassment, such as migrants in Russia, whose paperwork is subjected to more or less scrutiny depending on whether the bearer looks Slavic enough (Reeves 2013:517). In essence, if someone looks out of place, their fate hinges on the existence and believability of their paperwork. There is no better illustration of this kind of scrutiny in urban Sierra Leone than scruffily dressed youth on motorbikes, who "look like they have no papers," according to many adults. Similar to the drive to inhabit a structure, they are also obsessed with generating, acquiring, and displaying paperwork.

The Complex History of Paperwork and Social Position in Sierra Leone

In conducting archival research for this book I sorted through hundreds of boxes on Sierra Leone, which were stored in libraries and archives in Freetown and London. The archives hold a history of *who* has the power to produce paperwork, to state their opinion, have it read and responded to in some way, and to have it deemed important enough that it was logged and stored. Until the country achieved independence in 1961, British colonial officials produced most of the documents, which revealed a preoccupation with how, to what extent, and to what end to educate the "natives." That focus, which was based in the larger colonial project of spreading "civilization" in Africa, left a lasting trace in the archives and in the entanglement of documents and personhood today. The education system in Sierra Leone during the colonial era was designed to provide the British administration with an efficient, docile workforce. However, the moment it was instituted, Sierra Leoneans recognized its possibility as a private good, capable of advancing the goals of individuals and communities. Their belief that education produced distinction is evident in the battles that took place around literacy.

The most important divide existing in Sierra Leone's early colonial history is that between the colony—the Freetown peninsula where the Krio people were the dominant social and economic actors—and the protectorate, encompassing the rest of modern-day Sierra Leone, and home to its "tribal" people. The Krio had been beneficiaries of missionary education since the 1700s. The first primary schools were established in Freetown, and the Krio had been the first students at Fourah Bay College (FBC), which was founded in 1827 and is the oldest university in West Africa (Alie 1990). Tasked with educating lawyers, doctors, and other professionals, FBC solidified the Krios' position as the social elite. Education in the protectorate, which began a hundred years later, was guided by a completely different ethos, that of producing "better Africans," in the words of H. S. Keigwin, the first director of protectorate education. His philosophy, articulated in 1928, is worth quoting in whole:

> It must be remembered that we are educating Africans to be better Africans, not imitation Englishmen. The premature teaching of English, so ignorantly clamoured for by unrealizing people, is, especially when accounted by bad teaching, or by overemphasis on book English, is fraught with definite harm . . . it is clear that it may become a force for actual disruption of the home, a breaking down of home and local cohesion, and may be the cause of false pride, contempt for natural ties, and a disorganizing restlessness and insubordination among the growing youths. This has already been voiced by many chiefs and leading men. The future prosperity, health, and happiness of the people lie not in unreasoning migration to towns along the railway, or to other over-stocked centers of unskilled employment, but in an enlightened understanding of the values of local effort, local hygiene, and purposeful homelife. (CO 267/630/6 1928)

The goal of education in the protectorate was not professionalization or literacy—these were hallmarks of Western education and available only to the Krio. That young people especially were clamoring for English was because they understood the power of the English language in the colonial world. That chiefs and leading men would see this as a cause for concern resonates almost a hundred years later, with the illiterate artisans seeing the young accountant's request for work as insubordination and a threat to their social position.

In 1930 the document that formally established education in the protectorate officially undermined Keigwin's ideas that literacy would feed "insubordination" among the youth. With a dearth of British and Krio teachers available for the protectorate, local teachers were hired if they were functionally literate in the vernacular, meaning they could read and write Krio. The 1930 Education Ordinance also set the minimum age for teachers at nineteen for men and seventeen for women, making teenagers acceptable authority figures for their peers if they could read (CO 267/630/6 1930). The colonial administration took care to limit instruction in English outside of Freetown to only a privileged few, notably at the Bo School for Boys, which was described in the previous chapter (see Corby 1990).

The protectorate chiefs who had access to Bo School took great care to maintain their privileged position in the education hierarchy, and to link the schooling of their sons decisively with the advantages conferred by the elite status of Bo School. When a proposal was put forward in 1931 to merge the Bo School with Koyeima College, whose mandate was to train local youth as teachers in village schools, there was an immediate uproar (CO 267/632/12 1931). The chiefs were outraged that their own sons would be mixed with village youth who were not learning English, which would blur the class distinctions that had arrived with colonialism. Six years later, the standards at Bo School had deteriorated to the point where graduates were being denied civil service jobs. Most chiefs promptly withdrew their sons, sending them instead to Prince of Wales School in Freetown, where they mixed with Krio students (CO 267/661/14 1937). Chiefs configured formal education as a private good whose primary goal was distinction, in their case, maintaining their position, and that of their sons, above illiterate Sierra Leoneans.

The issue came to a head in 1948, when the colonial administration considered creating a literacy requirement for membership in the Legislative Council. Paramount chiefs from the protectorate who wanted to join the council argued, according to one, that "it is a privilege and duty of government to appoint members to represent the Protectorate, but . . .

it is a betrayal of such privilege and duty for Government to appoint one whose educational standard is not above the inarticulate masses" (CO 267/691/3 1948:1). Many council members mocked the habit of illiterate chiefs of leaving their council document envelopes unopened and then taking them home as souvenirs (2–3). They argued that only formal education rendered a chief worthy of governing. This echoes the notion mentioned in the previous section that graduates are intelligent and hardworking, and dropouts and illiterates are lazy and stupid. Other councilors defended illiterate chiefs, noting that one could be educated and unintelligent, or uneducated and intelligent (4). The older paramount chiefs admitted that they were silenced by their illiteracy and had no choice but to allow younger, educated chiefs to speak, and hope that they spoke wisely. Simultaneously, they articulated fear that educated youth who were not "rightful rulers" might influence their neighbors to vote them onto the council, upending the centuries-old hierarchy of rule in the rural areas. These debates show that the question over whether education creates better leaders or causes intergenerational tension is very old, and that the contours of the boundaries around wisdom were just as problematic seventy years ago. Paperwork was becoming a fetish, but one that could not merely be undone by touting traditional wisdom. The effects of documents on a person's life chances and social relations were becoming real and consequential (see Burke 1996:6).

After independence in 1961, education was transformed to conform with local understandings of "wealth in people." Parents went to great lengths to enroll their sons, even if it meant sending children to live with relatives or strangers in distant towns, because children would enlarge the parents' own network of social and economic ties (Bledsoe 1990). An adult who invested in a child's education expected to benefit from that child's future success, as they had "blessed" the child with their assistance (Bledsoe 1992). Children would not succeed without these blessings, no matter their intelligence or capabilities. This meant the emphasis in formal education was not on learning or thinking, but on generating and nurturing social networks that could provide jobs. Teachers were respected because they had social connections and the power to grant or withhold school certificates, and not because school lessons had practical or social value (Bourdieu 1977:172, 1991:153). Only students blessed by their teachers could succeed.

The entanglement of school documents with students' life chances intensified in Makeni in 2010, when the first two private preparatory academies opened. Tuition at both schools was high, with the average elementary pupil paying Le1,000,000 a year, about $220, a price tag that delivered qualified and well-paid teachers and well-resourced classrooms. The academies only hired teachers who had bachelor degrees in education, while government schools required a much more easily attained teaching certificate. Government schools were also underresourced, overcrowded, and teachers were underpaid—often not receiving salaries on time, or not achieving the approval that allowed them to be paid at all. The results for students were striking. The private schools achieved the highest exam success rates in the city, with one school boasting the top two WASSCE scores in the country in 2012. These students were rarely configured as youth because their position as children of the relatively wealthy precluded the need for them to perform seriousness, as their postgraduate jobs were assured. They never needed to collect certificates like Ibrahim, because, by dint of the entanglement of the tuition their parents paid, their WASSCE results, and their social connections, they were already people of consequence.

Paperwork and Agential Cuts During and After the War

Though the civil war began in 1991, Makeni was untouched by major fighting for the first five years, and there was little disruption to education during that time. Makeni had a dozen elementary schools and two major high schools when the war began, and students made great sacrifices to stay in school even when the town was overrun by displaced people, occupied by hostile forces during a coup, and continually threatened by rebel incursions (Bolten 2012a). All government schooling stopped in December 1998, when the three-year RUF occupation began. Many of my interlocutors who were students during the occupation mentioned that keeping their documents safe was a primary concern. This was because paperwork facilitated a young man being identified as serious, intelligent, and committed to the existing social order—everything that rebels were assumed *not* to be. Any young man traveling outside his home area courted suspicion as a rebel, especially if his clothes were torn or he was injured. Carrying one's paperwork—school ID card, exam results, written schoolwork—facilitated observation not of a young man's distinction from others, but of his legitimacy as a civilian. Adults assumed that only "real" civilians cared about education, and if a youth with paperwork was also humble and soft-spoken—the opposite qualities of a brash, arrogant rebel—he might escape encounters with police or military with his life. It did not matter to most people that the majority of RUF cadres had once been students; what was important was the material proof.

The relevance of the stuff of civilian status was heightened precisely because the war was entirely indiscriminate in terms of who was brought into the fighting. Most of the former RUF members I spoke with talked extensively and with great longing about their time as schoolchildren, and invariably that their paperwork was lost during the war, forever foreclosing an identity they had hoped to occupy again at the war's end. One RUF member tried to return to school in Makeni in 2004. He wore his best clothes to a meeting with the headmaster, spoke English as proof of his educated status, and begged to be given a chance. He was told that without paperwork he would have to pay Le500,000 to take the primary school leaving exam—with ten-year-olds—and go from there. He could not bear the humiliation of being infantilized instead of helped, and so left education forever.

Young people risked plenty in attempting to maintain and recover their status as students. According to one, "I kept my school documents in a plastic [bag], and hid it under my bed, so that the rebels would not find it and I would still have it after the war." Without the certainty of the war's outcome, students knew they had to maintain some kind of stock in trade. Many young men tried to leave Makeni, cross rebel lines, and make it to government-held areas. Every youth I interviewed who attempted this took his school papers with him. A different youth I call Abdul described being stopped by soldiers at a checkpoint after he left Makeni. He had gashed his leg on a branch when skirting a rebel checkpoint, and was limping and bloody when the soldiers accosted him. They demanded proof that he was not a rebel, or they would execute him. Abdul's secondary school ID card and his junior high school exam certificate were two years out of date, but they were enough to convince the soldiers that not only was he the person he claimed to be, but that he was a serious student and not a rebel. He explained, "I demanded to know why I would be careful with my school papers if I was intent on overthrowing the government? I told them that I wanted to help lead Sierra Leone out of war, and I could only do that if I could go back to school once the fighting was finished." His documents saved his life, and he was able to present them to the headmaster of his old school in 2001, when the school reopened: "The papers were dirty and torn, but the new headmaster accepted that I was in Form Two [eighth grade] when the rebels came, and he returned me to that class so that I did not have to start over." His few pieces of paper were the only thing that stood between him and the humiliation suffered by the ex-combatant who met with a headmaster with the same goal and no papers.

Once the war ended in 2002, Makeni was flooded with humanitarian aid. This created new opportunities for youth who could utilize paperwork, and was a source of postwar tension between educated young people and their uneducated elders. Organizations from Europe and North America needed local people as cooks, drivers, program managers, coordinators, and liaison officers. Even knowing how badly Sierra Leone's education system had been disrupted, they had official hiring protocols to follow. All positions required an application and supporting documents, especially if the job was a coveted white-collar position as a clerk or manager. These office jobs were much better paid than unskilled work, and many of them went to young people who could complete paperwork and produce school documents.

One young man, Abubakkar, explained the tension that arose in his neighborhood when he and his neighbor, a much older gentleman, applied for the same job with an ex-combatant reintegration NGO. "We came to the office on the same day to apply for the job as a workshop leader to these young guys, and I sat at the table filling out the application and he sat with the pen just staring at the paper. He would look over at me and ask what details they were requesting, and I explained it all to him and he said, 'Why don't they just ask me these questions? I can answer them personally.' He didn't understand that to be an official application, they needed the piece of paper." Abubakkar was also able to produce a university degree and provide other supporting documentation, which his neighbor lacked. The interview process was rocky for the older man, as Abubakkar related hearing from the other side of the door of the office. "He kept repeating that as an elder it is his job to counsel the youth and make them act appropriately, that he has this wisdom, life wisdom, that earned him his respected position as elder. He couldn't answer their questions about qualifications or official positions that he held in the past. They kept asking him why he didn't fill in the application form, and he was ashamed to admit that he is illiterate. I don't think he has ever been ashamed of that before." Abubakkar, junior by twenty-five years, was offered the position.

Abubakkar was not the only youth to achieve coveted salaried positions with international organizations, nor was he alone in being chosen instead of someone older and ostensibly more experienced based on paperwork. In Marxist theory, paperwork is a fetish in that it develops an independent existence from the person whose labor produced it, and has significant power to alter their life chances, for better or worse (Marx 1906:83). In postwar Sierra Leone, regardless of one's intelligence, wisdom, or social standing, a person who could not present a piece of paper extolling their virtues and speaking the language of the employer—in this case, the application—had their personal worth diminished. To be an elder in Sierra Leone means that one's community recognizes his social achievements and his wisdom, especially when it comes to guiding the next generation (Lahai 2012). That a recognized elder would be shamed for his illiteracy and passed over in favor of a young man with papers was too much for their relationship to bear—it undermined, rather than merely shifted, all previously existing boundaries. Abubakkar had always been respectful and polite to his neighbor, but the older man was aloof and distant afterward.

The war and its aftermath created a double bind for young men who could produce paperwork. On the one hand, documents had saved many of their lives. On the other, youths' facility with documents colored encounters with adults who had never needed to materially mediate their performances. By 2005, when most humanitarian organizations began withdrawing from Sierra Leone, documents became a key focus for young men's performances of seriousness, their knowledge, their histories, indeed their entire worth as people. This nurtured know-your-place aggression as a boundary configured around youth who ostensibly used paperwork to try to jump the boundary into adulthood—indeed into elderhood, as Abubakkar was effectively doing by taking a job counseling ex-combatants. It did not matter that Abubakkar needed the job to marry his pregnant girlfriend. Local social codes required that the wisdom of the most senior person be recognized, and in this case it appeared that the youth was rewarded instead for his ability to write his address and phone number. This kind of social leap threw the boundary around adulthood into question, generating encounters where "uppity youth" emerged.

This begs the question of whether Abubakkar *was* more qualified for the job, and highlights the apparent incommensurability of formal schooling and life wisdom in the current moment of globalization. The emergent universality of formal schooling paperwork favors the individuals who can collect it, but still reveals nothing about who should be treated as a person of consequence. Is education just documents, or is it proof of an equivalent wisdom that is the fundamental marker of adulthood, making it possible for youth to be configured as adults? Abubakkar's neighbor was appalled that someone who lacked the life experience to counsel young people would be formally employed to do so—this was an inversion of the social world. The second problem is that the schools are flooded with serious students, creating problems of in/distinction. Abubakkar got the job instead of his older neighbor, but there were a hundred other applicants who were also turned down. The position required a high school diploma, and Abubakkar was the only applicant with a bachelor's degree. This kind of credential inflation (Dore 1997) hampers young people's ability to stand out unless they double down on acquiring more, and better, pieces of paper (see also Jeffrey et al. 2008:202). Adults reconfigure the boundaries around youth in many ways, most notably in this case by joining the credential race and emphasizing that one needs education *and* life wisdom to stand out.

Configuring Youth Through Credentials

In 2010 I was assigned to advise a student called Alpha as he finished his bachelor's thesis at a university in Makeni. His research involved survey-ing youth around Makeni about their employment experiences. Some of his survey results were important for education and labor policy, es-pecially the notion among youth with diplomas that it was the govern-ment's responsibility to create jobs for them because they had answered the government's call to pursue an education for the benefit of the nation. He found that young people wanted to be rewarded by the gov-ernment for doing what was asked of them, a clear indication that they were not trying to overthrow adult authority (see Sommers 2015:176). This was especially interesting considering that the dominant political conversation at the time revolved around how educated youth believed they were above manual labor and wanted to jump into elite status. I asked Alpha what he was planning to do with his research results once he finished his thesis.

"I will use the thesis to get my degree," was his answer.

I persisted: "But these are important insights into the thinking of youth, that they aren't trying to overthrow elders, they just want the elders to put a hand under them. Don't you think the Ministry of Youth and the Ministry of Education should know this?"

He seemed not to understand the question, and elaborated, "Well, the thesis will go to the university library and I will get my degree, and then I can get a good job, maybe with a ministry. Then I can give them my recommendations."

Alpha was completing his degree in development studies, a hybrid social science that the vice chancellor, a Sierra Leonean priest educated in Italy, designed to respond to Sierra Leone's lack of indigenous social policy researchers. The course combined qualitative and quantitative methods with development theory to train students to tackle the country's most pressing problems. Alpha had chosen the major because he thought it was the most likely route to obtaining a job with an NGO: "If the organizations see that I was a development studies major, they will know that I am the right person." He saw the job landscape a decade after the civil war as one where humanitarian NGOs were simply replaced by development NGOs, and they would be most likely to hire someone with his particular qualification. He had not thought further about why he was pursuing the development studies major. Alpha's perspective was typical among college students in Makeni at the time, with development studies second only to accounting in popularity, because, as many students articulated, "all businesses need accountants."

If Alpha did get a job at a ministry, it is not clear whether he would be able to perform the job well, or if his serious self-presentation would instead be seen as a bluff—misdirecting and deliberately misleading his employers—because he had not developed critical thinking skills (Goffman 1959:60). He had produced survey results without thinking about their worth as data. Instead, he focused only on being able to maneuver well in the credential race. Alpha was clearly serious about graduating—he had passed his examinations, was writing his thesis assiduously, and cultivated a professional disposition—and thus would make a good initial impression on employers. However, as Goffman articulates, "The attentive pupil who wishes to *be* attentive, his eyes riveted on the teacher, his ears open wide, so exhausts himself in playing the attentive role that he ends up by no longer hearing anything" (1959:33). In other words, Alpha, and many students in Sierra Leone, are so caught up in performing seriousness—epitomized by attaining documents—that they struggle to articulate or undertake other goals for their education. This, as adults affirmed, is why they are foolish instead of wise, and why adults disdain young people brandishing paperwork when they encounter them.

Paperwork is fundamental to serious students' conception of education, and paperwork is precisely why their holders, all pursuing the same goal of employment, are *indistinct*. Students taught to cram for exams, repeat information verbatim, and write to please professors fail to stand out because they share this skill set with every other student (see Bledsoe 1992; Bolten 2015; Bourdieu 1996; Dore 1997; Labaree 1997). This mass pursuit of credentials also fuels negative encounters with adults because serious students often fail to internalize knowledge in their pursuit of credentials, but mistake one for the other. According to one adult, "These youth get their papers but they cannot engage in debate as to why corruption is bad or development should benefit everyone. And then if you correct them they defend themselves saying they have degrees. They are educated but they know nothing." Adults who had returned to school often spoke of youth lacking the sense to get anything worthwhile out of their degrees, whereas adults had the wisdom to make use of them.

Of the many encounters I had with the credentialing fetish while teaching at the university, none better epitomized the entanglement of paperwork with youth than what my fellow professors derisively referred to as "this pamphlet business": teachers compressing exam information into a few pages of notes that they either gave or sold to the students. In doing well in his exams, Alpha had proven his adeptness at memorizing information for the purpose of getting the answers right. During the time I worked with him I also taught an undergraduate course on mass communication, and the students asked constantly when I would give them their pamphlets. I emphasized that they should read the books and take notes. I reiterated that studying in groups would help them retain information for the final exam. Distraught, the students arrived early for class one day (this was not normal), and formally presented me with a petition they had all signed politely requesting that I provide pamphlets within a week. The petition stated that the students were happy to pay for copier costs, and that they collectively wanted to do well on the exam, hence the need for pamphlets.

The student who presented the petition on behalf of his classmates stood before me as I read it silently, eyes slightly downcast as he reiterated their plea: "We, all of us, want to do well, Dr. Catherine, to please you and get good marks so we can get our degrees. Do you not want that?" As someone who had the power to grant or deny a coveted degree, I was the person to whom they turned for the blessings that might have a profound effect on their future encounters with adults (Bledsoe 1992). A poor grade was not a reflection of their knowledge as much as it was me judging them unfit to recommend to others, or to "put a hand under them." Giving students exam notes is anathema to education from a perspective of instilling critical thinking for empowered citizenship and innovation. It allows no possibility for understanding the level of student knowledge or engagement, only their capacity for rote memorization (see Bolten 2015; Jeffrey et al. 2008:47). However, from the perspective of students who want to please their professors by doing well, the pamphlet was the only thing that mattered. Any effort expended in ways that might not be reflected on the exam—and thus might have no bearing on my judgment of them as serious or competent—was wasted effort. Achieving perfect exam results accomplished two goals: a higher level of commendation on their degree, and ostensibly greater admiration from their professor, both of which might influence the encounters they had with employers and other elders. There was nothing outrageous about their desire for pamphlets, given the landscape in which educational qualifications had become fetishes.

The substance of encounters between formally schooled young people and their elders was also shifted by adults acquiring their first degrees after the war. This trend emerged alongside the humiliation suffered by older men when they were outcompeted for NGO jobs by youth with BAs. Between 2010 and 2012 about a third of students enrolled at the university were adults, in the sense that they were treated as independent actors of consequence by others. Their configurations of uppity educated youth are epitomized in the opinions of a man I call Tejan. In our conversations, Tejan was adamant that education was only useful when accompanied by wisdom, as a functioning society required a division of labor where wild and inexperienced youth undertook the manual labor that would tame them, humble them, and make them respect and appreciate their elders—especially their educated elders. Only those people who had finished "running around," had a family and had to pay their own way, were serious because they had experience, a drive to succeed, and the wisdom to transform formal schooling into impactful careers. For everyone else, including all young people, it was a waste of money.

Tejan had himself parlayed his high school diploma and informal business training into an auto parts store in the early 1990s. He got married and supported his family, but lost the store when rebels looted it during the occupation. Tejan had saved his account ledgers, which allowed him to secure a loan and reopen his store after the war. It was robbed and burned in 2006 in an incident Tejan was convinced was engineered by one of his competitors: "You see, Catherine, the landscape of business here in Makeni was getting very competitive after the war, and some people will do anything to pull you down if you are successful." He again sought and received credit to reopen the store but decided that the cutthroat nature of the business made it too risky.

Tejan decided to return to school even though he was in his forties. He enrolled in paralegal studies, which he chose for the same reason young people did: "This was the first course in paralegal studies offered in the country, so I thought that if I pass this course, my degree must be in high demand. There are only ten of us this first year, only ten paralegals in the country! Not too difficult to get a job!" Though he was only a year into his program, Tejan was confident he would find employment. He wanted to get his degree while he was still "vigorous"—not too old to stand up to the rigors of the work—but also believed that his older age made him a better fit for an office job than his younger classmates:

> I am a bit advanced in age, but I am still vigorous, and I am still determined, and I get cross when the youth say we should give these opportunities to them because even with the same degrees, they have better energy for the job. Pah! You see lecturers at this university and they are in their seventies, and with this job, I don't need to be going up and down [the road] all day. Let the youth who has so much energy go up and down all day. They will one day be old and then they can sit behind a desk. Even if I am infirm, then at least I can write paperwork and lecture to other people. Law is a field that keeps you reading until you die. So at least I can be sitting in my office, passing good information to my children, as long as I want to be alive in this profession.

Tejan believed that to be an adult conveyed the right to have one's degree recognized because one had replaced physical vigor with intellectual vigor. He emphasized that youth should be performing manual labor because they can—indicated by the ability to "move up and down all day" as did Mohamed the cigarette vendor in the previous chapter—and being taken seriously meant one recognized that this vigor cannot last forever. Tejan's agential cut on vigorous young people was that they were performing youth, rather than consequence. Credentialing for adult students is a matter of enjoining their degree with life wisdom, earned rest, and articulating those who can do manual labor as youth, qualities that have long been attributed to the rights of elders more generally in Sierra Leone (see Richards 1996; Ferme 2001; Shaw 2002). It was adults' abuse of young people's labor that many scholars attribute to fueling the civil war that so unsettled intergenerational encounters (Archibald and Richards 2002; Hanlon 2005; Lahai 2012), with Peters arguing that many rural youth joined the rebels because they were fed up with living in conditions of "modern slavery" (2011). Tejan's argument resonates with a pattern of encounters where sedate wisdom and energetic foolishness configure adult and youth.

Tejan believed adult students were more serious than their young counterparts who lacked true life experience that would lend them gravitas. He expounded readily on his greater willingness to study for exams than younger students because he had a family to think about:

> Young students have not experienced life, and they are not feeling the pinch of paying their bills, someone pays it for them. Their clothing: somebody does it. Their feeding: somebody does it, and they are not feeling the pinch. How does their money come? From their mother. So at the end of the day, you see some of them taking to drugs, taking to alcohol, taking to those societies [fraternities], not minding the effect of those things on their parents. I share the view that mature students, especially those who come back after some struggles and still want to make their way academically, they are more focused, they are more serious. So that is the facts.

Tejan configures college-aged students as social children—not to be taken seriously in encounters because they depend on their parents for everything and could not possibly have the life experience to teach them to be sober. This renders them simultaneously degenerate and uppity. For many adult students I spoke with, the struggle of accruing life wisdom was the only thing that rendered a degree meaningful and valuable. They also believed that parents suffered only moral and social injury if their children goofed off, with no consequences for the children. Adult students, on the other hand, had to consider how their reputation affected their children. Though there were a few lucky students whose parents paid their fees, Tejan made no effort to differentiate between them and the young who scraped pennies together day by day to acquire their degrees, with no assistance from family members.

Adult fear of "degenerate" students was founded in worries that popularity had the power to overcome the authority of wisdom. One young man Tejan cited by name had graduated two years earlier and was employed by the university as a supervisor at the age of twenty-three because of his stellar qualifications. The young man had boasted that his staff loved him, which an administrator commented occurred because he maintained low expectations for them, and often failed to show up for work himself. He quit his job to run for local political office, which was a relief to administrators who hesitated to fire him because of his popularity—and their fear that outrage over his firing would overcome their will to raise employment standards. One day in the canteen I deliberated his suitability for political office with several students who knew him. After twenty minutes discussing the relative importance of popularity, wisdom, and education, they concluded that he was, in fact, a good candidate for public office. The reason? In short, "He is educated." In spite of everything they knew of his behavior, nothing was more a more powerful mark of his qualifications and credibility than his credentials. And nothing places adult arguments that wisdom should be taken more seriously than credentials in a clearer light.

This episode was ample reason for Tejan to dismiss younger students. He also cited the fact that many of them failed to show up for their exams as proof of their laziness, when in fact university policy barred students with unpaid fees from taking exams and receiving their degrees. He interpreted the empty exam room, after a semester of a full class, as proof that the young students had not studied. "When exams are coming, I don't mind coming here and spending all night preparing myself. So I always tell people, if I fail an exam, people will always ask: If you knew you weren't going to make it, why did you go? So I go the extra mile! The students who don't show for the exams know they will fail, and they do not want to disappoint the lecturers." Tejan grasped the will of students to gain blessings from their professors but had conflated that will with the financial ability to do so. Those students who had the most to gain from attaining a degree, and the most to lose by sacrificing everything they had to still fall financially short, were the ones who could not, in the end, be taken seriously. Adult students configured their encounters with their younger counterparts through the empty exam-day classrooms, generating agential cuts of laziness and lack of wisdom based only on absences and silences.

Documents and Il/legitimacy

Students were not alone in fetishizing paperwork; documents were deeply entangled in whether businessmen were taken seriously, and youth emerged as both dangerous and uppity in this realm. Mohamed the box trader was effusive in his praise of one particular man whose business "lifts my spirits," as it was proof that finding the right niche could bring security to uneducated men. Di Fambul Tile Shop (The Family Tile Shop) was located on one of the town's main roads and was owned by an elderly man I call Umaru, who was widely known as shrewd, hardworking, and illiterate. His workers referred to him as "the big boss," and his story epitomized the problems that capable, respected, uneducated adults have when engaging a system requiring paperwork. It illustrates how the ability of young people to use documents to mediate—sometimes malignantly—between their elders and bureaucracy feeds the configuration of uppity youth illustrated by the metal shop owners at the start of the chapter.

What immediately differentiated Umaru from the majority of my interlocutors was his discomfort with Krio, the most common language heard on the street of this large town. It indicated that his illiteracy extended further than documents; even a language spoken by most urban residents was out of reach. We conducted our conversations in KaThemne, Umaru's native language, with his son translating. Umaru had started the tile business thirty-five years earlier with two bags of cement, and through hard work had been able to support his two wives (Umaru was a polygamous Muslim) and their children. However, the success of the business was not a result of steady profit. Umaru relied on contracts, which waxed in the dry season and waned in the rainy season and came and went with business boom and bust cycles. This prevented him employing people full time, and he was concerned that his product quality was not consistent because he was forced to rely on casual laborers. Their work was of a variable standard and they worked on their own schedules. He also struggled to maintain sufficient capital to make enough cinderblocks to secure contracts from large businesses that only paid when a job was completed.

Umaru had approached multiple banks requesting loans to stabilize his business. Every bank in Makeni turned him down, because, in his own words, "It is not enough that I am a man of experience, that I have been doing this since I was twelve years old and I know the business.

They ask me, 'How will you keep the accounts? How will we know the way you are using this money? Do you know how to do sums and figures?' Because I cannot answer these questions, they say it is impossible. If there is no paperwork, there cannot be a loan. It isn't enough that they can see the shop here, it hasn't moved, that they know me by sight." I suggested that he hire someone to do his books, and after a few years of ledgers they should be able to get a loan. This caused murmurs of consternation among his assembled family. One of his wives disappeared into the house and returned with a photo album. She flipped through it, found the page she was looking for, and passed it to Umaru.

He frowned when he looked at the picture, which he then passed to me. Staring unsmiling at the camera was a man in his twenties in a suit, a watch and gold ring displayed prominently on his folded hands. "Sheku," Umaru said, "was my secretary after the war. He did me very, very badly, very badly indeed." Umaru hired Sheku, who had an accounting degree, as he ramped up his business to take advantage of the building boom that accompanied the postwar aid swell. Sheku started account ledgers for the business, showing Umaru pages of numbers as proof that he was working, knowing that Umaru could not assess the meaning of the paperwork, except that it looked good (see Riles 2006a:19). Sheku had written false receipts and purchase orders, and had cooked the books to hide the money he was funneling to his own business. After embezzling from Umaru for two years, he absconded from Makeni with what remained of the tile shop's cash and was never heard from again.

Umaru sighed. "I need someone to do the books, a young person who won't demand money that I don't have, but there is no way I can verify. What if he is using me? What if he makes all of this paper and I take it to the bank for a loan, and they tell me it is all bad paper? Then I will lose face publicly, and no one will help me." Umaru's concern about bad paper reveals the mystification of paperwork among uneducated adults, and the justified fear they have that tainted documents, which they cannot tell from good documents, can have lasting negative power over them (see Gupta 2012). If Umaru sought a loan with falsified paperwork, a loan officer would refuse him and potentially blackball him. Umaru would limp along with foreign contracts that he could afford to take based on his cash reserves, and any competitor who could get loans would likely force him out of business. For Umaru, paperwork and accountants had transformed from a path to legitimacy to the documentation of his illegitimacy. He felt safer simply operating the business "from my own small money" than finding another educated youngster to produce documents. For illiterate adults, young men who could create paperwork were dangerous, and encounters configured with them reflected this danger.

The metal shop owners who were so dismissive of their would-be accountant at the beginning of the chapter had a similar problem. The brothers needed to build an addition to their workshop, after which they could seek the official government recognition that would allow them to issue certificates to their apprentices. They needed a bank loan to do this, and an accountant. Though their needs were at odds with their maligning of the young student who spoke "big English," they saw no contradiction. This was because the certificates they issued would be attached to skills rather than "paper learning" and would come from the old structure of the community: its wise adults. As one explained, "This welding work is much better than formal schooling, because at the end of the day, you can prove that you can do the job. If one of these guys [waving generally at his apprentices] asks for a job somewhere and the person says, 'Okay, prove that you can make a door,' then you give them the metal and tools and by the end of the day you have a door! They can do the work! But if we had government recognition as a place that teaches the skills that youth should be craving, we could make our workshop known! And then we could find the money to grow the business. The business is here! It just needs to grow."

The logic of the argument rests in an understanding of wisdom and permanence as adult qualities that can be rendered to resonate with the expanding requirement for paperwork that seemed to be the handiwork of the young. The argument that welders can prove their skills reveals that the brothers reject the documentation acquired by formally schooled youth as proof of skills and competence—rather they see it as reams of paper and arrogance, with no substance. Wisdom is acquired painstakingly over time, through the guidance of a community of practitioners led by artisanal masters (see Lave 2011). The brothers believed that if they could convince more youth to become welders with the promise of government recognition of their skills, they could expand their workshop and earn more respect. If they could produce that paperwork, they could procure a loan. However, the requirement to have paperwork in order to acquire paperwork was an obstacle. The brothers were prevented from registering themselves as a government-approved workshop, and also from getting loans, because they could not produce account ledgers, tax receipts, and finished contracts. They had a receipt book for materials and services rendered, but that was not sufficient to prove the shop's history. One brother handed me a blank receipt, a small yellow slip that had the workshop's name, First Stop Metal Workshop, address, and cell phone numbers on it. He explained the importance of the receipts: "You see, we exist, permanently. This land belonged to our father, and the workshop will always be here. If you keep this you will always be able to reach us here. Our apprentices are working, and even when they move on they still show their appreciation for us." The receipts did not give insight into the quality of the business; they were merely another form of proof that it was real (see Heimer 2006:103).

Echoing the importance youth attached to cinderblocks and plaster, the brothers saw the shop as legitimate because its physical and social presence echoed the historical entanglement of adulthood with the land, buildings, and equipment they owned, and the loyal apprentices they trained. Their approach adhered to a model of "wealth in people" (Miers and Kopytoff 1977; Nyerges 1992), where these material entanglements specifically configured adults, a goal to which serious youth were perpetually striving. In this case, wisdom has concrete dimensions—visible in the land, the workers, and metal products—that were absent from paperwork, however carefully laminated or however elaborate the government stamp. The conception of adult and youth emerging between artisans who lacked formal schooling and youth who clung to their paperwork existed in the tangible proof of wisdom: its permanence. Documents, as opposed to workshops, were thin, fragile, easily lost, and easily contested.

"If I Had These Documents, They Would Save My Life"

For okada men, public legitimacy and physical safety could be achieved with documents. In one of my first interviews with an okada rider, he described riding as a last-resort occupation. His explanation was cogent and striking: "Riding is not easy work. It is soldier's work. Too risky. Like a war you are fighting against society. You always have one foot in the police station, and one foot in the grave. If I could afford the documents that would save my life—the riding [driving] license, the registration for my bike—I would have enough money that I don't need to do this business." The association's headquarters was one way it fought riders' configuration as dangerous, lazy, and criminal. Their desire for and use of documents was another.

My work with the riders reinforced the experience of the artisans who lack formal education by highlighting that there are two kinds of documents: the official paperwork issued by institutions and their agents, which often has profound legal, social, and economic consequences for its holders (see Hull 2012; Gupta 2012; Reeves 2013), and the paperwork that people produce themselves, like the metal shop receipt book, which, though lacking legal weight, may be vital for individuals striving for recognition from others (see Goppert 2013). For the brothers, the receipt book connected them with their customers and merely symbolized a business that was permanent in every other way. For the okada association the struggle to obtain legal documents, particularly drivers' licenses and motorcycle registration certificates, was tied to their ability to become legally legible to the state and its actors, notably the police and the courts. Acquiring these documents would enable new performances of legitimacy as public service providers, rather than criminals who were arrested at police whim and were refused treatment in local hospitals because their injuries resulted from alleged illegal riding. The paperwork they generated themselves—most notably account ledgers and riding tax receipts—were key aspects of cultivating legitimacy (and warding off accusations of embezzlement) with the national union and among their own members. This was true even as the ledgers revealed extensive illegal activities and the price paid for them, notably in bribes to police officers and funeral costs for riders who died in accidents. That they showed me these accounts reveals the desire to prove that they were not profiting off their riders but were instead assisting and defending those riders, even as they showcased their legal illegitimacy. The irony of the bribery paperwork was that it also highlighted the illegitimacy of police practices; however, the power to utilize this stuff of bookkeeping to exclude others lay entirely with those who were already actors of consequence—the police officers themselves.

The okada riders' problems began with the motorcycles. The vast majority of MBRA members rode bikes that they rented from masters, as I mentioned earlier, and most riders had to accept whatever bike they were offered, even if it was smuggled from Guinea and was not registered. Registration was Le700,000 per year at the time, and most masters did not bother because the riders were legally responsible for the documents if pulled over. With a single ride fare set at Le1,000, and over eight hundred registered association members in 2012, the margins riders made were extremely slim. The market for okadas was saturated, and most riders reported only twelve to fifteen fares in a ten-hour day. Coupled with the expense of a Le300,00 a year riding license, the master's rental fee of Le10,000 a day, and the daily Le1,000 association tax, riders' ability to make ends meet every day was as questionable, and their finances as precarious as their physical lives. One rider I call Ibrahim summed up the situation of having his survival depend on absent documents eloquently:

> This driving license issue is the biggest problem. To collect enough money for the license is impossible. After you pay the daily tax, you still have to find something to eat, somewhere to sleep, and medicine for your pains. It isn't easy. There is never enough to save for a license. You have to give the 1,000 every day. To get the 300,000 for the license, it is impossible. This is the main thing that worries all of our brothers. People who don't have to do this say that it is fine employment because it is always there for us, but it isn't fine if there is anything else to do, anything else at all! If I can ride all day and get so much money that I have 10,000 at the end of the day to feed my kids, then it is great. But that is only if every day is the best day it can be.

Ibrahim explained that the police "give us trouble for absolutely everything." Other riders chimed in, listing the offenses for which they had been arrested: riding in flip-flops, overloading the bike, not wearing a helmet, not giving their passenger a helmet, and so on. A rider pulled over for any reason had to produce their license and registration, and without them, was arrested. Someone would have to alert the association of the rider's plight, and it would be up to the association to gather a sufficient bribe to release them. The fine was always more than the cost of a license but a bribe was always less—Le100,000 was a standard bribe—rendering it cheaper to enable continued informal police corruption at their expense than to ride legally (see Weiss 2009:53; Sommers 2012:170). The bike masters were another part of adult abuse of okada riders, as in addition to collecting bike rental fees, the police returned impounded bikes to the masters if they could prove they owned the bike. The riders I spoke to reported that masters were happy to let the rider languish in jail, with many riders finding that their bikes had already been rented out to someone else by the time they were released.

In October and November of 2012 the precarious lives of unlicensed, unregistered okada riders took a violent turn when six riders were murdered in Makeni. It was the riders' undocumented status that left them vulnerable, as it was generally the consensus among my interlocutors that unlicensed riders could make more money and avoid the police by riding at night. Fares doubled once the sun set, and as the police day shift ended, riders were less likely to encounter patrols. Those riders most desperate to earn money—to eat, to pay the masters, and to save money for documents—sometimes slept overnight next to their bikes in the public squares while waiting for fares. They became easy targets for thieves, who killed them in their sleep and rode away on their bikes. The outcome of these murders was not greater protection for okada riders, but a more complete police crackdown on undocumented riders and manipulation of the association to suit police purposes. The police articulated riders as the source of the problem, and the acute vulnerability of the riders ensured they were powerless against the new policy.

After two murders occurred in two weeks, the police proposed a solution, which involved targeting unlicensed riders who attracted bike thieves, instead of the thieves who committed deadly crimes. The police instituted an okada curfew, with unlicensed riders banned from the streets after nine p.m., while licensed riders were sanctioned until midnight. The police mandated joint patrols with the association, where riders teamed up with motorcycle police after dark to visit the parks where riders typically waited for fares. Not only did the association have to pay for the gasoline for these patrols; the only arrests that came from them were of unlicensed riders who, while being questioned by police if they had witnessed or been victim to bike crime, were unable to produce their own documents. The other spate of arrests was of riders who had been caught breaking the curfew. In appealing to the police for assistance with and compassion for their plight, okada riders received yet more aggression from adults, configuring them, and not their would-be murderers, as dangerous and illegal.

One of the few ways the association met the problems of their documented illegality was by producing their own paperwork. They believed this paperwork linked them to larger legitimate structures of taxation and accounting, and also proved to their own members and to outsiders that their performances of good management were honest. Just as occurs around young people building, decorating, and occupying structures, performances designed to produce a notion of legitimacy had the opposite effect. Their honesty created even greater friction with the police and the public because they revealed the full extent of police bribes, rider deaths, and accidents that injured or killed civilians.

I pored over the logbook one afternoon with the treasurer, asking him about what the various expenses represented. "De bang" was any payment made to a civilian who was hit by a rider and represented the standard admission fee to the government hospital. Funerals for riders killed while working varied in cost, with riders who had been association members longer receiving more expensive funerals. Those who had languished with injuries, which the association often tried to help with by paying hospital fees, were given more basic funerals if their treatment had already been expensive. One of the most common line items was "to police," which involved jail fines, court fines, bribes to avoid jail fines and court fines, and bribes to officers who had witnessed crashes to convince them to walk away. Much less frequent were line items for the purchase of helmets for riders, one of the few pieces of equipment the association could afford after bribing the police, nursing the injured, and burying their dead.

The push to keep accounts emerged from concern among riders that the administrators were embezzling the daily tax. The membership was 500 riders in 2010 and over 800 riders in 2012, amounting to hundreds of thousands of leones ostensibly collected every day, with riders who were unable to pay having their bikes impounded. The riders continually demanded to know where it went, intimating that the leadership was "eating" the money off their own riders' sweat and blood. The treasurer was hurt by these allegations, as he explained, "The police will make whatever changes to the laws that they want, and institute fines for everything, and we have to do everything in our power to keep them off our backs. We continue to pay them, for every little thing, so that we can keep our riders on the road."

In furtherance of this quest, the association attached itself to the national bike riders' union in late 2012, from which they began purchasing "official" union tickets for the riders' daily tax (see Figure 3.2). This move was meant to encourage the police and local government to interpret them as legitimate, as they were being taken seriously by a government-recognized union. The fee the Makeni association paid for the official union's paperwork cemented them to the larger, ostensibly legitimate structure of a union that had links to official political structures, but this

FIGURE 3.2 The new daily ticket issued by the national bike riders' union.

meant that even less of the tax collected went into their own coffers. As they paid more to the national union their operating budget suffered, leading to cheaper funerals, more trouble with bribes, and further allegations from their own members that they were being cheated. Stoking the fire were reports that emerged in October 2012, just one month after the association joined the national union, that the national chairman had been arrested for corruption and embezzlement. Apparently the union leader, once a bike rider himself, could not resist taking advantage of his younger counterparts once he himself had made it.

The association's internally generated and circulated paperwork documented the violence of a life of riding, and the impossibility of achieving the legitimacy that it sought through the very act of producing paperwork. Rather than the documents being proof of honesty and good business sense that the administrators could take to the bank for loans, development programs, or humanitarian assistance, their honest performance of their accounts instead revealed their abuse by the police, the legal system, and their own national union, and that they met these practices with bribery, payoffs, and complicity. Il/legitimacy speaks to the aggression that emerges when powerless youth address their exclusion and abuse through documentation. Instead of being taken as actors of consequence in encounters with adults these documents instead contribute to, reproduce, and represent the boundaries of "dangerous" and "criminal" configured around them by adults.

What is in a piece of paper? From the moment that colonial administrators generated paperwork about Sierra Leoneans, they initiated a process of entangling people's identities with documents—whether educated or not, licensed or illegal, truthful or deceptive—that was emerging around the world. From the war, where young people's lives literally depended on their paperwork because of those documents' power to reveal them as civilians, to the postwar period where laminated certificates from NGOs denoted one's suitability for employment, paperwork has been a key site for the performance of one's serious identity vis-à-vis others. Because of paperwork's origins in Western systems of education and bureaucracy, every encounter that begins with documents entangles a young person within long-standing global trends of how seriousness is known and standardized. It is a medium for perceiving and judging others, and for presenting the best version of one's self. As such, it also contains the inverse power of revealing weaknesses, and potentially making visible aspects of one's identity—illiteracy, bribery, failure—that undermine rather than support one's performances of seriousness.

The difficulty for young people of performing their serious selves through their documents is the inability to control the agential cut, namely how that documentation—and thus their identity—is observed, understood, reacted to, and acted upon by others. Whether a young aspiring accountant is congratulated on his achievements and given a job as a serious young person, or is berated for attempting to humiliate his elders as an arrogant youth, or scolded for his lack of life wisdom as an uppity youth, is singular to every encounter with another person, each of whom possesses their own unique entanglements with paperwork. What is the same in each case is that documents are *fundamental* to the configuration of these boundaries of exclusion, and that these documents are embedded in long global histories of performance that first became important in Sierra Leone through formal schooling and literacy.

CHAPTER 4

Cloth

In/visibility and the Social Skin

My friend Wusu always carried a backpack, and one day it became a site for a literal unpacking of the entanglement between a young man's social identity and the materials of his everyday performance of self. In 2004 and 2005, when Wusu began high school, it contained his notebooks, pens, books, and study guides. In 2010, when he started his job hunt, it contained his exam results, secondary school certificate, and documents certifying his status as a final year student at the local polytechnic university. The backpack was merely heavy in 2010. Two years into his job search, in 2012, the pack was bursting at the seams. Though he spent many months unsuccessfully looking for a permanent position, the impending election made him hopeful, as politicians were hiring youth for their campaigns and foreign organizations were also hiring election programming officers, with possibilities for long-term employment offered. The employment opportunities did little, however, to explain why a bookbag suddenly looked packed for a camping trip.

We walked quickly between a series of appointments—from a local think tank hiring researchers to conduct an election survey to a local mosque whose Imam was hiring youth to run his nonviolence outreach campaign—and Wusu was trying hard not to break a sweat. He was going through his collection of clean bandanas rapidly, mopping his brow repeatedly and wiping his back under his shirt to prevent his freshly laundered polo from looking damp and crumpled. As we approached the think tank's offices he stopped briefly to compose himself, and spent a few minutes smoothing down his shirtfront and attempting to pinch new creases into his linen trousers. Wusu scrubbed half-heartedly at his muddy leather shoes with a damp bandana and called to a small boy inside a nearby shop to bring him some water and a brush. The boy obliged, and Wusu washed and buffed his shoes. After five minutes of preparation, we proceeded to his first appointment. The interview went seamlessly but ended on what seemed an odd note, as Wusu inquired of his interviewers if there was an empty room in the compound he could use briefly. His interviewer pointed him to an empty guard hut near the gate, and he disappeared, emerging a few minutes later transformed. Gone was the Western outfit, replaced by an indigo *shalwar kameez*—a traditional Islamic outfit of a long, embroidered shirt and loose pants— and a white *kufi* cap covering his head.

Our next appointment was at the mosque, but it was not a Friday, the Muslim holy day, which would have accounted for the clothing change. It was also not an hour of prayer, which would have also made sense if Wusu had planned to pray before or after his appointment with the Imam. He noticed my quizzical look and smiled shyly, gesturing to his backpack, which he revealed contained yet another change of clothes. "It is vital that I look my best for these meetings." I acknowledged the importance of making a good impression, but pressed him on this point: "I think everyone in Makeni understands that you can be a good Muslim without always wearing Islamic dress, and you can be a good researcher while being Muslim, so why not just choose one outfit and stick with it?"

Wusu's answer revealed the importance of presenting adults with committed performances of his identity, which he believed gave him more control over his interviews. "I have to make exactly the impression they want from me, and not ask them to dig for my motives. If I come to this secular think tank dressed in a shalwar kameez, maybe they think that I have no room in my worldview to be a scientific researcher, that I am not as serious about election surveys as I am about the religious side of politics. If I go to the mosque dressed in my urban [Western] clothes, maybe the Imam thinks that I am not a good Muslim and would hire someone with my same qualifications who is." We walked to the mosque, and the Imam, who had just finished his other job as a school-teacher, greeted us dressed in gabardine trousers and a button-down shirt. Wusu joined him inside for his interview, and emerged half an hour later, grinning. As we left the mosque, Wusu anticipated my question with the comment: "I do not regret going in Muslim dress, even as he was wearing Western [clothes]! Everyone knows he is an Imam."

The backpack was not just stuffed with clothes; it contained a wealth of information about the role of "the social skin" (Turner 2012) in influencing the agential cut adults make when observing young people in their encounters. A decision about how someone looks is not just an observation; an agential cut is what gives the observation substance—that looking over how someone is dressed generates actions that lead to their inclusion or exclusion. Though there was nothing socially inappropriate or unserious about Wusu attending either appointment dressed in any of his outfits, by mapping his clothing onto distinctions between his social environments, he acknowledged both the importance and the thinness of his own social skin (see Cole 2008:103; Greenberg 2014:76). A thick social skin is a good metaphor for understanding the entanglement of clothing with discourse in the configuration of youth. The Imam is socially thick-skinned because of his visible, repeated public performances of his role, and thus is created as a powerful elder in encounters with others no matter how he is dressed. The young man, socially thin-skinned and unable to command space for visible, repeated performances, can be produced as serious or unserious, uppity or lazy, professional or useless depending on the form of observation made on his clothing by an adult. As "youth" is an inherently indeterminate identity, clothing is the most visible and consistent material entanglement that influences how young people emerge as a phenomenon through encounters with others. Wusu presented an image that left little room for interpretation, granting him as much control and predictability over his encounters as possible (Goffman 1959:10). Young people's clothing is what Goffman calls their "personal front" (25), namely the performance they carry with them at all times. A young person might not always have his paperwork or be in the building through which he displays respectability, but he is always in his social skin, which is the most immediate mediator of his self for others.

Clothing is the most critical part of youth's self-performance for several reasons, the most important aspect being that it can be misleading (Goffman 1959:59; Diouf 2003:9). It is the first impression that a young person makes on an older observer, before his speech or his mannerisms and the more "ungovernable aspects" of his performance—such as a regional accent or uneducated language—can be gauged and assessed (Goffman 1959:7). It is the opportunity a young man has to be judged legitimate and serious and opens the door to a longer encounter, even if he has nothing else to back up this first impression. Clothing requires none of the intellectual or time commitments of paperwork, none of the physical toil of erecting a structure. It only requires enough money to purchase a few pieces of attire, just as one would pay for membership to an ataya base. There is nothing stopping a homeless, unemployed youth from owning a suit and creating the impression of being serious. A tailor is not interested in whether his client is a white-collar professional. A youth who can pay for his suit is free to make any impression he wants, even a misleading one, and this is also why clothing is such an important material entanglement generating "dangerous" youth.[1] In Sierra Leone it is known as "bluffing." Bluffing can be any form of showing off, whether it is adding a strut to one's step or wearing clothes far costlier than one should be able to afford in an effort to look more successful than one is. Between 2004 and 2012, with education costs rising and little possibility in the overcrowded, run-down town of building their own structures, many youth invested instead in their wardrobes.

Clothing is vital to young people's ability to influence the agential cut made from their encounters because of the degree of control they have over their social skin. Their bodily performances can court respect, thus making them adults, even if only in some encounters. More than just performing one's seriousness through education and physical permanence, clothing can combine with other materials synergistically to produce a lasting impression on others. A young man may possess a dozen professional qualifications, but no one he encounters will know this initially. A young man can stand inside a government building without anyone assuming he works there. However, for a young man with credentials in a suit standing in a government building, his encounters with others will be generative of being treated with consequence, as all material mediations of his performance lead to the conclusion that he belongs there.

Youth become visibly serious when they dress professionally, and they can act with confidence around adults because they are projecting the image they wish to inhabit. Bluffing through clothes is how young people influence the boundaries configured around them, and, as importantly, present their willingness to sacrifice to do so (see Newell 2012:38). It is a "locus of a language of aspiration" (Nuttall 2004;

HasHemi 2015:273). For serious youth, the cost of acquiring a professional wardrobe—a youth may go without food to acquire a suit for job interviews—can be prohibitive and may damage their health and life chances if their bluff results in them being thought of as dishonest. However, the boundary configured around them if they are dressed shabbily will always be negative, therefore the risk—a defining feature of youth—is *always* worth the potential result. For youth gambling on a nice suit getting them a job there is little to be gained by *not* striving to enact an expensive display. Any youth who wants to succeed must, in some way, use clothing to create a "phantasm" to influence his reality (Hoffman 2017:42), to reincarnate himself in his desired image (Gondola 1999:24).

Young people pay a price for enacting seriousness through clothing, and this occurs in two ways. First, every young man who purchases expensive clothes strives for visibility through distinction from his fellows (Bourdieu 2010). Individuals like Wusu dress impeccably for each occasion, but with so many young men adopting chameleon-like dress habits to make good impressions, clothing generates similar agential cuts of in/visibility as do ataya bases and school certificates. Second, the mass adoption of professional dress habits and exploration of global fashion trends have unpredictable results with respect to how adults observe and act on those observations. Current fashions have diverged enough from traditional clothes that they have generated moral panics, initiating a contest between young people and their elders to define the social contours of appropriate dress. Youth and their elders struggle over whether Western clothes such as denim jeans and tank tops denote global connection or nostalgia for the war; whether modern European suits reach the political and social prestige of handmade, colonially inspired safari-style suits; whether jerseys from English football teams denote misplaced energy and hooliganism or a transformation of sports loyalties into political loyalties. A final consideration is that initial impressions do not last; young people must maintain respectability even if they have a single suit and are literally unable to change clothes. As the suit wears thin, so does their social skin.

This chapter begins by framing young people's drive to dress "well," in their own words, within larger trends of fashion, respectability, and bluff in West Africa and elsewhere in the developing world (see Gondola 1999; Newell 2013). Though the social skin they adopt is different depending on location and circumstance, there is a universal movement toward aspirational self-fashioning, namely dressing as the people they want to be, and thus want to be seen as. The chapter then analyzes the important role of clothing in generating the identity of the "rebel" during the war. In Sierra Leone and next-door Liberia, urban street fashion inspired by rap music began to take hold among young people in the late 1980s and was adopted by some rebel factions in the 1990s, firmly linking global fashion with rebel social worlds. In the aftermath, young people's adoption of "cool" global fashion heightened social tensions. These fashions were associated with the town's burgeoning postwar clubbing scene, a scene that survived the war because rebels liked to have a good time. Johnny Boy Boutique played a critical role in fomenting this fear and feeding panic around nattily dressed youth, as it was the town's first purveyor of urban street fashion. Johnny insisted that there was nothing sinister about people wanting to forget the war by dressing up. His opinion is supported by post–World War II fashion trends in the United Kingdom, specifically the phenomenon of the Teddy Boys. These were working-class London youth who adopted Edwardian-era outfits as a way of reinventing themselves after a childhood of war austerity. They were then marked by their dress as hooligans. There are striking similarities between the Teddy Boys and postwar Makeni youth, which highlights that young people incurring hardship to feel good may simply be reacting to their circumstances, but they are observed and excluded as dangerous. This is a hallmark of il/legitimacy, as a performance of "fresh urban youth" is just as easily demarcated as degenerate, wasteful, or rebellious when enmeshed in an otherwise austere social world (see Van 'T Wout 2016:2).

The fashion arms race is illustrated best within the town's custom clothing industry, because tailoring is not solely the pursuit of older artisans. As older tailors create elaborate traditional dresses for well-to-do women and colonial-style safari suits for men, younger tailors and apprentices look to European fashion houses for inspiration, imitating European designs for wealthy patrons who want to add modern fashions to their wardrobes. Many young tailors explore the boundary between the two, using local and regional fabrics to make their Western patterned creations and combining imported second-hand clothes with local fabrics, provoking a conversation about what comprises neat, serious, and professional dress. At the other end of the spectrum are young people who cling to professional respectability despite having no money for clothes. I focus on the unpaid "unapproved" teachers who wear the same threadbare suits day after day, with no income to improve their professional wardrobes. They are caught in a bind of needing to demonstrate class control and good exam results in order to get their approval from the Ministry of Education—and thus a salary—but struggle to maintain discipline and learning among students who do not respect them because of their shabby wardrobes.

The chapter finishes with one of the most visible examples of how youth is a phenomenon of risk-taking and globalization: professional soccer team jerseys as political symbols. Bars began televising English Premier League soccer matches in the decade after the war, and along with betting on matches, young people began wearing the jerseys of their favorite teams. Many members of the APC youth wing embraced Arsenal—who wear red—as their team, and a sea of red jerseys became commonplace at political rallies. Young people's desire to be taken seriously as political players meant they "threw their eligibility to the wind" (see Simone 2011:267), not caring that wearing the jersey entangled them with accusations of being lazy and hooligans, hoping just to be noticed at all. They contrasted with politicians, who countered the power-in-numbers of APC youth and instead wore their most elaborate, expensive hand-tailored costumes and imported accessories. During the 2012 elections, politicians openly advertised their luxury accessories and worldly connections—the very globalization they disparaged in youth. As young men felt their strength and visibility politically was in their numbers, they were countered by adults who created a boundary of "youth gang" by emphasizing the danger of blending in as soccer hooligans, rather than standing out as European fashion connoisseurs. This highlights the importance of seeing youth as a material entanglement configured in an encounter, rather than a defined trend. Whatever performances they adopt, adults erect an exclusionary boundary around them by adopting an opposing performance, and observing, commenting on, and making real that difference.

Clothing as Identity Formation

As the social skin is a primary site of observation and judgment in encounters between people, it is also fundamental to the creation of exclusionary boundaries. Especially in urban areas, where global fashion is common, clothing is a site of friction between generations, as young people try on new ways of being through their clothing choices

(Ocobock 2017:9). No longer tied to the wardrobes that defined their lives in rural areas, urban African youth since the colonial era have used fashion as a performance of maturity, as the ability to purchase their own wardrobe was a signal of their impending independence (Ocobock 2017:86). As most young people receive their clothing from their parents, a young person selecting their first outfit is a watershed moment (Bastian 2005:37). If their style is an extreme deviation from the social norm, as Stanley Cohen noted with Mods and Rockers in 1960s England, the symbolic resistance of the young to their subordination is often read by adults as provocation (1980:x).

Clothing as symbolic resistance takes many forms. For example, blue jeans in London are the uniform of the working class (see Miller and Woodward 2012), and resisting their ubiquity is a symbolic rebellion against the unremarkable life they represent. Mods and Rockers— epitomized in *The Who*'s rock opera *Quadrophenia* (Humphries et al. 1979)—were semiskilled and unskilled young men in unstable low-wage work, glaring outliers to the post–World War II narrative that everyone was upwardly mobile (Cohen 1980). These youths' outrageous styles—from pinstripe suits and tricked-out scooters among the Mods to leather, chains, and motorcycles on Rockers—were a direct rebuke to the conservative styles of early 1960s Britain, even as deviant style did not translate to social or economic mobility (Cohen 1980:x). In addition to resisting dominant narratives young people also resisted their circumstances, spending the bulk of their income on expensive clothes to demonstrate the people they would be if their situations allowed it (Gondola 1999; Newell 2012:1).

The Global South is replete with examples of young people producing their aspirational selves through clothing. Poor youth in urban Cote d'Ivoire spend their incomes on suits and parties. Their consumption behaviors signal membership in the modern world, even as they are rarely able to inhabit the jobs, homes, or vehicles that would be an "honest" performance of that membership (Newell 2012). In Northern India, unemployed educated youth dress professionally to signal their unsuitability for farming, the profession of their parents (Jeffrey et al. 2008:98). In Ethiopia, unemployed youth who yearn for government jobs wear neat office dress, hanging out in movie houses and at home in the clothes that reflect the lives and jobs they want for themselves (Mains 2012:6). This trend became extreme in late 1990s Madagascar, where youth regularly starved themselves to purchase the latest fashions and mocked youth who were too poor to do so, as ownership of fashion was equated with power and masculinity (Cole 2005:896). In all of these places, office dress entangled youth in globalization and served as embodied performances of their challenge to adults configuring boundaries of "serious" and "professional" only around themselves.

In Zambia in the wake of the collapse of the international copper market, the country's main export, style was how individuals demonstrated their orientation to the outside world. Cosmopolitan dress became popular among urban youth who saw Zambia as perhaps regaining membership in the modern world, even as rapid economic decline indicated a withdrawal from that world. People who adopted "village" style made a contrasting moral statement about Zambia's future, namely that the only logical and moral path was to embrace rural life and livelihoods (Ferguson 1999). Young people move in and out of styles, depending on the circumstances in which they are trying to make an impression, gaining mastery of their situation through exactly the right dress (Jeffrey et al. 2008:24). Achieving a little control over circumstance through one's "personal front," even at great cost, is understandable in places like Sierra Leone where an individual's long-term success depends on the depth and breadth of their relationships (Bledsoe 1990), which begin with first impressions.[2] However, a young person's ability to cultivate social networks also depends on how much their personal front evokes sinister memories of the civil war for the very adults they are trying to impress.

The Social Skin of Rebels

In the preceding examples, a country's uneven development—often leaving young people jobless and without clear direction in their lives— is met by individuals who resist their circumstances through fashion. Resistance cannot change the social landscape in Ethiopia and India, and further damages young people in Madagascar and Cote d'Ivoire, where youth sacrifice basic necessities to buy fashionable clothes. In Sierra Leone, youth who reject their circumstances through clothing face a very different set of constraints on and interpretations of their behavior. Their globally inspired variations on neat or professional dress can kindle fear and approbation by adults, whose lingering memories of the distinctive dress habits among RUF rebels color their perceptions of fashion. The adoption of a global urban style among many rebel cadres, especially in the cities, was linked inexorably in people's minds with the particularly brutal marks that violence left on individual bodies. If a person's body was mutilated by a young man wearing mirrored sunglasses and acid-washed jeans, it is not easy to resist drawing those connections with similarly dressed urban youth even many years later. This is why Karen Barad describes agential cuts as "touchstones": history can be fundamental to how interpretations persist (in Kleinman 2012:80).

Sierra Leone's conflict became world news in part because RUF terror tactics marked people visibly and viscerally. Thousands suffered amputations that irrevocably changed them (Cole 2014). In addition to the physical agony, victims were subjected to a twisted assault on the social world, as rebels sometimes announced that they were tailors, and asked if their victims would like "long sleeve" or "short sleeve," namely if they would like their arm amputated at the wrist or above the elbow (Penketh 2013). This brand of sinister attack began during the Liberian civil war, where warlord Charles Taylor's minions claimed that Taylor was "a good tailor" who gave people what they wanted. In addition to long and short sleeves, Taylor's rebels offered "body fit" amputation, at the shoulder (Utas 2003:38). These tactics transformed everyday life-affirming objects into materials of terror that up-end the normal social world (Nordstrom 1997). By consistently linking mutilation with tailoring, rebels severed the relationship people had with their bodies, their clothing, and their social selves.

Rebels who performed amputations were rarely clothed in the traditional rural dress of country cloth or in nondescript second-hand clothes; rather, they displayed their dissociation from rural and otherwise "normal" life through outrageous sartorial choices. In Liberia and among some RUF cadres, bizarre costumes—women's dresses, Halloween masks, and heavy makeup—were adopted to instill a sense of altered reality among their victims (Ellis 2006:26). Rebels also displayed their dedication to global urban style, with many sporting sunglasses, jeans, and tank tops as their uniform (Utas 2003:5), while others continued the sense of unreality that accompanied the war by wearing the uniforms of soldiers they had killed (Bolten 2014a). Young rebels deliberately and actively linked themselves to the modern world as they understood it, and much of the looting that took place in Makeni during the occupation targeted clothing stores such as Johnny Boy.

Memories of rebel fashion were alive and particularly raw in 2004. When I walked around town with adults, they took pains to point out former rebels in our midst. These conversations often began, "Do you see that youth wearing sunglasses/jeans/high top sneakers/gold chain/ white undershirt?" Even if the individual pointed to was not conclusively known as an ex-combatant, he rarely received the benefit of the doubt. As a follow-up to my question "How do you know he is a rebel?" a common response was that there was no reason for a young man to dress like a rebel unless he was one. Why would one "fake" one's membership in the RUF, knowing the social costs? A young man who wanted to be taken seriously by adults would never align himself, even in dress, with people who had turned the social world upside down (see Bolten 2012c). That young men sporting sunglasses, baggy jeans, and high tops often lived together was proof of their enduring RUF membership and their disdain for adult authority. It never occurred to adults that for rebels to adopt urban style during the war, the fashions and movies that inspired them had to already be available in stores. In spite of urban fashion emerging *before* the war through Sierra Leone's existing global linkages, it was indelibly linked in popular imagination to the RUF.

The first time I met with a group of RUF ex-combatants, I noted their clothes carefully. Some were dressed as though for job interviews, sporting pressed slacks and collared shirts (Bolten 2012a:85). Others were more casually dressed, in jeans, t-shirts, and the occasional gold chain or watch. Several were wearing mirrored sunglasses, even though we were meeting inside. One young man in particular caught my attention, as he paired mirrored sunglasses with a gold earring, a Wu-Tang Clan t-shirt, and baggy jeans. If there was an individual who appeared to confirm popular fears about the linkage between clothing and rebel danger, it was certainly that young man. When I interviewed him one-on-one, a different truth emerged. Joseph wore sunglasses to hide a disfiguring injury that had blinded him in one eye. He had been kidnapped by the RUF early in the war and was hit by shrapnel during a firefight. Joseph had become an RUF celebrity when Foday Sankoh personally funded a trip to Cote d'Ivoire to try to save his sight and repair his face, and Sankoh had praised his bravery. The surgeries were unsuccessful and Joseph suffered permanent blindness and facial scarring. His disability led to an outpouring of sympathy among his cadres, and they showered him with gifts when he joined them in the invasion and occupation of Makeni. A friend who looted a clothing store gave him a desirable pair of jeans, another a bit of gold jewelry, until he amassed an enviable urban wardrobe. Joseph was not trying to dress "tough," as he stated; these were merely the clothes that he owned.

Another important detail that must be remarked upon is that Joseph was not singular in Makeni; in fact his wardrobe represented the bulk of the clothes that came into town in the burgeoning used clothing market. One of Makeni's main roads was lined with vendors selling a wide array of used clothing that they purchased by the bale from vendors in Freetown. Ripped jeans, concert t-shirts, sports team jerseys, costume jewelry, and accessories of every kind arrived in the country on container ships. Many of these clothes were donated by well-meaning citizens in the West, most frequently the United States and Canada; however, the saturation of local used clothing markets means that thousands of pounds of clothes are auctioned in bulk to trans-Atlantic used clothing vendors (Cline 2012; Strutner 2016). Sierra Leonean vendors choose the highest value items out of the bales and put these on display. Though items like family reunion t-shirts and oversized cargo shorts do get sold, a large percentage of items the vendors sold after the war were the newest and flashiest items, and these were the clothes that young people preferred. This meant that young people being feared as rebels, hooligans, and criminals because of their wardrobes was a direct result of the fashion choices of Western teens. In addition to availability, second-hand clothes were *much* cheaper than traditional outfits made to measure by tailors. A simple dress from a single piece of cloth cost me $20 in 2004, while a similar dress in the used clothing market would be a third of the price. Youth wearing jeans, pop culture t-shirts, and wide-brimmed baseball hats were taking the best quality clothes for the lowest prices they could afford. Inevitably, however, they all risked being configured as rebels by adults who connected the war and the vanguard of urban fashion in the 1990s with the flood of similar items into Makeni's postwar used clothing market.

Johnny Boy Helps People Forget Their Problems

When Johnny opened his boutique after the war, he did not know what would sell in a decimated, impoverished town. However, he believed the prewar love of fashion among Makeni's young people would reassert itself. When I spoke to him in 2012, he said, "Sierra Leoneans like to buy clothes, young people especially. If they have any money, they will buy something to wear because, sometimes, it is the only thing they can do for themselves." Echoing the habits of young people around Africa from the colonial era, a young person's first expression of independence is their wardrobe. Johnny had what young people wanted, and as people began buying, he stocked more luxury items. "The young people started with just a few things, jeans, t-shirts, boots, but then when the [disarmament] money started coming into the town, young people had a little more money. I started keeping watches, chains, and perfumes, and they sold." Johnny found profit in postwar recovery, as ex-combatants had transition allowances granted when they demobilized, and spent some of it on dignity.

As Matthew Desmond uncovered in inner-city America, poverty never precludes the possibility of enjoying beauty or wanting nice things (Desmond 2016:218). Desmond's interlocutors believed they would never escape poverty, and instead vowed to "survive with some color" (220). The disarmament allowances given to former rebels were a few hundred thousand leones a month (about $100 a month in 2002), and after dedicating the bulk of it to basic survival, young men splurged on beauty: a watch, a gold chain, a new pair of jeans. Johnny saw different young people all the time, some with money they had saved for months to purchase something small for themselves. At first it was ex-combatants who patronized his business, but once people began moving back to Makeni, his clientele expanded. They were almost exclusively young people between thirteen and thirty who came even if they could not afford it. It was not Johnny's job to dissuade them from buying fashion; he needed to pay his backers and so he accepted their money, but "I didn't think it was right that there would be no dinner for a youth who bought a gold chain. But he wanted the chain enough to do it."

What prompts behavior among youth that seems to counter to daily survival, let alone the ability to appear serious? For Johnny, his regrets were tempered by the knowledge that he was helping people forget their problems. He said, "Bluffing . . . it is a way of thinking that if you try hard enough, you will be successful. Some of them, when they used to wear nice clothes and bluff, and go dancing, I believe they want to clear their minds, to reduce the stress from the war. Some of them had houses before, and during the war they lost their houses, and from that point until now, they don't have good housing. For them to forget, they have to wear good clothes, they have to go to clubs, they listen to music, they watch [football] games." As Desmond discovered, in the United States the barriers to owning a home, or getting a degree, or securing a bank loan are so prohibitive for the poor that they focus on the aesthetic details that improve life just a little: clothes, costume jewelry, perfume, and distractions. He explains, "They aren't poor because they throw away their money, they throw away their money because they are poor" (Desmond 2016:219). For young people in postwar Makeni, part of escaping was dressing and partying like the movie stars and musicians they saw on television in the clubs they frequented. They did not think about the linkage between global urban style and their own elders' fears; they were rebelling against the past and forgetting their circumstances in the present.

One of the best parallels is the Teddy Boy phenomenon in post–World War II Britain. In the late 1940s, tailors in London's elite Savile Row reintroduced the long drape jackets and distinctive trousers of the pre–World War I Edwardian Era. The flamboyant style featured large amounts of fabric and complex tailoring and was a sartorial reaction of the upper classes against the austerity and rationing of the war years (Bell 2014). The style was adopted first by Oxford students and army officers, but eventually found its way to the working-class neighborhoods, where lower-class youth in draped coats hung around on bombed-out London streets. The moment nonelites adopted Edwardian dress it was abandoned by the upper class, one of whom remarked, "the whole of one's wardrobe immediately becomes unwearable" (Sinfield 1989:153). Tailors scrambled to produce new elite styles, and universities banned Edwardian dress on their campuses, referring derisively to the "Teddy Boys" as degenerates in dandy dress. The clothing had not changed, but "its wearers had immediately translated it into a stigma" (Edwardianteddyboy.com 2017). Edwardian dress configured dangerous youth in London just as urban hip-hop fashion configured a rebel in postwar Makeni.

Johnny never imagined that style was a threat to postwar reconciliation; he merely thought it was good business sense. He began specializing in denim jeans, hip-hop t-shirts, and accessories before the war because they sold better than more conservative styles, and he knew he could corner the market in postwar Makeni by providing them. That these expensive fashions attracted mostly impoverished youth rather than his prewar clientele of flashy upper-class youth was not odd to Johnny, even as the poor had access to second-hand versions of his goods. He noted that youth bought most of their wardrobe second-hand; however, "everyone wants just one new thing, one shiny thing for their own." Though Johnny did not make the link himself, it is plausible that well-to-do youth veered away from urban fashion immediately after the war precisely because of its rebel connotations. Poor youth did not see this; rather, as Johnny explained it, "They needed to dress differently than in their rags from the war." Newspapers noted a similar sense of ennui among the Teddy Boys, whom they described suffering "a nagging dissatisfaction" with their lives that resulted in "a need to draw attention to themselves" (edwardianteddyboy.com 2017). Both Teddy Boys and young men in postwar Makeni looked to shed the war years and introduce something bold, beautiful, and interesting into their lives.

Poor Makeni youth and Teddy Boys faced the same formation as being identified as dangerous in encounters with their elders. A group of Teddy Boys killed a youth during a fight in 1953, and the style went from being associated with poor youth to articulating delinquency (Edwardianteddyboy.com 2017). Police and political councils decried the "snappy dressers" as thugs, initiating widespread panic around them in the United Kingdom (Bell 2014:5). In line with Johnny's assessment of most poor youth, including ex-combatants, wanting to forget their problems, most of his clientele spent their evenings in nightclubs located on a road called "Ladies' Mile" because of its historic associations with prostitution. The bad reputation of Ladies' Mile long preceded the throngs of snappily dressed youth who flocked there after the war; indeed newspaper reporters from Freetown in the 1970s and 1980s were intimidated, shocked, and awed by its thrumming, teeming club scene (*Daily Mail* 1980), where one could get the best palm wine in the country and dance with scantily clad women "who should be at home discharging their matrimonial duties" (*We Yone* 1979). That the country's postwar elders were part of the generation of prewar clubgoers is lost in current conversations about the wayward, unproductive, and dangerous habits of the young, and how global fashion is entangled with moral decline (see Gondola 1999:27; Guyer and Salami 2013:208).

The clubs at Ladies' Mile were popular with rebels during the occupation, and so they were spared the looting and destruction that faced other businesses. As one ex-combatant told me, "Even rebels need to forget their problems." Drinking and dancing during the occupation dulled the pain of his tragic experiences. Kidnapped into the RUF at fifteen and forced to watch his parents die, he had endured nearly a decade with the rebels, and had come to Makeni after his girlfriend and infant son were killed in an ambush. He was not the only one who wanted to forget; the clubs were packed during the occupation because so many rebels had suffered similar tragedies, and spent most of their money on beer that had been smuggled in and whatever music could be coaxed out of the town's dilapidated stereos. The clubs' popularity swelled after the war, attracting displaced people, especially young women, looking for emotional diversions and potential partners with money. Though the need to forget may be universal in postwar social worlds, the Teddy Boys and youth in postwar Makeni reveal that the young primarily embody the lingering fear of violence in their encounters with others. One of the ways youth navigate their sense of self and the fears of adults is through custom fashion, as the town's tailors whimsically span traditional and modern through their own creations.

"I Can Sew Anything"

The configuring of young people wearing European and hip-hop fashion as dangerous is complicated by Sierra Leone's long history of globalization and the new forms of entanglement emerging between local and global. For example, safari suits were once worn only by British administrators but are now considered marks of elite tradition. Clothing being designated as either Western or traditional is further muddled by Makeni's creative young tailors, who mix local and global influence in their designs. While older tailors understand the safari suits as the garb of chiefs and politicians, young tailors look to European designers for inspiration, mixing local and Western fabrics to produce new styles and new ways of thinking about what "serious" looks like. If a young person arrives at an interview dressed in an impeccably tailored suit of locally dyed cloth cut in the style of Giorgio Armani, is he not serious? What kind of image is projected by a young man wearing a handmade outfit of reclaimed second-hand clothes?

My first visit to Kamara Brothers Tailoring Workshop was motivated by my own sartorial desires. The elderly tailor who had sewn dresses for me between 2004 and 2010 had passed away, and I visited Kamara Brothers on the recommendation of several loyal customers. In addition to their master tailors, Kamara Brothers also had a regular roster of apprentices, an arrangement the owners had with a technical college to offer students experience and mentoring. Every wall of the brightly lit shop was covered with bolts of colorful fabric. Each tailor sat at his or her station with an example of the clothes they made hung near their sewing machine, so that potential customers could choose the tailor with whom they wanted to work. I was greeted by the boss, Mr. Ibrahim Kamara, who was busy cutting a pattern for an elaborate dress on the large front table. He gave me a tour and introduced me to the tailors, saying a few words about each of them. Mr. Kamara articulated each tailor's preferred sewing style, and it quickly emerged that there was an aesthetic divide between the younger and older tailors, with older tailors sewing from older influences in global fashion, and a newer hybrid aesthetic represented in the clothes made by young tailors.

I met Mr. Conteh, who became a tailor in the early 1990s after losing his leg in a farming accident. Mr. Kamara explained, "Mr. Conteh couldn't farm anymore, and he was looking for a way to sustain his life, so we taught him the business. You can see he makes the finest safari jackets! You will not find a tailor in town who makes them better, and people are lining up for these even though they are costly." He showed me a jacket made in the characteristic style in olive polyester, with short sleeves, four pockets, and four buttons down the front. "This one costs Le300,000 [about $70 in 2012]. Isn't it beautiful?" I nodded, even as the style has colonial origins (see Figure 4.1). The safari style originated

FIGURE **4.1** Safari Suits on the Freetown Civilian Defense Corps, World War II.

with British officials in nineteenth-century India. They wore the jacket with either trousers or shorts, knee socks, and pith helmets as an alternative to the traditional heavy wool uniform used in cooler climates (Farwell 1991). The style then spread around the British Empire, from Asia to Africa (see Ocobock 2017).

The safari suit was considered the best dress for maintaining a polished official look, as it was adapted directly from the jacket cut of British military uniforms. African tailors began making the style when local officials were also called upon to adopt it, and many government boarding schools required the suit as a school uniform (Ocobock 2017:135). When Bo School for Boys was opened in 1906, a photo of British officials and regional chiefs gathered for the dedication shows all the British officials and one local chief wearing a pith helmet, a remarkable moment that captures when colonial fashion began making its way into local traditional dress (Sierra Leone National Archives 2017). Many current chiefs own several safari suits, with the two paramount chiefs in Makeni wearing them as their daily official dress when I moved to the town in 2004. Safari suits are performances of elderhood because of their expense and their association with political power. That they are so expensive is the primary reason that men in other parts of Africa who wore them were mocked by European administrators. They were chided for wasting money and imitating a modernity from which they were supposedly barred. Administrators "put these men in their place" by reminding them that the character, and not the clothes, made the man (Burke 1996:102–04). However, they missed the local importance of the social skin and advertising one's position and worldly wisdom through dress (Gable 2000:197).

The next station was occupied by a much younger man Mr. Kamara introduced only by his first name, David. Next to David's station hung a button-down shirt and waistcoat, which would have been conservative except that the body of the shirt was blue, the sleeves were pink, and the waistcoat was a pink-lined blue with pink pockets. Mr. Kamara made it clear that David was a college-assigned apprentice in his probationary period, and that he was "finding his way" in his sewing. I asked Mr. Kamara when the apprenticeship ended, and he was clear on his arrangement with the college: "The students can stay at their station for one year with no charge, as they learn the ways of professional tailoring. After that, they start paying [rent] for their station, or they need to find a new place." David told me in a later conversation that he was not planning to stay: "I have my own ideas about clothing, and what people want to buy. There are so many tailors who can make these old [safari] suits, but if I make things that are different, the young professionals will want them, and I can create my own business."

David's creativity matched that of another tailor a few stations away, a young woman I call Kadi. Her display outfit was a long sheath dress reminiscent of European runway fashion, which she had sewed out of locally dyed batik cloth. Stunning in oranges and yellows, the dress was in itself global hybridity, as she combined disparate patterns and fabrics into something new. Mr. Kamara praised the fine quality of her sewing but was clearly abashed by Kadi's work wardrobe, which was comprised of her own creation. She wore a shimmery silver Empire waistline dress, cut high up the thigh and with a local touch of a ruffled hemline above the bust and bows on the skinny straps that held it on her shoulders. I commented on the beauty and innovation of the dress and she lit up, stating, "I can sew anything. Just show me the pattern and the fabric you want and I will make it." Kadi's clientele was primarily elite young professionals who wanted the status of hand-tailored clothing but still felt "young" enough, in her own words, to want color and innovation. When I asked to what occasions they wore her creations, she was adamant that her fashion could be worn anywhere. "I have seen one of my dresses in church. I have seen one of my suits on a man at the bank. If they want to wear them, they will wear them." The dress she was wearing would cost Le300,000, the same as the safari jacket, if she sold it.

That Kadi could cultivate a clientele that would pay so much for her clothes was not surprising. As I mentioned earlier, not all young people are poor—wealthy young people do not have to worry as much about first impressions if they are not configured as youth in most of their encounters. For those who can afford a social skin that diverges from the customary uniform of their social world, it reveals their power, rather than bringing into question where they stand (Turner 2012:491). For Kadi to wear her most striking creations as she sewed—even with her boss's clear consternation—was an expression of the esteem in which she was held by the local elite, and thus the power she had to dictate the terms of her work. Kadi had the means to keep her station at Kamara Brothers; she was equally able to set up her own business, taking her clientele with her. She could afford to be visible, and to render her clients socially visible, because they all had the economic means to influence their social engagement with others. This is not bluffing in either the

Goffman sense of misrepresentation (1959:59), or in the Sierra Leonean understanding of making one's self out to be more than one is (see also Newell 2012). Rather, in confidently displaying an unusual but recognizable style—a twist on acceptable dress, rather than a departure—wearers show that they are not affected by the impressions of others, or can dictate how others perceive them (Goffman 1959:17, 25). In their encounters with others, they are the ones drawing the boundaries—in essence, they are adults. They can afford to be visible, to stand out in ways that would cause boundaries of "uppity youth" to be configured were the wearers to lack the other qualities—the profession, the building, the paperwork—whose entanglements produce them as adults.

Kadi was also making "patchwork fashion," finding second-hand clothes whose fabric was still durable, working in strips of local cloth left over from her commissions and combining them into whimsical, useful fashions that were cheaper, while still showing a tailored aesthetic. While we chatted, she was working on an outfit combining scraps from a church dress she had made with second-hand jeans and an old gray flannel shift. Kadi explained her plan to rip out the central panel on the jeans, which were elastic to accommodate pregnancy, and replace it with the fabric scraps, which she was also using to add detailing down the leg seams. The rest of the local fabric would make spaghetti straps and a flower bow for the shirred, tight-fitting tank top she was making from the stretchy gray flannel, which was probably once a tube top. This creation was socially bold: the outfit was clearly for a woman, but few adult women wore trousers in public, and the spaghetti straps on the top were also risqué. However, she would market the outfit for Le60,000 (about $15 in 2012)—much more affordable than anything using whole cloth or high-fashion patterns, but also more aesthetically pleasing than items from the second-hand market. Its destination was a boutique near the local university, where middle-class students formed a market for her combination of value and whimsy. Indeed, I saw the outfit on the mannequin on display in front of a shop a week later, and within a few days, it had sold.

The hybrid fashions made by young tailors, the rising popularity of patchwork design, and the persistence among the elite of older global forms of tradition reveal Sierra Leone's history of globalization clearly. It also highlights the importance of global influences in fashion in visibly defining generations, and the entanglement of clothing with identities given to the young in their encounters with adults. However, clothing does not map comfortably onto agential cuts of in/visibility and in/distinction established thus far. Young people must dress to render themselves visible but not too visible, especially if they lack the social power to perform novel fashion without repercussions. They need to both stand out and blend in to be taken seriously but are also constrained by their financial circumstances and the clothing available, with the second-hand market determined by the cast-offs from the West. A thousand youth can dress in urban hip-hop fashion because of Johnny Boy and the second-hand clothing market, but it does not mean adults will view it positively just because it is common. Indeed, it might spark the opposite reaction, that youth are forming an urban army of the disgruntled, inspired by gangster rap the way RUF cadres were inspired by Rambo movies (see Richards 1996).

If the same thousand young people wear patchwork fashion, a very different statement is made, as the entanglement of clothing and seriousness, or locality, is more open to interpretation. Patchwork makes important concessions to established tastes and fashions—local design elements, colors, and fabrics are prominent—incorporates the global clothing market, engages the creativity of tailors, and emerges with something new and different but also familiar and comfortable. Patchwork fashion is *bricolage*, a putting together of what one has on hand in novel ways to create a new cultural form (Levi-Strauss 1966; see also Diouf 2005:34; Nuttall 2004; Weiss 2009:18). It is, as anthropologist Brent Luvaas describes for indie fashion in Indonesia, the social skin as "cut 'n' paste" (2010:2). Patchwork unapologetically displays its lack of elite status through its second-hand fabrics. These second-hand fabrics inspire the form, pattern, and cut of the clothes, rendering them uncompromisingly global in their character. The clothing becomes local in the tailors' own bold touches, which draw the eye from the whole to the particular: the colorful fabric that comprises patches, sleeves, pockets, and detailing, the replacement of t-shirt sleeves with ruffles, the deliberate nods to local history and traditional fashion that render the wearer's identity indeterminate in its commitments, thus also making the agential cut of those who engage them difficult to predict.

A young person wearing patchwork demands to be taken seriously as a global citizen and a loyal member of their social world. They must be viewed as thoughtful and deliberate about their personal front, but also unafraid of being distinct; impossible to pigeonhole. As Luvaas argues for indie design, young tailors who make patchwork, and the young people who wear it, are not just projecting a certain social image to the world; they are positioning themselves as empowered social actors in the global milieu, and also producers of local form (2010:2; see also Howes 1996; Nuttall 2004:433). That young people commission clothes from tailors means that others must take them seriously, as someone whose performance is designed to be seen. That a young man has the confidence to wear patchwork can spark admiration among the old, who, in spite of the boundaries enacted between them, can recall the moment they first paid a tailor to make them something new. Unlike paperwork and structures, clothing has the power to connect people as quickly as it can enact boundaries between them. As one's personal front, it is the first moment at which forms of observation on others enact either boundaries or connections. Just as the social skin can have lasting positive effects for the wearer on those who see him and are impressed by him (Goffman 1959:3), if an individual is unable to change their social skin according to the dictates of the social world, that effect can quickly change from positive to negative, and negative impressions can last.

"This Is the Suit That I Teach In"

Schools were fascinating places where the phenomenon of youth was produced, not just because of the material entanglement of people with paperwork—which we would expect—but also for the importance of clothing to interpersonal encounters. It was not just adults who judged young people as youth; children also engage in agential cuts, observing, judging, and generating real consequences for their teachers. For young teachers, clothing epitomizes the paradox of il/legitimacy. This was illustrated one day when I sat down with six teachers for a conversation on schooling. I had asked older and younger teachers to come together so that I could assess the range of opinions they held on issues from educational testing and corporal punishment, to the state of teaching and learning (see Bolten 2015, 2018). The youngest teacher in the room was the best dressed, wearing a dark grey wool suit, a white dress shirt, maroon necktie, and polished black patent leather shoes. He held himself erect, never once relaxing into his chair during the animated conversation. After discussing testing standards and the dearth of classroom resources, conversation turned to salaries, which had not risen in ten years and were habitually late. The young teacher, who I call Abu, stared into space as the others spoke passionately about the need for a raise, and then he suddenly drummed his middle finger on the table, indicating that he would like to speak. The room went silent.

"I am sympathetic to the trials of my fellow teachers, whom I agree need raises to reflect their devotion to their students," he said. The other teachers exchanged glances but were silent. "But we must also differentiate between the teachers who receive salaries and those who do not. I am an unapproved teacher, and I receive only what my fellow teachers and the headmaster can collect for me." He nodded and smiled gratefully at the others, who returned his smile. "I cannot get my approval until the Ministry of Education decides that I am qualified, and so this is my teaching apprenticeship. I must make a good impression on the headmaster, who can fight my battle in the Ministry, and also my students must produce good results. If they are successful in their exams, maybe the Ministry will approve me. But the students must be attentive to be successful, and for that they need to work in the classroom." Abu gestured to the oldest teacher at the table. "Mr. Koroma's students do well, they respect him and so they do as he asks. I have to get the upper hand on my students because I am young. I need to establish my class control and never lose my grip on the students. This is the suit that I teach in." He stood up and pivoted slowly around. Upon closer inspection, his suit was more worn than I initially thought. The cuffs were fraying, his shirt neither as crisp nor as white as I had initially imagined. He sat down.

"I used all the money I had after getting my teaching certificate to purchase this suit so that I could make a good impression on the headmaster. And I wore the suit to the first day of class, to make a good impression on my students. They were very good at the start of the year, very good. And I wore the suit again, and again, because I was afraid if I changed into my other clothing, they would not take me seriously. But then they realized that I was always dressing the same, and they began mocking me: "Teacher has only one clothes [sic]! See how he wears them!" And soon I lost their respect, and then I also had problems with class control. If they do not respect me, they will not try to learn, because they see their own teachers are not doing well. If they struggle on the exam, maybe I don't get my approval. It may be that I never become an approved teacher because this is the only suit that I teach in." Clothes could be the difference between Abu being approved or losing his job. Thus is the power of agential cuts to generate exclusionary boundaries.

Abu had invested three years to acquire a teaching certificate, but it was no guarantee of job, even in that time of teacher shortages. Wearing a suit for his first classes was a type of impression management that Goffman refers to as "getting the upper hand on a situation." One starts out with an extreme self-presentation—Goffman uses the example of a teacher who is tough on the students at the beginning of the year and then lightens up—because it is much easier to lighten one's image than it is to toughen it (1959:10). However, Abu's relative youth, the extreme overcrowding in classrooms that led to widespread indiscipline (see Bolten 2015, 2018), and his need to cultivate his image as serious among fellow teachers and students led to him wearing the same suit every day. It is likely that his next-best outfit was such a marked step down that it would have destroyed his image immediately, and he could not risk such a drastic alteration in his appearance, lest he lose control of his classroom quickly. The act lasted for a while, until students realized that he had only a single suit, and Abu's carefully cultivated, fragile performance fell apart. Abu's suit illustrates clothing as il/legitimacy: a performance that generates "adult" at first, but with repeated encounters configures the poor, shabbily dressed youth. The teacher becomes a farce.

This kind of misrepresentation has important consequences for boundary configurations of youth. According to Goffman, "When we think of those who present a false front or 'only' a front, of those who dissemble, deceive, and defraud, we think of a discrepancy between fostered appearances and reality. We also think of the precarious position in which these performers place themselves, for at any moment . . . an event may occur to catch them out and baldly contradict what they have openly avowed, bringing them immediate humiliation and sometimes a permanent loss of reputation" (Goffman 1959:59). However, Abu, like so many other young teachers in Makeni, had no intention of defrauding others. Rather, dressing up for work and hoping to gain approval that will earn a paycheck is better characterized as "fake it till you make it." There was no possibility of Abu, or any young teacher in his position, gaining the initial respect of students without looking the part (see Bolten 2015), and yet that respect was possible—and Abu's case it was granted—before the performance was shattered. What Abu had hoped to gain before the thinness of his social skin was revealed was *enough* respect from the students to overcome his wardrobe constraints. In essence, he thought his teaching acumen would eventually make it impossible for his students to configure him as a youth, whatever he wore. As Wusu explained at the start of the chapter, one's wardrobe was always critical to cultivating respect if one was not already a respected elder, and one cannot gain respect from adults if one lacks the respect of the children. If children do not respect you, you are no more respectable than a child.

This emerged in a conversation I had with a teacher I call Sheku, who had a bachelor's degree in education and was more qualified than anyone with a teaching certificate. He was also more qualified than any other teacher in the school in which he taught geography, and he arrived for class the first day in the neat but unspectacular button-down shirt and khaki trousers he had worn as a student. He initially held the respect of his fellow teachers because of his degree, but the students were less impressed. Sheku had four changes of clothes that he rotated between, and within a few weeks his classroom discipline was falling apart. The students began to challenge him. He reported a conversation where a student explained to him the relationship between education and power, and how it is revealed in one's wardrobe.

Sheku explained, "I asked the boy who was being rowdy, "Do you not want a good education, and to go to university?" And his response was, 'If you have a degree, why can't you get better clothes? Is this all that education will get you? If so, I would rather die than get an education! I would rather ride an okada than get an education!' And then he walked away. It was too terrible to hear this!" Having realized that students drew a direct link between his classroom wardrobe and the value of an education, Sheku scrambled to assemble more impressive work clothes. It was not only that he wanted the students' respect for its own sake, or for the sake of their will to learn. He was also concerned with how the other teachers would react to his deteriorating classroom control. As a young, new teacher with a degree, he was singularly qualified and energetic but also singularly vulnerable to criticism. His degree could not protect him from the approbation of other teachers if his classroom fell apart, and that required whatever it took to maintain his students' respect. It did not matter how intelligent Sheku was, or how good pedagogically. None of these things mattered if he did not manage his personal front to the standard of what an educated person *should* look like, what the students should aspire to be, and thus whether they configured him as an adult. In this case, clothes really do make the man.

The Arsenal Effect: In/distinction and the Global

The first hand-tailored outfit I bought when I moved to Makeni in 2004 was a fitted blouse and long skirt. My elderly tailor, Santigie, sewed it out of a gorgeous hand-dyed red fabric that contained swirls of orange that made it look like molten lava. Santigie loved the fabric, commenting on its beauty multiple times, and insisted he use as much of it as possible in my outfit. I had wanted a loose knee-length skirt for ease of movement, but he insisted that a fitted ankle-length skirt would show off the fabric to best advantage. I donned the outfit one Saturday and walked into town for lunch with my friend Sorie. We met in the square, and he grinned when he saw me. "Ah, today you wear the colors of the sun!" I had no time to respond as from behind us came an enthusiastic shout from a group of young men: "Osay-eee!! Owayee!!!" Sorie responded in kind, pumping his fist as they waved at us. He asked me to twirl for them, which, bewildered, I did, and they hooted and clapped. They spoke briefly about a meeting, then the young men walked off, and I turned to Sorie, demanding an explanation.

He was happy to enlighten me about my fortuitous wardrobe deci-sion. "Did you see they all had stripes of red somewhere?" I nodded, and he pulled a strip of red cloth from his pocket and tied it around his arm. "Today is an APC rally day. The party emblem is the rising sun, and red is the color of that sun. They were shouting that you were letting the sun come out!" I was annoyed with myself for making such an obvious and unintended political statement, embodying support for the All People's Congress, but Sorie thought it would be a great for my research. If I invested in a hand-tailored outfit displaying party loyalty, it would bring positive attention from the party elders. All young people who professed APC loyalty were subject to scrutiny by elders based on their dedication to, and willingness to sacrifice for, the party. The more one spent on good red fabric and tailoring, the greater the possibility of distinction and being known as a serious political person. Through my outfit I was configured as an APC supporter, in spite of my foreignness and my inability to vote. Indeed, I was showing the community that the power of the APC was global, that my body was signifying an associa-tion that no explanation to the contrary would refute (see Greenberg 2014:62). This was not the impression I wanted to make, but the conse-quences were fascinating.

Sorie urged me to wear the outfit to the town council inauguration to establish my credibility with the party. I demurred, wanting to keep as low a profile as a white woman could expect to do. Sorie grudgingly agreed but suggested I bring my camera to record some of the greatest outfits that I would ever see. The town hall on inauguration day was a sea of red, as new councilors, party elders, and audience members wore their loyalty. Women were clad in red dresses with huge frills, red headwraps, red earrings, and accessories. Men wore red suits with red handkerchiefs and caps. The outfits were particularly outrageous among young people. One young man wore red Capri pants with red knee socks, a red waistcoat over a red shirt, a red top hat, and shoes he had painted red. Another had a onesie he had tailored out of a single piece of red cloth. Teenagers wore red sunglasses, red head sashes, and red sweatshirts, the sweat pouring off them in the midday sun. The inauguration ceremony was a sea of in/distinction: everyone dressed so spectacularly that there was no possibility of standing out, even as on their own each outfit would have been noteworthy. Party devotion had no price, and to be configured as APC in this moment was to have an opportunity to deepen one's entanglements with the party, as many young people without social connections aspired to be "discovered" at political functions.

Young people who could not afford to purchase APC-inspired outfits hoped to acquire official swag given out on event days. People who showed up at the party headquarters early enough were rewarded with a red t-shirt silk-screened with an official party slogan or an informal party motto (see Figure 4.2). When President Ernest Bai Koroma sought reelection in 2012, the most common phrase on t-shirts had been popularized by young people impressed with his record of building infrastructure: "*Di Pa de wɔk*," meaning "the Pa is working!" As 2004 was not a presidential election year, the t-shirts at the town council inauguration were standard APC designs of the rising sun. For many young people this was the only piece of party-specific clothing they owned, and they wore it with pride at events. However, in a sea of silk-screened shirts, young people were nothing more than part of the large mass of supporters present at parades and rallies. It was good for general political morale, but did little to advance young people's desire to be noticed by politicians who might employ them as political aides: errand boys, security, or other low-level jobs through which they hoped to secure stable employment.

FIGURE **4.2 APC campaign parade dress.**

By the time I returned to Makeni in 2010, foreign investment had eased the poverty of the immediate postwar period slightly, with many young men working for biofuel and iron ore companies (see Millar 2015). With this rise in employment came Mercury International, a sports gambling company that installed ubiquitous red betting machines around town. Young men hoping to translate their knowledge of soccer into cash often bet on professional matches, which they would watch on the screens of the town's relaxations: bars that charged a small cover for admission, with matches and times posted on chalkboards outside. The rise in sports betting coincided with young people advertising their support of professional teams, and one of the most popular among young people in Makeni at the time was Arsenal, the English Premier League team whose jersey is the same bright red as the APC. The rise in popularity of Arsenal meant an increased demand for the jerseys in the clothing marketplace, which meant both the boutiques and the second-hand clothing dealers began sourcing Arsenal gear. Many adults found the ubiquity of Arsenal jerseys irritating, with several commenting that the jersey highlighted that youth were not serious, and that they would rather spend all their time and their scant money betting on soccer than bettering themselves. Any young person in an Arsenal jersey was immediately configured as lazy, a gambler, or a hooligan, even if that young person was a student, or had a job, and was donning the jersey to watch a match on a Saturday afternoon.

Schoolteachers were the first to articulate this critique, with older teachers noting a change in the tenor of recess from a decade earlier. According to one teacher in his sixties, "The students used to use their breaks between class to play football, to talk about their subject interests and to try to outdo each other in terms of their brilliance at certain subjects. Now they use that time to argue about professional teams, and to show off their knowledge about players. It is a total waste of brainpower." The other teachers in the room agreed, with another noting that the oldest students now had two uniforms, the one they wore to class and the one they wore on weekends, when they "sit down doing nothing" watching matches in the relaxations, rather than studying or working "to become somebody," in the words of one teacher, implying that a soccer fan was a nobody. By 2012, many other adults that I spoke with in Makeni agreed with them, seeing an Arsenal jersey not as proof of a hobby or global linkages, but as an advertisement of laziness and idleness, especially when these jerseys were worn in the town's ataya bases, which they often were on game days. The conflation of the clothing with the building reinforced for adults that the youth went out of their way, spending money they did not have, to publicly advertise their will to do nothing.

I was curious whether the popularity of Arsenal as a team was a coincidence or correlated with their striking red jerseys. In interviews with several young men, it emerged that one's support of a soccer team was based in part on its star players, and in part how the team—and their uniform—reflected that person's character and politics. One fervent Arsenal supporter denied that his support was contingent on his party affiliation; however, he often wore his jersey to APC events, and over the course of several years rose to importance in the party's youth wing. His best friend was also a member of the APC youth wing but was not himself politically ambitious. He supported Chelsea, whose uniform is blue. When I asked why he did not support Arsenal, his answer was cryptic, but also revealing: "Well, I am quite an independent person." He acknowledged that there was social pressure among youth wing members to support Arsenal, but he was unmoved by it. Considering that he harbored no desire to become a politician or find educational sponsorship through the party, he felt his fandom was not constrained politically.

Over a series of interviews with youth about soccer team preferences, the importance of Arsenal—or rejecting Arsenal in favor of another team—became entangled with how an individual perceived his social vulnerability; in essence, the thickness of his social skin. The more precarious a politically minded young person thought his position in the party—whether he was ambitious or merely trying to convince people of his loyalty—the more likely he was to be a vocal Arsenal supporter. Rather than distinction, these young people sought solidarity (Cole 2008:104) through what Miller and Woodward call "the art of the ordinary": fitting in as the first and most important step in being recognized as somebody (2012). In situations where decisions about who succeeds and why appear to be increasingly arbitrary and unpredictable, fitting in, rather than standing out, may leave individuals more likely to be "left standing" in the end (Simone 2011:267–68). Among poor young people in Makeni, it was not enough to support the APC. To be an Arsenal fan and to march in an Arsenal jersey signaled two things: a lateral social network of Arsenal fans, and that supporting the APC outweighed any negative connotations of football hooliganism that came with wearing jerseys. Arsenal was a critical node of social organization in Makeni. Though it was risky to stand out as a fan and potentially a hooligan, this was a risk that APC-supporting youth were willing to take.

The sea of red Arsenal jerseys at APC events during the 2012 elections prompted adults to reconfigure the boundary around youth in novel ways. The first form was the overt critique described earlier; the second was participating in a sartorial arms race with the youth. APC elders shifted themselves in encounters with the young by adopting expensive and elaborate costumes. They countered the sameness with difference, transforming APC supporters from a sea of red clothing to a social and political chessboard, with Arsenal jerseys on the pawns and custom outfits on its kings, queens, and knights. The trends in fashion among adult APC members in 2012 was a marked change from previous years, when affiliation could be denoted with something as simple as an APC hat. I took photos of Ernest Koroma in 2004 at the town council inauguration, three years before he became president. He wore only an APC t-shirt and hat. By 2012 there was an increase, according to several Kamara Brothers' tailors, in requests for elaborate red outfits costing several hundred thousand leones. Commissions used mostly imported fabrics, involved hand-embroidered APC logos and designs, and added any ruffle or sequin that might draw someone's attention, proving that politicians and party elders were going out of their way to distance themselves from the Arsenal-jersey-wearing youth. I saw my first red safari suits in 2012 at an APC rally, red shalwar kameez outfits complete with red kuftis and red shoes on several men, and dresses that clearly required a hundred hours to make. These outfits were competitive, with adults also trying to outdo each other in displaying party loyalty in addition to drawing attention away from the Arsenal supporters (see Weiss 2009:152).

Global fashion also became a node on which the concept of adult versus youth was configured. Youth wore uniforms. Adults donned European accessories, showing off their international connections and mobility. I had multiple encounters with party elders who articulated a preference for items they believed would never be available locally. I spoke to a man just before an APC rally who had returned from living in New York to run for office. He was adamant that I comment on his special edition red New York Yankees baseball cap, his designer label red slacks, and his red Italian leather shoes. He said several times, "None of this is available in Sierra Leone! I am the only man in Makeni who has them!" I noted my admiration for his fashion choices, and he continued with a list of APC-inspired items that made him stand out at rallies: a red fedora he found at Nieman Marcus department store, red Giorgio Armani shirts, a red Swatch watch. One candidate had a dozen designer handbags that she rotated between for public events. My friend Sorie informed me that Madam Forna had family in London, and her sister sent her new handbags frequently even though they were not wealthy. Configuring a boundary of distinction between herself and the party masses was so important to Ms. Forna's status that her family sacrificed needed income to support her. The Arsenal effect generated an inversion in the boundaries typically made around youth and adults, with adults pushing and sacrificing to distinguish themselves from the vast sea of red jerseys.

The day I spent with Dauda, the chairman of the Sierra Leone Alliance for Advancement whose bid for distinction involved commissioning a statue of the president, was interrupted by a visit from Ms. Forna, who wanted to tour the statue. Her retinue of seven wore identical red t-shirts sporting the face of the president. Her accessories included red stilettos in which she carefully picked her way along the potholed road from her car, a gold necklace dotted with rubies, a red felt cowboy hat, and her red handbag. She swept in to Dauda's storeroom, where he unveiled the statue to many small gasps of admiration. After gazing at the statue for several moments, she turned around and apparently noticed me for the first time. I smiled and greeted her. She returned the smile, and then gestured to her handbag, saying, "Gucci." Unsure of what to say, I responded, "It's nice." She nodded and swept out of the room, followed by her retinue. When I returned to the United States several months later, an Internet search revealed the handbag cost $800. Entangling her personhood with the global elite, Ms. Forna emphasized a boundary between herself and everyone else through my acknowledgment of her handbag. These performances, in large ways and small, overt and subtle, are part of the continuous configuration of boundaries between people in their encounters, and bring global materials into intimate moments of adult and youth, elite and common.

From rebel dress to patchwork, Arsenal jerseys to Gucci handbags, clothing is a critical aspect of personal performance that has a significant effect on the boundaries fashioned around adult and youth. Whether youth are hooligans when they wear soccer jerseys, rebels when they wear baggy jeans, or imposters when they wear a single suit over and over, the identities of the young are continually configured by—and are profoundly sensitive to—how they don their social skin. These exclusionary boundaries of youth are thoroughly entangled with a long history of global influence, with the boundaries around adult shifting to older and often more expensive expressions of global connection both through the passage of time—what counts as serious expression is tied to one's own generational experience—and through reactions to what the young are doing and wearing. Innovations like patchwork fashion and the Arsenal effect, for which there is no precedent, is where these boundaries are most threatened, and where they are more clearly reconfigured through adult actions in their encounters with the young.

Notes

1. If every young man invests in a suit, it becomes remarkable as a trend, and potentially a reason for moral panic, as occurred with the Mods and Rockers in 1960s England (Cohen 1980), rather than a reason to notice any individual young person positively.
2. One of the most important and widely known example is the Congolese *sapeur*, whose elaborate bespoke suits and accessories are embedded in a colonial history of the wealthy dressing their servants in second-hand suits to enhance their own prestige (Gondola 1999:26). For an example, see https://www.youtube.com/watch?v=W27PnUuXR_A.

CHAPTER 5

Politics

Fashioning Il/legitimacy in the Material World

In June 2014, I was passing through Freetown and caught up with two friends, Ibrahim and Foday, over lunch. I had known and worked with them in Makeni for a decade, and at the time of our meal they were both students at Fourah Bay College. We chatted about the political situation in the country, the worrying rise in Ebola cases, and the continuing struggles of students who had passed the WASSCE but had no job or university prospects. The complaint I heard from many teachers in 2012 was that the students "had no brain for the work" because the exam requirements had become so relaxed that it was possible for a student to attain a diploma without reading an entire book. My friends believed the declining school standards would have a tremendous effect on the ability of students to be taken seriously by adults who had achieved much higher standards of secondary education in previous decades.

I combed my memory for the 2005 exam curriculum, which my friends had taken, and asked: "Are the students no longer reading *The Beautyful Ones Are Not Yet Born*?" The classic of African literature, written by Ayi Kwei Armah in 1968, was set in the waning days of Kwame Nkrumah's presidency in Ghana. The story follows a nameless bureaucrat who lives honestly and refuses to accept bribes amidst a world rife with corruption. His moral steadfastness angers his wife as it condemns them to a life of poverty. A military coup throws that world into turmoil, but it is eventually revealed that the soldiers are just as corrupt as their civilian forebears. The book had been taken off the curriculum, which saddened Foday and Ibrahim because they thought it held critical lessons for young people.

Foday posited that the most important aspect of the book was the ending. In the last few pages, the protagonist has an opportunity to turn in a corrupt former politician, and instead helps him escape by pushing him down a sewer, and then following him down to avoid being caught himself. He explained, "Even though the man makes a point of publicly not participating in the system, still, he is psychologically affected by it. He is part of the system because it produced him, and he only reveals it at the end." Foday asserted that people might perform their distance from the system, but they cannot escape it and always eventually show their true colors. This was why the protagonist throws himself down into the sewer after the politician—an overt metaphor for his acknowledgment of his complicity with corruption. Ibrahim added, "Everyone should know that they are part of this system of performing for elites and asking for their favor. The youth who don't read Armah think they are the only ones who are trying to advance by being serious. That they are the only ones who deserve a slice of the national cake through their hard work. But the thing is, everyone works this way. Thousands of youth are being serious!"

In this final chapter, I bring together the material stuff of all the previous chapters—the structures, papers, and textiles—into a discussion of politics, the sphere in Sierra Leone where young people are most frequently and publicly subjected to exclusionary boundary formation. The Truth and Reconciliation Final Report in 2003 highlighted youth as people who needed a place at the national table via political representation, prompting attention as to who exactly comprised "political youth." Unlike "lazy" youth hanging out in ataya bases, "arrogant" youth showing off their paperwork, or "hooligans" in soccer jerseys, the boundaries configured through political campaigning and elections generated youth as an opportunity: to gather their votes, their work, and their passion, and also as an immediate and persistent danger to adult supremacy; in essence, youth were needed and legitimate as political supporters, but dangerous and illegitimate as politicians. This boundary certainly did not sit still, but is something that can be grasped. Using their clothing, structures, and documents, young people engaged in public performances of solidarity, leadership, and patronage that were but together held the possibility of blurring the boundary between them and adults. Political youth acted like adults, replicating their habits and politics, and thus proved dangerous to the clarity of the boundary around adult. This resulted in more concerted, coordinated, and overt acts of boundary configuration by adults, bringing the legitimacy of such practices, and thus the system upon which they rested, into constant question.

What is clear from the preceding chapters is that the consistent delegitimizing of young people's efforts, in ways both banal and overt, means performances of adulthood are not immutable. By patrimonial logic this makes youth revolutionary, in that their risky public perfor- mances *can* translate into successful challenges to social difference. Adults act as though youth, like Armah's tragic protagonist, are oper- ating outside of the patronage system, attempting to usurp it through what appears to be socialist solidarity. And yet as Ibrahim and Foday made clear, no one who was raised in a social world with a particular history, values, morals, and interpretive frameworks live unaffected by them, whether they are aware of it or not. Youth are just as much a part of the system of social politics in Sierra Leone as was Armah's main character, and their use of materials in their deliberate public perfor- mances are geared toward being configured as adults. The social danger occurs when it is unclear whether young people are endeavoring to have boundaries of adult generated around them, or are acting to destroy explicitly ageist boundary construction; in essence, whether they are re- inforcing or delegitimizing what counts as adult.

As will unfold in this chapter, serious young people are, whether they know it or not, endorsing and replicating the hierarchies, tensions, and inequalities of their world as part of participating in it, and it is the form of observation adults make, the agential cut, that subject young people to exclusion even though the practices are the same. For exam- ple, when adults recognize the lack of difference between themselves and youth politicians, they interpret student politics as a threat, ban stu- dent politicians, and cancel their elections. It is the sameness of serious youth to adults, rather than their difference, that renders them danger- ous, so they must be "cut" to appear different. The more serious young people are, the more likely they are to have forceful, negative boundaries configured around them, and the more likely they are in turn to force- fully differentiate themselves from "half-baked" youth.

Politics is where Sierra Leone adulthood is most clearly config- ured in the form of "big" men and women (see Utas 2012), and also where the agential cut of il/legitimacy of serious youth appears most clearly. We begin with the contentious history of youth politics in Sierra Leone, and how the founding of the West African Youth League in the early twentieth century established youth politics as inclusive, progressive, and a threat to establishment power. We then delve into how student politics presaged the National Provisional Ruling Council (NPRC), the youth military coup that seized power from the APC government in 1992. The NPRC touted their difference from their corrupt forebears, but their rule ended in disillusionment and a palace coup just a few years later. Twenty-two years after the palace coup the ousted youth leader is an impoverished laughingstock, and his ouster is the sitting democratically elected president of Sierra Leone. This illustrates that the agential cut of who is a youth and who can be a legitimate leader shifts with performances, and reveals the mutability of boundaries.

The chapter then moves to student politics, highlighting student leaders as "politicians in training." Their performances as politicians replicate adult practices—from elitism to tribalism to corruption—and these revelations of the overt corruption of politics inspire drastic acts of boundary configuration by their elders. The chapter then returns to the ataya bases, and how their memberships are contained and appeased by the APC as central but unimportant political actors with the illusion of inclusion and legitimacy feeding their practices of seriousness. We finish with the United Democratic Movement, which emerged as the "youth party" in 2010, whose members dedicated themselves to getting youth elected in the 2012 elections. UDM members in Makeni used every material and linguistic practice available to make themselves legible as serious political actors, but were undermined by their leader, Mohamed Bangura, who colluded with the APC to improve his own political position by selling out his own party members and stealing their campaign funds. Ibrahim and Foday predicted the downfall of the UDM before the election, stating that the members must lack knowledge of the system if they believed that the big parties would let them be independent, and that the party would never outgrow its status as a manipulated underling—a material, linguistic youth. They predicted this without emotion or irony, merely with the knowledge that any leader would use his party to secure his own connections and network, and would sacrifice his members if he must. For Bangura, his own configuration as a "politically serious somebody" mattered most.

The Political Origins of Youth

> We, the Youth of Sierra Leone and of West Africa in general, in order
> to form a more united body, in order to watch carefully and sincerely
> matters political, educational, economical, and otherwise, that may be
> to the interest of the masses of the motherland, to sacrifice, if need be,
> all we have, for the progress and liberty of our Country and Race, and
> to ensure happiness to ourselves and to our posterity, do hereby form
> ourselves into the body designated as YOUTH LEAGUE.
>
> *Manifesto of the WAYL, 1938*

The first use of the appellation "youth" in Sierra Leone's archival record
was explicitly political, when union leader I. T. A. Wallace-Johnson
founded the West African Youth League (WAYL) in 1935 in the Gold
Coast (now Ghana). He brought the party to Sierra Leone in 1938, and
it quickly gained popularity. Wallace-Johnson chose the word "youth" to
announce a political orientation toward independence for West African
colonies, rather than to designate the membership composition. Instead
of mapping onto a demographic cohort, a life stage, or a marginal or
subaltern social position, the word "youth" was a fresh, vigorous challenge to the repression and exploitation of colonialism. It was a contrast
to the "softly-softly" approach to ending British control adopted by his
fellow Krio politicians. Instead of establishing a social category, the activities of Wallace-Johnson and the WAYL generated the phenomenon
of youth through political opposition, setting a precedent for "youth" to
generate and reflect a bold challenge to the existing order.

Wallace-Johnson was born in 1894 to poor Krio parents in Freetown. He excelled in school but his employment history was checkered
with resignations and dismissals due to his determination to organize
black workers in opposition to colonialism. He traveled around West
Africa as a union seaman and labor organizer, founding the WAYL in the
Gold Coast in 1935. While there, his activities as an illegal trade union
organizer and Communist sympathizer led to a sedition trial and his sub-
sequent departure. He returned to Sierra Leone in 1938, where he built
the party's membership in Freetown (Wallace-Johnson 1938). Wallace-
Johnson was forty-four years old when the youth party came to Sierra
Leone, a party which he announced would counter the Krio politics of
acquiescence with colonization. For a veteran union leader and worker
rights agitator to found a youth party makes it clear that youth did not
apply to the age of participants so much as an orientation to "young"

politics, which was encapsulated in the WAYL's motto, "liberty or death." The implication of violence in the motto was met with alarm by the colonial government, even as he never openly advocated for revolution.

The party was an instant sensation with local people (Spitzer and Denzer 1973). Wallace-Johnson held regular meetings in a public hall in Freetown, and his deputies habitually published the transcripts of the meetings in local newspapers (Craig 1938). The WAYL's consistent progressive populism eventually soured its relationship with local newspapers, whose editors maintained connections with the elite. Lacking other mouthpieces, the WAYL published its own newspaper, the *African Standard*, giving the party exposure that no current youth political organization could hope to achieve without significant pushback. The ease with which Wallace-Johnson penetrated and upended traditional politics was by inviting everyone—young and old, rich and poor, skilled and unemployed—to his banner. This generated a fear of the sheer number of disaffected people in Sierra Leone, which resonates with the country's obsessive focus on addressing "the youth bulge" in the present day (see GOSL 2003, 2007). Numbers mattered then, and continue to matter in the present. The power wielded by the WAYL, and the obvious fear and attempts to squelch their activities by the colonial government, belies the overwhelming feeling of powerlessness that characterizes individuals configured as youth eighty years hence, but the fear and questions of il/legitimacy with which elites meet their activities are resonant.

Wallace-Johnson's politics with respect to youth were prescient to the concerns of the current day. In a 1938 letter to Sierra Leone's governor, Douglas Jardine, he demanded free and compulsory education around the colony and protectorate, stating that people have "a right to knowledge" (Wallace-Johonson 1938:10). Simultaneously, he accused the government of "exploiting the vitality of the Youth" as parents paid their sons' school fees, only to see their sons employed by the government at poverty wages (11). He accused the government of running the colony on the backs of exploited youth, while leaving a vast majority unemployed. Though these accusations and demands seem confused and contrary, they echo the contradictory experiences of young people today who struggle to be taken seriously. Education is both knowledge and a potential threat to one's elders, something that is sacrificed and paid for with few concrete benefits even as it is touted as the key to advancement, with young people berated and exploited when they show some initiative and creativity. Unemployed youth, on the other hand, produce fear and condemnation because of their inability to navigate these competing and contrary demands. In these early letters and transcripts, Wallace-Johnson revealed a framework that still governs how the concerns of youth in Sierra Leone emerge politically. Every encounter produces a new youth, simultaneously unemployed and exploited, having a right to knowledge but being exploitable precisely because of his knowledge, represented by a party that seeks liberty at any cost. In short, whatever is done to young people to generate them as youth also renders them dangerous to the existing social order (Cohen 1980).

Youth were never the sole focal point of Wallace-Johnson's politics; the WAYL welcomed anyone who was receptive to its progressive message, and the party continued to gain adherents. The rise of a "militant working-class consciousness" in Sierra Leone alarmed Governor Jardine and ruffled the feathers of the Krio establishment, whom Wallace-Johnson denounced as clannish and dedicated to leadership only from the "high circles" (Spitzer and Denzer 1973:575). Patrimonialism extant among the "big men" of twenty-first-century Sierra Leone politics clearly has deep roots. The WAYL's wide support revealed that populism could in fact overcome traditional elite politics, which occurred in the 1938 Freetown election when WAYL candidates swept the vote across the board, sending the colonial government into panic (Spitzer and Denzer 1973:580). The government instituted a rash of anti-sedition laws specifically aimed to curtail Wallace-Johnson's activities. He was arrested in 1939, convicted of criminal libel, and spent the next five years in prison. By the time he was released Sierra Leone's attention was firmly on World War II, the WAYL was largely in disarray, and Wallace-Johnson had lost political momentum.

Long-term absence had effectively crushed this first "youth" political party, and the colonial government proved that progressive politics could be dismantled simply by removing their leader. That the "youth league" was not the sole interest or quarter of the young did not matter as much as the revelation that "young" politics were a frightening challenge to the established elite, even as Spitzer and Denzer assert repeatedly that Wallace-Johnson's politics were not revolutionary, but were "within the best traditions of democratic reformism" (1973:583). For youth politics to be so broadly popular meant that boundary configurations around young people had nothing to do with this moniker and its later negative associations. Rather, "youth" was a way of imagining a future of liberty, democracy, and freedom from colonialism. That it was an explicit and direct contrast to old politics and the elites who benefitted from traditional forms of power is the threatening undercurrent that follows youth to this day, especially where politics are concerned. "Youth" is people and politics that menace the existing political order, even as their opposition may not be revolutionary at all.

From Student Journalism to the Children's Coup

After the quiet death of the West African Youth League, the involvement of young people in progressive national politics was limited largely to protests by university students at Fourah Bay College in Freetown. The 1970s especially was a time when students—but not necessarily youth—became a phenomenon of political opposition and threat to the existing order, and were routinely harassed and repressed by the country's dictator, Siaka Stevens. Through his ruthless treatment of student activists, Stevens highlighted that young people *were* consequential political actors, and in meeting their protests with violence and incarceration, revealed that he did in fact take them—and the potential popular consequences of their actions—seriously.

It was not until a 1992 military coup comprised of young officers and led by a twenty-five-year-old captain, Valentine Strasser, that the moniker "youth"—rather than students—became explicitly political, and around which configurations first of youth as idealistic and progressive, and then highly corruptible and power-hungry, emerged. The idealism that dominated the early days of the coup gave way to popular disillusionment and calls for a return to democracy. A palace coup followed in 1996, and the new head of the NPRC, Maada Bio, initiated a transition to democratic rule. In 2012 Bio re-emerged in national politics as a presidential candidate, and though he was beaten by Ernest Koroma, his 2018 bid for the presidency was successful. That a "youth coup" member could eventually be elected president does not mean that youth is merely a category that can shift (Durham 2004). Rather, it highlights that particular historical moments entangle with novel performances and encounters and generate entirely new boundaries around individuals through new agential cuts (Nyberg 2009:1,184). In essence the agential cut, the form of observation, judgment, and action around Bio, changed. This profound political development resonates with Karen Barad's argument that boundaries do not sit still. He is Sierra Leone's president, and this is a difference that matters in the world (Barad 2007:90).

The Siaka Stevens dictatorship between 1967 and 1985 was marked by consistent repression of student dissent, which occurred mainly in Freetown. Though I lack the space for a detailed history of the relationship between Stevens and young activists, one example is particularly enlightening for illustrating how students were configured as a threat during this era, and it occurred through the material medium of paper. I spoke with two journalists in 2005 who regaled me with tales of their work on *The Tablet*, a student newspaper at Fourah Bay College in the 1970s that routinely challenged Stevens over his ruthless political tactics, and often demanded a return to true democracy (see Rashid 2004:77). One of the men commented, "We went to jail for that once in a while," which elicited gales of laughter from his friend, who reminded him, "We were founding members of the Pademba Road Boys Club!" This was a gallows humor reference to the fact that the two of them, among other politically outspoken students at the time, served multiple sentences in the notorious Pademba Road Prison as "enemies of the state." They took pride in this because it proved that Stevens *was* treating them as actors of consequence. Explained one, "I didn't know that our little paper could have so much of an effect on the man! Look at this powerful president, president for life, and he can't handle that *The Tablet* is printing caricatures of him!" They explained that it was the frequency with which Stevens sent his security detail to harass them that strengthened their political resolve. After concluding a story about Stevens's personal bodyguard kidnapping him from the Fourah Bay campus and hauling him into the State House for interrogation, one of the journalists commented, "If we were not hitting a nerve, if we were not having some kind of effect on the other students and the people of Freetown, then why would he bother with us?" He continued a career as a journalist after his graduation, and at the time of our conversation was editor-in-chief of one of Freetown's most important and widely circulated newspapers.

These men's experiences reveal that students became people of consequence the moment they were arrested during the Stevens regime, and this boundary was configured around them through their material entanglement with the newspaper. If they had been ignored, or their repression had been a quiet, internal matter, there would never have been the possibility of seeing them as any more than troublemakers or as their behavior as typical of their age or status. It was Siaka Stevens observing them as a threat and treating them as such that generated this boundary of "dangerous students." A decade later another group of Fourah Bay College students dabbled in politics, only this time their goals *were* revolutionary. Rather than overtly demanding democratic reform from the government, which was headed by Siaka Stevens's stooge Joseph Momoh, they encouraged young army officers to stage a coup. In a previous publication, I wrote about these student revolutionaries holding secret meetings with the officers in Freetown in 1991, urging them to install the student leaders as cabinet members in the new government (Bolten 2009b). The coup occurred in 1992, but to the disappointment of the involved students the successful officers established a new government on their own, the National Provisional Ruling Council (NPRC), and failed to appoint any of the activists to key positions. As one of my interlocutors, the ringleader for the ostensible student coup, remarked bitterly, "It was supposed to be an opportunity to turn the government over to us, the intelligentsia. Instead it became the children's coup." In this case weaponry, and not paperwork, forced people to take the young seriously. However, unlike young rebels terrorizing the rural areas, the NPRC initially generated a very different agential cut, one of optimism, patriotism, and support. This reveals that not all boys with guns are the same; that the moment of encounter generates novel boundaries depending on the form of observation enacted by observers.

There are many theories about what happened to bring the NPRC and its twenty-five-year-old leader, Captain Valentine Strasser, to power, but very little concrete knowledge of what actually happened on the day of the coup. What is known is that a group of young officers abandoned their posts at the eastern front of the civil war and arrived in Freetown on April 29, 1992. Some accounts state that the officers originally came to demand better pay and conditions of service from Momoh's government and seized power when Momoh refused (Zack-Williams and Riley 1993; Richards 1996:9), others that the coup was planned as an urban "lumpen" youth takeover (Abdullah 2004; Rashid 2004:84). There was no disputing that the NPRC was chaotic. Hoffman called it "a haphazard affair" (2011b:34), and Gberie, "a mutiny that escalated into a coup" (2005:68). In 2014 a reporter found Strasser, now an alcoholic hermit with a violent temper, and described him as a man who "accidentally seized power" (Mark 2016). Despite its inauspicious start, many scholars were initially optimistic about the potential for the junta to successfully end the war and usher the country into a new era of democracy (Da Costa 1992; Opala 1994). Young people were especially enthusiastic, undertaking street cleaning and mural painting in Freetown to express their support (Rashid 2004:84; Richards 1996:9).

The NPRC was not immune to a shift in the agential cut, from support to disdain, once the substance of their materially mediated performances changed. It became apparent quickly that the soldiers were more interested in fast cars, large houses, and parties than they were in running the country. Stated one officer who served in the army under the NPRC, "At first they preached all of the good words about reform and democracy, but then they realized that they wouldn't have the Mercedes Benz, the women wouldn't pay attention to them if they kept their promise and had an election and handed over power. So they became just like all the other politicians, and they bought more cars and designer clothes." This shift away from serious behavior eroded public confidence. Monica Mark writes, "Meetings were often presided over by men trailing the scent of weed. Strasser sought . . . to make the disco classic 'Ain't No Stoppin' Us Now" the national anthem, and Valentine's Day and Bob Marley's Birthday were both celebrated with official festivities" (2016). This was a far cry from the youth politics of the WAYL. Indeed, instead of rejecting the corruption of the old guard, the new guard simply replaced Stevens's brutality with impulsive frivolity. The corruption remained the same (Gberie 2005:12; Kpundeh 2004:91; Rashid 2004; Richards 1996:xix), and soon the form of observation that Sierra Leoneans enacted on the NPRC cast them as no different from their forebears—merely replicating those politics in different clothes. It was only the material form of the young officers' indulgences and corruption that differed, reflecting the global resonances of the world in which they grew up.

By 1996 it was clear that the NPRC was making no headway in the war against the RUF, that the spending habits of its inner circle were draining the already struggling country dry, and that Strasser had no plans to transition the country to democracy. Disappointment and disillusionment with the youth government was rampant, and citizens and the international community were making increasingly urgent demands for elections. Reacting to Strasser's foot-dragging, his second in command, Maada Bio, deposed him in a palace coup. After gathering a platoon of troops loyal to him, Bio marched into Strasser's office, held a gun to his head, and bundled him into a helicopter bound for Guinea (see Bolten 2012a:59). Bio initiated elections with the help of the United Nations, and on March 29, 1996, handed over power to Tejan Kabbah. Bio was reconfigured as the mature leader of the NPRC, though he was only three years older than Strasser and had himself benefitted personally from being the country's ostensible vice president for four years.

His brief time as head of state was followed by his retirement from the Sierra Leone military, from whence he applied for and was granted political asylum in the United States, where he remained until 2005. While in the United States he earned an MA from American University in International Relations, got married, and had three children.

In returning the country to democracy and stepping out of the spotlight, Bio had crafted the possibility of being taken seriously by the political establishment, even as his sacrifice led to a comfortable life in the United States. In choosing anonymity he could be fashioned as a legitimate politician, in opposition to other NPRC members, who navigated different paths to either shame and exile, as occurred with Strasser (Mark 2016), or returned quietly to military careers. His path echoed what Shepler found for child combatants returning home after the war. The successful cases were "spontaneous reintegrators" who returned home without NGO assistance, and adopted a mentality of humility and conformity in their communities (2005:205; 2014). However, Bio's long-term intentions were clear when, upon returning to Sierra Leone in 2005, he immediately challenged for the leadership of the Sierra Leone People's Party (SLPP). He remained in the party even though he failed to win the leadership, and was nominated as the SLPP's presidential candidate in 2012. The boy captain who had salvaged his reputation from the children's coup by humbly handing the country over to an elder was recognizable as a serious somebody by his party, and was now in a position to achieve the presidency democratically. This moment illustrates perfectly the indeterminacy of identities and their ability to be fashioned anew in novel encounters.

Presidential candidate Bio visited Makeni in early November 2012 for a public forum at the University of Makeni (UNIMAK). There was a tremendous buzz of excitement over what the SLPP candidate would say in this heavily APC-supporting area, sitting President Ernest Koroma's hometown. I watched students and staff spend hours setting up chairs and benches in the university's main courtyard to accommodate the anticipated crowds, as a makeshift stage went up and the university's temperamental public address system was coaxed into life. Hundreds of people swarmed into the courtyard—students, traders, artisans, professionals—clamoring for a glimpse of the candidate. A few young men dressed in elaborate green outfits showed up, and one dressed like a leprechaun began serenading a small assembled crowd on his accordion. Bio took the stage without fanfare and sat quietly at the table, flanked by the Catholic Bishop and the vice chancellor of the University.

After the vice chancellor, affectionately known as "Father Joe," got the crowd noise down to a hum, he invited the accordion player on stage for a song, to the amusement and appreciation of the crowd. The young man, throwing caution to the wind, mounted the stage and, hands shaking, performed a song he called "Maada Bio" (see Figure 5.1). Encouraged by the thunderous applause, he stole a quick glance at the candidate, who smiled and nodded at him. Bio then signaled to a man standing behind him and whispered something in his ear. The man beckoned to the accordion player to follow him. The young man stumbled and nearly fell over, surprised that his gesture was indeed successful in gaining Bio's public appreciation. It was proof that youthful risk-taking can pay off (Simone 2004, 2008), even if under the circumstances of a young man acting in a subservient and obsequious manner. Unlike Ousman and his statue of Ernest Koroma, a youth risking looking like a fool and being hounded out of an official event could be given a pat on the back—and some small financial reward—for making clear his inferior social position vis-à-vis others.

An undergraduate student introduced Bio, fashioning him as a particularly legitimate candidate to the audience. The student emphasized Bio's Catholicism (UNIMAK is a Catholic university), and that he "gave

FIGURE 5.1 Maada Bio (seated in front of the microphone) is serenaded before his speech.

service" to the nation in the armed forces. No mention was made of the NPRC except that "he served briefly as head of state." Bio took the stage, an air of expectation hanging over the crowd. How would the former youth statesman, a member of Sierra Leone's militariat, the military-proletariat (Kandeh 1996), perform his new role as presidential nominee? Would the audience interpret him as such? His address, titled "A New Direction for Sierra Leone," was polished and articulate. He measured his remarks to allow for polite applause between comments, and the address culminated in a focus on education, catering to the largely student-based crowd. He proposed discarding an APC-initiated change to the education system that would have added an extra year of secondary school—to thunderous applause from the students—and received equal enthusiasm for each proposal to strengthen the education system and ensure it was both free and compulsory.

If Bio's public addressed had finished there, it would have been unquestionable that the agential cut made on his performance would configure him unequivocally as a "big man" (Enria 2015), an adult who had the backing of his party and his people, a determinate identity in that encounter. However, the forum had a question-and-answer session, which opened the space for quite different agential cuts to be made. A student asked the first question: "In 1992, together with a group of other young military officers, you ascended the presidency through the bullet. On November 17th, you want to ascend the presidency through the ballot. How will you manage this extreme political transition? Thank you." Laughter and hoots of appreciation rippled through the crowd, which were quickly quelled by the moderator, who insisted, "Please limit your questions to The New Direction!" Though the event was brought firmly back under control, the question illuminated the indeterminacy of this politician: that he could still be configured as a youth and a "coup-monger" and his performance of adulthood was fragile.

What reconfigured Bio as an adult and a statesman was that he chose to answer the question, seizing control of the encounter and establishing his relationship with his interlocutor as one of respectful but firm discourse, rather than one of entreaty and a need to be taken seriously. He emphasized that he had initially determined that force was the only way to end twenty-three years of one-party rule, but then himself turned the country over to a democratically elected leader. He concluded, "At a very defining moment in the history of this country, I chose to sacrifice all the benefits of leading a nation just so that we can have democracy and peace." He moved seamlessly to answering the next question, and the rest of questions posed addressed only issues emerging from his speech. In spite of the challenge to his history as a youth, being responsible for a coup *and* a palace coup and somehow ascending to the rank of brigadier general despite serving only ten years in the military, Bio was not uppity, a charlatan, hooligan, or troublemaker. His audience responded with only education-related questions from that point, reinforcing an agential cut of respect; thus generating a phenomenon of the reformer, the savior, and somehow also the future. His identity was not fixed with clear boundaries; indeed its very indeterminacy was encapsulated in the first question, and he emerged at the end with a very different identity than he had upon first ascending the stage.

In 2017 Bio once again gained the SLPP presidential nomination, and narrowly beat APC candidate Dr. Samura Kamara in a runoff in March 2018. He was inaugurated as the country's fifth president on April 4, 2018. In actions typical of his predecessors in the State House, he moved quickly to establish his presidency, dismissing public servants with spotty attendance records, halting all foreign business contracts that had been forged by Koroma's government, and initiating corruption investigations into most departing members of the APC government. This housecleaning was not a novel approach to the first hundred days; indeed Bio's two predecessors had initiated similar processes of eviscerating the previous government in establishing their own presidencies. However, Bio did abolish application fees to all government tertiary institutions in one of his first acts, fulfilling a single small promise he had first made to university students six years earlier. Despite initially being a member of the children's coup, Bio's performance of the democratically elected presidency revealed his adherence to, rather than distance from, previous performances of the same office. Youth politics in this instance were just politics with a slightly different global valence.

That a member of a haphazard coup that descended into corruption and condemnation could then ascend to the presidency democratically reveals that configurations of youth are malleable, performance-based, and prone to reconfiguration in future encounters. It is not merely that Maada Bio was older, waiting nine years before trying his hand at politics again. Many would-be politicians with much cleaner histories of maturity and lack of corruption failed where he succeeded. It was not that he was respected for completing the life-course transition, fulfilling qualifying tenets of adulthood such as marriage, supporting a family, and achieving widespread respect in his community. In fact, Bio faced heavy criticism from opposition factions after the 2012 election for various charges of domestic violence and bigamy (Cham 2013; Kanu 2013). It was that Bio had transformed his material entanglement from guns to paperwork, opening the door to new agential cuts, and had assembled a strong enough network of powerful allies and supporters that his performances did not comprise risk on his part. He did not have to engage in overt entreaties to more powerful people in order to generate respect. Instead he could calmly address or refute configurations of militariat, youth, and coup-monger, among others, expressing powerful agency in his encounters with his audience and proving that his identity did not pre-exist his relationship with that audience.

What does it take for an individual to emerge from repeated configurations of "dangerous youth" to become respected and powerful? How can one subtly shift from indeterminate young person—known as politically illegitimate before he disappeared—to being taken seriously, to being able to take risks without being consistently configured as revolutionary or an upstart? Bio articulated during his speech at UNIMAK that his time in the NPRC opened his eyes to the importance of democratic governance, which he solidified with his degrees in International Relations, and recently, a PhD in peace studies from the University of Bradford.[1] Critics contended that he undertook a PhD to polish his credentials, as they claim that illiterate Sierra Leoneans treat anyone with that degree "like a demi-god," and he had to draw attention away from his brigadier status being declared "fake" by serving officers in the armed forces (Anonymous 2014; Thomas 2014). These critiques certainly bolster the argument that Bio self-consciously undertook performances to distance himself from his past in anticipation of future encounters that may still configure him as a coup-mongering youth, grasping for power and trying to overthrow the system. For other young people who hope to be taken seriously by configuring themselves as politicians, their materially entangled performances calculated to reveal them as actors of consequence are often the very reason they are configured as dangerous, illegitimate, and thus unfit for adulthood.

"University Is Our Training Ground for Politics"

The majority of national politicians began their political careers in student government, which is fruitful ground for discussing how self-fashioning and repeated material performances influence encounters. In this case, those encounters were between student politicians and university administrators. I had in-depth conversations about the relationship between student politics and national politics with students from three different universities: Fourah Bay College in Freetown (FBC), and UNIMAK and Northern Polytechnic in Makeni. UNIMAK is the only private university among the three, and the only religious institute, having been founded by the Catholic Church. These conversations revealed critical insights into how and why student politics is where agential cuts of il/legitimacy occur, where students are simultaneously taken seriously by adults as political actors, and are consistently configured as nonadults who do not deserve the rights and privileges of self-governance or a say over larger governance structures, precisely because their actions replicate those of adults so closely. The relationship generated in repeated encounters between student politicians and adults also matters, as they encounter each other either as enemies, threats, challengers, or co-constitutors of the nation.

The boundary configurations around student politicians are clear outgrowths of recent national politics, but are also manifestations of colonial policy, which transformed chieftaincies from accountable structures to fiefdoms. Thus, student politicians—and all aspiring national politicians—embody historic processes of globalization that enabled and rewarded patronage and corruption. The abiding entanglement of student politics with national politics, the fear and repression that greets student politics, and the fascinating outcome of a university that chose to ban its student union all reveal youth politics as il/legitimacy; that the politics of the young are taken seriously as threats to the boundaries around adulthood partially through their replication of the corruption of political big men in the colonial period. They are a phenomenon generated by a colonial policy that allowed previously accountable chiefs to become tyrants. They highlight that new boundaries are constantly being fashioned around the young, who utilize existing material and linguistic structures to erect challenges to those boundaries.

In September 2012, I interviewed six FBC students who had forced the closure of the campus the month before and then traveled home to Makeni. The student body had burned tires and changed the padlocks on building doors to keep faculty off campus. It was a violent response to the administration forcibly ejecting thirty-one students from residence hostels for allegedly residing in them illegally (Fofanah 2012). One of the ejected students sat across from me, and he claimed that the rustication was a campaign against student leaders who opposed the administration. This set the stage for a discussion of what seriousness looks like for young people in politics, and under what circumstances students are either configured as actors of consequence, or whether—like the NPRC—they seize power and work on the details of public opinion later. The discussion focused on how learning to be a politician was about continually shifting one's identity to suit the needs of the moment—that to be an adult was when a boundary of legitimacy was constructed around a person in spite of their actions—and that university was where students learned how to do this. The idea that one's indeterminate identity could be "worked on" to produce consequences emerged in our discussions of how they related to their elders in encounters.

"University is our training ground for politics. Most of what happens at FBC isn't the classroom education, it is navigating student union politics with respect to the administration." The student who spoke first, whom I call Umaru, admitted that he attended FBC to be a politician. For him, university was the appropriate setting for his training not just because of the student politics but because so many faculty members were politicians; indeed the college was "a place to land" for politicians who were out of power. He continued, "Everyone says that if you are successful in the student union at FBC, then you will be a successful politician, and we have seen that, quite recently. If you can fight your fights at Fourah Bay, you can be successful. So the educated ones from FBC who know the problems of youth, they . . . have had to fight for so long, this makes them good politicians." In essence, learning to continually fashion one's self vis-à-vis established politicians is what creates new politicians among the young—that they have to hone their performances in repeated encounters to influence the agential cut made on them.

The more the students talked about their actions—performances they described as "serious politics"—the more it appeared that these actions combined national party squabbles with the tactics of the NPRC, where forcible action was followed by requests for legitimacy. Students who felt that they were consistently treated as illegitimate actors without recourse chose material means other than filing grievances and writing articles to provoke encounters where they would be treated as consequential. This begins with the student union at FBC not representing a unified student voice; instead it has party representation, just like "downtown" politics outside the campus. The main issue the student politicians articulated in 2012 was the administration taking student union fees for their own use, and refusing to recognize the union as a pressure group dedicated to student welfare that was protected by the school's constitution. This was mostly because the party in power in the union, the "black" party widely described as the university's APC, represented opposing political associations to the majority of administrators, who sympathized with the "white" party associated with the SLPP.

Because their continued protests, demands to see the student union account book, and requests for meetings were rebuffed, the "black" students chose another materially mediated route to being deigned actors of consequence: forcibly occupying structures. Though class was not in session and the hostels chosen were empty due to their poor condition, the students squatted in them as a way of being seen, publicly, as actors whose demands must be addressed. The supposed substance of this protest was the inability of poor local students to stay in the hostels over holidays while wealthy foreign students were allowed to remain. This was a material response related to the problem it highlighted; however, all thirty-one students who engaged in the protest were members of the "black" student party. The administration pronounced their protest—because it did not take the form of respectful negotiations with their elders—as illegitimate, and physically removed them.

The students' performance of occupation, of requesting treatment as legitimate political actors who can inhabit spaces on behalf of their poor brethren, must be qualified by its "backstage" aspects (Goffman 1959). The protest and the reasons for their rustication were less pure than initially stated, and in fact revealed their similarity with adult politicians, and thus the reason for the administration treating them as outlaws rather than as serious political actors. Umaru explained, "Students at FBC, probably because they can be resident on campus, it makes it easier for them to converge to take decisions, they have more time to concentrate on politics, it gives them more energy and time for politics than students at other campuses across the country. Politics at FBC is a very serious thing, it is really the only practical you get! After class the only thing you do is mix with friends and play politics!" In essence, it was the ability to be in residence that enabled student politics. These students, who continually accused the administration of corruption, did not hide that their own motives were not merely supporting poor students, but maintaining their own staging ground. Just as the NPRC quickly became the corrupt regime it so decried when it came into power, so do student politics at FBC proudly and openly replicate downtown politics in their student union. However, the success of Maada Bio makes it clear that practicing politics as a young person does not determine one's identity as forever a troublemaker—on the contrary, it is a series of performances through which they can shift the agential cut; the observations made on their encounters with others in the future (Nyberg 2009:1,184).

Student government emerged as a matter of grave consequence within the larger political landscape with the elections at Northern Polytechnic University in 2012. Northern Polytechnic is a government institution like FBC, but its location in Makeni is geographically distant from the downtown politics cited by FBC students as an enrollment draw. It did not have former politicians on the faculty, and the primary educational focus was vocations such as teaching and agriculture. These would appear to produce a school whose student elections are inconsequential; in fact, as the student body president, Abdul, explained to me when we spoke, "all human beings are political beings." He was referring to the fact that even the student government elections at a small college could be a cause for concern for downtown politics.

My conversation with Abdul occurred in the wake of the mayor interfering in the student body election because he supported another candidate. This is an interesting twist on know-your-place aggression (Mitchell 2013, 2015), as it indicates the mayor's acknowledgment of the blurry boundaries between adults and young people in politics. He opposed Abdul not on the basis of his age, but because he was a member of the Fula tribe from Mile 91, a town located about a hundred miles southwest of Makeni. Abdul emphasized that the student government had worked for a transparent election process in order to be treated as legitimate by the administration (see Greenberg 2014:171). He explained, "The polling went smoothly and the ballots were being counted in a room full of people with all three aspirants present. Legitimate polling practices! I was ahead by 51 votes and the mayor arrived and stopped the counting, and then confusion started." Panic erupted among the students, who poured out onto the quad shouting that the mayor had canceled the election. The police were called, and they fired tear gas canisters and live bullets at the students. Abdul explained, "It was not a riot! It was a protest!" He believed the mayor thought that bringing in the police would delegitimize the students as political actors. "Had they dealt with us like adults who were running an honest and fair election then we would not be in this position."[2] Abdul's vehement defense of the students highlights how the agential cut can be manipulated in an encounter. Calling a public disturbance a protest, as opposed to a riot, only reveals whether or not the activity was considered a legitimate form of contestation (Murphy 2011). That everyone assumed the students had been violent reveals that the typical cut made on young people is that they are illegitimate political actors.

The furor forced the mayor to allow a second election to save face, and Abdul was allowed to stand for election again. The result was, as Abdul put it, "a tsunami victory!" He more than doubled his nearest opponent's votes, making it impossible for the mayor to intervene again, and he set to work immediately. He explained, "I am a practical politician, not a theoretical politician. Action passes intention!" In invoking President Ernest Koroma's own mantra about physical changes being more important than words, Abdul linked his performance to that of Makeni's hometown hero. His focus was material changes that the students could see and benefit from every day: "It is because of me that we have a working photocopier and our copies are the cheapest in all of Makeni. I also had 106 scientific calculators donated for our technical students to use. And we had this one classroom building that was not finished, so I bought five bags of cement and we paved the floor and the fittings, we finished it! You see, a word spoken will never come back, you cannot build your politics on what you say." Paperwork, technology, and structures were what Abdul wanted, because he believed that only material proof of his seriousness, and not arguments with the mayor about constitutionality, would establish him as a serious person.

Unlike FBC and Northern Polytechnic, UNIMAK is a private university, and has no constitutionally mandated student government. Between when the university was founded by the Catholic Diocese in 2005, to 2012 when I conducted this research, student government had been started and stopped three times. The registrar, a law professor I call John, had a keen interest in exposing the students to the workings of legal democracy, but argued that every time student government was dissolved it was because it violated those tenets. As a legal scholar, he wanted a government that reflected his idea of true democratic frameworks, even as that definition is an open question in anthropology (see Bolten 2016; Comaroff and Comaroff 1997; and Paley 2002). It emerged that the students had locally grounded understandings of democracy, and considered their activities nothing more than an honest replication of national politics. John's argument, however, was that these activities were corrupt because they stemmed not from the democracy of pre-colonial Sierra Leone, but from the tyrannical despotism that emerged as democracy under colonialism. This renders student politics, at FBC and elsewhere, neither a reflection of new progressive politics nor of old forms of local governance, but of hundred-year-old global inputs that became locally embedded and *de*-democratized public life. Ironically, precolonial Sierra Leonean politics, though elitist, contained powerful forms of public participation that we associate with contemporary democracy. These were repressed, and in many ways destroyed, by colonial administration and what followed. In essence, John was seeking to awaken precolonial democratic echoes, not institute Western democracy (see Moran 2006).

The student government was banned twice for engaging in "corrupt" activities, which the school administration argued revealed the students as too immature to be treated like adults. This was the case even as the students' activities closely mimicked national politics and the fights that FBC's student government was so proud of. This was youth performance generating both moral panic (Cohen 1980) and know-your-place aggression (Mitchell 2013, 2015). John described the first student government as "cultist," meaning they held meetings in secret without informing the administration, and membership was restricted. This cultism—which John saw as undermining democracy—resembled the "black" and "white" parties at FBC, as well as echoing older forms of local governance where a few selected people deliberated and made decisions on everyone's behalf (Ferme 1999, 2001; Fanthorpe 2005). The student government was abolished for a second time after it initiated a disruptive campus strike because it did not receive its funding on time. The administration was delayed collecting tuition and fees that year, so it was not a case of the students having their money deliberately withheld; they were merely suffering empty coffers on par with every campus unit. According to John, it was their hubris in demanding money they knew was unavailable that prompted the ban. The students I spoke with claimed that the strike was called "on moral grounds," and that the administration's own failure to collect fees should not be passed on to the students. However, the students were made to know their place in the hierarchy, which, as John put bluntly, "is at the bottom."

After these two misfires and a government that was dissolved for lack of activity, John devised a council where students elected representatives without parties, tickets, running mates, or ballots. Every candidate was a write-in, so there was no chance of coercion or tamper-ing. He described how these measures produced entirely different forms of governance than had existed before: "The lack of parties means there is less internal control. It is harder to gain obedience and people falling in line without a base of party support. And the executive did propose measures that failed, for example that members of the executive should have full scholarships paid for from the student council funds. The rest of the council shot this down because there wasn't enough money for every council member to have one. On the downside, the council lacks the built-in discipline that parties provide, and no institutional memory. When everyone stands individually, they have to expend a lot of energy staying popular, and even then, the last election returned only 25 percent of the incumbents. And there is always a shifting coalition within the council of those who support the executive and those who do not, which means we can't know what the council might accomplish." The students played by the rules and embraced the council structure in spite of those rules preventing real movement on their priority welfare issues. Why?

John drew a contrast between the council workings and chiefdom politics under colonial policy. British administrators drew lines around chiefdoms and forced people to stay put and be governed by an ap-pointed chief. This was a direct counter to older forms of governance where people "voted with their feet" and deserted unpopular chiefs (Alie 1990; Ferme 2001). In this case, instead of increasing mobility and exposure to other ideas, global inputs rendered people less mobile and cosmopolitan, more docile and easier to exploit because of their inability to move (see Shaw 2002). Because the student elections were a simple, individual popularity contest, the candidates had to fairly represent their fellows to stay in power. As John explained, "There is no room for despotism to creep in." John saw UNIMAK as a precolonial chiefdom, with the vice chancellor, Father Joe, in charge: "I think all of this comes down to the fact that the students really trust Father Joe. They believe that Father Joe is benign and well-intentioned, whereas they expect bad things to come from the FBC leadership because they are all political animals. It is more than the fact that Father Joe is a priest . . . they always call him 'Father Joe' and don't refer to him by any of his other titles. He's not 'Professor Joe,' he's not 'Vice Chancellor,' he's 'Father Joe.' The 'Pa' aspect of his character is more important than his official capacities. This is Father Joe's chiefdom, but they are all welcome to leave if they don't want to be here. I think they all want to be here."

The history of student government at UNIMAK, which has been under Father Joe's guidance since the school opened, reveal that young people pushing boundaries does not result in them always achieving— or even desiring—treatment as adults. John believed they saw Father Joe as a benevolent chief, essentially "unlearning" their own colonial history. From my years working at the university, whether as a student or lecturer, John's words rang true: the students all wanted to be *bien*, or "behind" Father Joe, initiating a relationship of dependence where they felt stronger being configured as his students, and his children, than they would fighting for political gains at a different university (see Ferguson 2013). The phrase "*yu boboh de*," which I spoke of in the introduction as meaning "your boy is around," is suggestive here. Understanding themselves as Father Joe's supporters, who were under his protection and benefaction, reveal that in Joe's chiefdom, the roles were not generated so much as adult and youth, but as benevolent parent and nurtured child. When the parent is a priest and his "children" in their twenties, it reveals that boundaries are not always negative; they can be adopted by people who feel socially stronger for occupying them. This was an overt nod to preglobal forms. The conservatism revealed here of adhering to unequal dynamics within an encounter was not singular to UNIMAK— in fact it was replicated by young people in the town's ataya bases.

Accommodating In/equality and Inclusive Exclusion

As occurred with the WAYL at the start of this chapter, being treated as someone of consequence and included by those in power requires that one's efforts be familiar and nonthreatening—this is the heart of young people performing conservatism rather than progressive or radical politics. And as I have emphasized throughout the book, social position is always relative to encounters—there is no demographic cut-off point demarcating youth and adult in African social worlds. What comprises progressive versus conservative orientations, as adult manipulations of student politics in the previous section revealed, is also down to who is performing the agential cut. There was no better example of how the young performed deliberately for APC politicians than in ataya bases, where slightly better-off young people were configured as adults relative to their fellows. They became club administrators, providing counseling, advice, and money to their unemployed brethren, and became "big" within the clubs, closely replicating the patronage politics that has characterized governance in Sierra Leone since independence (see Reno 2008). Any individual can acquire "wealth in people" by acquiring debts of gratitude among those they assist (see Miers and Kopytoff 1977; Nyerges 1992). Ataya politics were not new or radical forms of youth organization, but performances replicating existing forms of hierarchy and advancement on a more intimate scale. The better-off members provided resources for poor members, and relied on them for support in their own bids to be taken seriously as people who had others behind them. Rather than a new form of collective organizing, ataya bases were serious in their faithful adherence to the social framework of status-seeking, and using the clubs as a staging ground for small-scale adult politics.

Politics in Sierra Leone is less about policy platforms and appealing to constituencies based on the public good than it is about the benefits that accrue from personal connections. Politics *is* personal, in that supporting one candidate over another is entirely a matter of who will provide individuals with the greatest reward. Young people thought of themselves as a constituency specifically referred to as "youth", and, as the preceding pages have made clear, they *were* bound together by common experiences, common aspirations, common disappointments, and being painted with the war-affected brush that categorized them as lazy consumers and short-term thinkers. However, this sense of a larger public disappeared within the conversations in ataya bases where youth expressed the substance of those hopes, dreams, and disappointments. In place of a public arose the same hierarchies, relationships of power, and *yu boboh deh* as characterizes politics writ large, even as individuals, just like the bureaucrat in *The Beautyful Ones Are Not Yet Born*, failed to realize it. In essence, the agential cut they made was believing that they had the power to take themselves seriously, rather than recognizing that this power lay with others, whose forms of observation could—and did—exclude them.

Ataya bases were not simply gathering places where all youth were equal. Part of the appeal for unemployed youth was the mixing and mingling of diverse young people, where the unemployed might be lifted up by their better-off brothers—a different version of the Father Joe phenomenon. The bases all boasted members who were employed or university students, who had material means to be taken seriously even if it had not yet occurred. These young men, who called themselves "youth" from their own experiences of exclusion, served informally as mentors, counselors, and cheerleaders for their unemployed brethren, thereby "accompanying" the unemployed in their struggles. The officers of the bases acknowledged these existing hierarchies without drawing power from them: the chairman, secretary, and treasurer were administrators rather than office-holders, and held no coercive abilities over other members. These positions were considered honors bestowed on admired youth by their brothers, and highlighted and reinforced the extant inequalities among youth. Unemployed youth drew hope and inspiration from their "elevated brothers," many of whom in 2012 were using their visibility to run for local office (per the tenets of the Truth and Reconciliation Commission recommendations that required parties to commit 10 percent of their nominations to youth). Many of the visits of these young candidates to their own ataya bases were treated like constituency visits, as the would-be politicians listened sincerely to the troubles of their fellows. These enactments of difference within ataya bases reinforces the idea that youth comes into being in performances and encounters, in this case with youth candidates talking to their youth constituencies.

Concurrently, as youth politicians cultivated constituencies among their fellows, they competed for attention with the "big" politicians—candidates for parliament—canvassing for votes. Big politicians frequented bases to survey the youth—essentially casting their eye over them—extolling them to membership of their party, wooing young people with promises of more jobs and fewer barriers to education. Big politicians occasionally hired a token young person from an ataya base as temporary staff, enacting a performance of inclusion to stimulate political support. The last point was something that youth politicians, even those with family support for their campaigns, could rarely afford, making it a source of distress because they were known as candidates without resources, and thus without consequence. For the youth who were singled out for employment by big men, these hopeful moments were also moments of know-your-place aggression, as they put the youth politician in his place, and, eventually, the chosen youth staff member as well. One young man described his friend's experiences, which represented that of dozens of individuals, during the 2007 election:

> One of my friends was a strong guy; he was built powerfully! One of the politicians found him just as the campaign season started, and said, "Hey, my friend! Why don't you come work for me?" My friend agreed, and became the politician's chief of security. He went with him everywhere, day and night, making sure that the situations were safe for this politician. He was paid a daily rate, and he spent months thinking that he was proving himself so well. He was loyal to this politician, and then this guy was elected. The election was over

and my friend was so happy, because he had succeeded! Days went by and he waited for this guy, now honorable [the local moniker for a member of parliament] to contact him and give him a place on his permanent team. Nothing. Weeks. Nothing. He went to his office and the door was always closed to him. And then one day he saw this honorable passing his ataya base in his vehicle, and he ran out to the car. It stopped, and the back window came down. The honorable gave him Le10,000 [about $3], and said, "Now leave me alone."

These stories reinforced boundaries configured around youth: that they were people who could be excluded without consequence. As one youth explained, "The politicians are coming, telling us to be their dogs so that they can misuse us. They think we want to remove them from power, so they don't give us a position of trust. But we are trying to be conscious now!"

This consciousness took the form of institutionalized suspicion of politicians bearing gifts and favors, but it did not extend to a critique of the system of political exclusion itself. In fact, many serious young people thought they were making great strides in 2012 in joining the system. That year the APC brought youth into the system by establishing its own Electoral College. Candidates for office would be nominated within the party through the votes of delegates, with different segments of the APC's constituent base offering their support en masse to one candidate or another. The individuals I spoke with about this were excited, as they saw the movement toward delegates as an acknowledgment of the importance of youth to the future of politics—that they were being taken seriously. In fact, they were suffering an insidious and quiet form of know-your-place aggression. All the ataya bases together had a single delegate, as did the poyo sellers, the motorbike riders' association, and other in/visible groups of youth. Collectively the youth had a dozen party delegates, out of a total of thirty-five. They never formed a majority of delegates, nor did those delegates have any power beyond the nomination of the candidate. It is a prime illustration of the in/visibility and il/legitimacy of political youth, as they were bounded as special interest groups, barely differentiated masses of humanity noticed and acknowledge because of their numbers, but without power. Among the youth I spoke to about the Electoral College, however, there was universal approval of the new system. Said one, "Before this time, issues of youth were not discussed at length. Politicians would just say, 'Leave them there, they are just drunkards, they are just *jamba* smokers,' when they would talk about the youth, considering us all half-baked. With the electoral college, the elders saw that indeed the youth need to be encouraged and incorporated."

In essence, the big politicians did not use ataya bases to config-ure youth differently for jobs or politics; instead they were created as "lumpen" groups more intelligible and slightly more visible to existing processes. When I interviewed ataya base members about the youth candidates who were running for office from their bases, the most im-portant thing mentioned when offering their support to their elevated brother was their personal connection and the benefits that would come from it. The youth politicians did not articulate bold visions for change or areas of policy focus; instead they offered a simple replication of exist-ing performances and boundaries, but with their own rear ends warm-ing the city council seat, rather than those of adult politician. One young man extolled the virtues of his friend, who was sitting next to him, and was running for a local council seat: "This man is a brother to me. If he wins, I can go to his office, and I know he won't lock the door on me, he will say, 'This man can enter.'" He was not describing a transforma-tion of political processes or an end to ideas of youth and adult through politics, or the material structures through which performances are en-acted and observations made. This was simple recognition that youth could be an inclusive boundary in those encounters—and only those encounters—rather than one of exclusion and difference. It was politics just as adult politicians practiced it, but with a younger face behind the desk, doling out favors to his own friends. As another youth chimed in, with no sense of irony, "The political system is not fragile at all." What appeared as novel configurations resulting from being taken seriously were, in fact, the same performances with a different cast of characters. As the final section makes clear, when youth participate to be taken seri-ously, they are at their most vulnerable for adult abuse and aggression.

"We Are the Youth Party"

Part of the faith that young people have in politics is the robustness of the party system, where democracy lives in the ability of people to change parties and alliances, enacting older local forms of democratic governance (see Bolten 2016; Comaroff and Comaroff 1997; Moran 2006). This is reflected most strikingly in the frequent birth of new par-ties and coalitions. Young people are not forced through ethnicity or region to be members of the SLPP or APC. They also move between the main parties, and occasionally flock to small parties who purport to see them as political actors whose voices, candidacies, and votes matter. Though they are replicating precolonial local forms of democracy in doing so, the idea of leaving a nonbenevolent chief to adhere to another does not always result in inclusion; instead it can merely make one's failure to be taken seriously, and one's exclusion from the boundaries of serious politics more abundantly, and painfully, clear (see Greenberg 2014:37). One such party whose history illustrated that process during the 2012 elections was the United Democratic Movement (UDM), the self-branded youth party.

The UDM was referred to by many young people in Makeni as the "grandbaby" of the SLPP, which nodded to the genealogy of the party and also enacted its exclusion from political adulthood. It came into being after two iterations of disagreements among big men (Utas 2012:6). The first was in 2007 when Charles Margai, upset that he had not been given the SLPP's nomination for president, broke off to form his own party, the People's Movement for Democratic Change (PMDC). The PMDC, like all political parties, rapidly adopted the materials of its performance: the color orange (in defiance of the SLPP's green) and a palm broom and palm fruit cluster for their banner. As one PMDC member explained to me, "In forming the party, Margai said he was cutting down the palm tree that represents the SLPP and taking only the most useful parts!" The PMDC became the spoiler party in the 2007 presidential elections when Charles Margai split the vote between the APC and SLPP. Because Sierra Leone's constitution requires an absolute popular majority to become president, Margai became the kingmaker in the run-off election, throwing his support behind Ernest Koroma in exchange for political favors. In 2010 Margai's deputy, Mohamed Bangura, was snubbed in his own quest to receive the PMDC's presidential nomination. He too voted with his feet, and founded his own party, the United Democratic Movement. Signaling his distance from that party, he chose the color purple (as purple emerges from combining the red of the APC with the green of the SLPP), and the cotton tree as its symbol. Selecting the cotton tree was particularly important, in no small part because of its association with Sierra Leone as a nation.[3] The cotton tree in downtown Freetown has been standing for over 250 years, and other full-grown specimens tower over the more common oil palm tree. Explained one enthusiastic UDM member, "It also blocks out the sun for anyone standing beneath it," referencing the APC slogan of a rising sun. Bangura chose "Yes, we can!" as the party's motto, connecting the party explicitly with Barack Obama, who was wildly popular among young people at the time. Bangura was casting a wide net, melding global appeal with local history, striking imagery, and strong metaphors (see Figure 5.2).

Bangura pushed the UDM as the youth party, and the moniker attracted young people from across the political spectrum who were disillusioned with their inability to gain positions in the main parties that would reflect them as actors of consequence. Bangura's credibility with young people rested on his own status as an "under-forty," even though, as one young APC supporter stated, "You are a youth when you have the sympathy of other youth. These youth politicians, they call themselves 'youth' but they don't share our plight because they are not youth. They don't know our problems." Entangling performance and the form of observation in an encounter, the quote strikes the heart of how Bangura's performance did not result in exclusionary boundary configurations around him. Young people did not consider him youth, precisely because he was always taken seriously and had a large supportive

FIGURE 5.2 The UDM headquarters sign in Makeni, 2012.

network. In fact, Bangura is the nephew of a famous politician and lived in Toronto during the war. He returned in 2005 as a political journalist, from whence he joined the PMDC. Always a member of the diasporic and political elite, Bangura would never be recognizable in encounters as youth, only as relatively young elite.

That being the case, Bangura had sufficient charisma to draw thousands of young people to his party and establish a national presence. The UDM rented out a small building on a main road in Makeni as its regional headquarters. My time conducting participant observation among the party revealed that politics was the place where young people leveraged all of their visible materials—structures, papers, and clothing—in performances that invited encounters where they were taken seriously. Simultaneously, they were being used by their own leader, who treated them as actors of consequence only in that corralling their numbers behind him in a voting block could induce the leaders of the APC and SLPP to take *him* seriously as a political contender. The legitimacy of his followers as political actors was in the material of their vote, which could leverage greater power for Bangura himself.

I attended my first UDM meeting in September 2012. As the party's regional executive secretariat gathered, the deputy regional secretary, whom I refer to as Mr. Kanu, introduced everyone and explained why they had all joined the youth party. He began, "We are the educated youth." Everyone around the room nodded, listing in turn their degrees and their age, and that they were unemployed. Most were in their twenties and thirties. All of them had been treated with disrespect, even mockery, in their job searches because, as he explained, "We are the unconnected." Every person in the room was a parent, but they were seen as youth in their everyday encounters. They joined the party because, as Mr. Kanu explained, "You do not have to follow the national policy to be a youth!" He was thirty-seven, and the policy he referred to bracketed youth as an age range between fifteen and thirty-five. The UDM is proof of youth as a diffraction pattern; a place where the effects of difference in the world are seen (Barad 2007:72). These were not just people who thought they would give themselves an identity label. To throw one's effort and resources into a new, tiny political party revealed that youth is not simply a category, it is a phenomenon of social-material boundaries, and that this exclusion generated new encounters—those that the UDM members hoped they could use to inspire others to treat them as actors of consequence. At this point a young man called Idriss, one of the party's aspirants (the local term for "nominee") arrived with campaign posters that he had just printed. His photo revealed an intense young man, dressed in a suit and staring into the camera. Everyone liked his motto, "Serve Humanity for Progress," with Mr. Kanu announcing that this was the kind of poster that would force everyone to take the candidates—and youth writ large—seriously.

Every party had been given designated campaign days during the election season, and the members were planning for their first day. Idriss's posters were held up as an example. Mr. Kanu extolled, "The UDM is real! How can anyone doubt our vision and our work when they see the posters? But you, the aspirants, have to be seen in the community, because this is not about your qualifications, it is about numbers, and we will have the numbers! And it is about issues, not policies!" He went on to emphasize that the party "was not tribal," like the others, as party leader Mohamed Bangura, his running mate, and the party deputy chair were from different parts of the country, and were qualified because they were all educated in Canada. He continued, "We have inclusion. We have a room for women, we have a room for the disabled, we have diversity!" As he spoke, he pointed to physical rooms in the house, each of which had designations of "Women's Wing" and "Disabled Wing" painted over the doorframe. It was not that the party had room for everyone; it had physical rooms for them. If the words were not enough to convince one of the party's commitment to diversity, it was certainly present in the physical spaces devoted to them, even as these rooms were empty of both people and furniture.

The evening was a performance that brought the UDM into being. The jumble of messages—that the party was not elitist but the administration was foreign-educated; that the party was about numbers and not qualifications even as they emphasized everyone's qualifications; that there was a difference, not enunciated, between issues and policies—revealed that the UDM was nothing that could be accurately captured and described in its political orientation. Just as "youth" does not pre-exist people's encounters, the meeting brought the youth party into existence through people sitting together in a purple-painted building, generating posters and the stuff of campaigns, chanting slogans, writing minutes, and planning, regardless of what was said or what it meant (see Coles 2004). It had designated rooms, everyone at the meeting had a title, and everyone knew the call and response, which was: "UDM?" "Yes we can!" and "Yes we can?" "UDM!" More than anything, the UDM existed in that every single person in the room could cast a vote that might matter in the election's outcome.

The second meeting looked much like the first, except for the absence of the aspirants. The regional chairwoman was running the meeting, and explained for my benefit that "they are running around trying to put modalities in place" for the campaign day. This turn of phrase meant that they were looking for money for campaign materials. What was striking about this was that the UDM, as an official party, had been provided with campaign funds from the Political Parties Registration Council (PPRC), whose mandate was to ensure peace and parity amongst the parties. Why had the aspirants not been given their share of this money? The deputy director asked where the stipend was for the building caretaker, and the chair responded that only the leader could pay him, as the regional chapters had never been given their own funds to spend. The chapter had also never been given the "official symbols", the party banners, to use in their campaigns. The primary materials of political performance—money, structures, banners, posters, t-shirts—were absent, rendering the candidates and the party unable to perform their seriousness with any real hope of success.

The material existence of the UDM mattered more than ever when the party's first campaign day arrived, and my husband and I were the only people standing outside the building waiting for something to happen. The building caretaker was on the porch, and he did not know where everyone was—the aspirants, the secretariat; no one had arrived. We eventually left. When I caught up with the public relations officer, Saio, the next day at a local relaxation, he was beside himself. "We never got out the door, we had to close the office and suspend the campaigns." After finding a place to sit down, Saio collected himself, and went on: "Mr. Kanu discovered that the leader [Mohamed Bangura] had given a small portion of the funds that were supposed to be given to the aspirants to the regional secretary [Mr. Kanu's boss] and he just chopped [stole] the money! And he won't answer to anything unless the leader is present. But the leader won't come up to Makeni, I don't think he has left Freetown since the campaign started. And where is the rest of the money? It is so embarrassing for the aspirants, because they believed in him and now he is just misusing them."

Saio then explained that many of the aspirants had so much faith in the party that they had sold their own possessions to fund their campaigns in the hopes of being reimbursed by Mr. Bangura. The executive was furious that the party was not funding its aspirants, and thought the chapter should go to the media with the story to shame Mr. Bangura into good behavior. Mr. Kanu stopped this from happening, saying that it would completely undermine the campaigns of the aspirants and embarrass them further, and he did not want them to look like fools. Saio explained that one aspirant was so committed that he had sold everything he owned to pay for posters, and Mr. Kanu did not want to dash his last hope. Mr. Kanu, for better or worse, was trying to salvage some dignity for his poor aspirants, whether or not Mohamed Bangura intended them to succeed. It was a moment where know-your-place aggression was abundantly clear. Young people enacted performances of aspiration, and their elite leader used the only form of consequence they had—their numbers as voters—to build a party to the point of legitimacy that it attracted government funding, which he used for himself and a few cronies, delegitimizing their vulnerable, poor aspirants, who had no recourse.

The legitimacy of the youth party and its members could not be separated from the materials of their performance, which, Saio explained, were never provided:

> This party was supposed to be for young people, and it was supposed to inspire them, and now here it is, making money off the backs of young people. None of these promises were fulfilled, the party is only two years old, but the leadership promised us that the benefits would be awarded to those who maintained their faith. He made so many promises! He promised that everyone would share in the benefits, and not just a few people, he had promised to capacitate the office with furniture and supplies, he promised to provide logistics for the campaigns, and vehicles for the party to move up and down in support of the campaigns. There was none of this! You saw that our executive was always moving with okadas. What kind of political party is this? And now Mohamed Bangura is just enjoying himself in Freetown, and he leaves all the suffering to us here.

A few days after this conversation, Bangura announced on the radio that he was withdrawing party support for its aspirants, suspending his own campaign for the presidency, and that the members of the erstwhile party should throw their support behind Ernest Koroma. As the official party membership at that time was in the hundreds of thousands in an election where only 2.1 million people voted for president, youth were a significant voting block, but also believed to be easily swayed between candidates because of their desire to be included.

UDM members in Makeni were devastated, but people outside of the party were not surprised at this turn of events. Foday and Ibrahim, with whom I had discussed *The Beautyful Ones Are Not Yet Born* at the beginning of this chapter, had predicted the party's downfall to me a month earlier, citing Charles Margai's actions in the previous election as precisely the blueprint Bangura was following. Said Ibrahim, "Everyone referred to these guys [the UDM] as 'the babies' [because] they are too small to know even as children do if they are being misused." Ibrahim went on to explain that Bangura needed to make the party legitimate enough to get it funded and attract a membership, and among the crowded field of small parties, being the youth party would attract thousands of young people who were desperate to be taken seriously. In the end, whether or not Bangura's support for Koroma swayed them, Koroma handily won re-election. After several years of quietly receiving financial support from Koroma, Bangura resigned officially from the moribund UDM in 2015 and was named minister of information in Koroma's government in 2016. In the end, what the UDM proved was that youth mattered as bodies, as votes—as an agglomeration of material performances—as their voter ID card was the one material entanglement making them consequential. However, once that vote was disentangled from its young person and firmly in the ballot box, that boundary could be configured once again.

Notes

1. It must be noted here that Maada Bio appointed his dissertation advisor, Dr. David Francis, to the position of chief minister in his new government. This is a position that did not previously exist, and it is not clear precisely what his powers are, except that he ostensibly advises Bio closely. This is an excellent example of the various ways that social connections can be leveraged in future performances.

2. In direct contrast, student governments elsewhere would stage public, nonviolent confrontations with the authorities in order to attract sympathy to their cause and earn treatment as innocent victims of police brutality (see Greenberg 2014:16).

3. A google search of "cotton tree" pulls up the Wikipedia page of Freetown's cotton tree as its first reference, rather than a focus on the tree as a botanical species.

CONCLUSIONS

In September 2018, entrepreneur and philanthropist Bill Gates gave a series of interviews about his new initiative, Goalkeepers, which provides financial assistance to the United Nations in meeting its new sustainable development goals (Gates 2018a, 2018b; Toynbee 2018). In each of these videos Gates highlighted the trends in global population, and the fact that most of the world's births in the coming decades will occur in Africa. He commented on the innovation, energy, and drive of Africa's youth, their facility with technology and their willingness to take risks, and noted that an investment in healthcare and education on the continent would ensure that the available potential talent was utilized to improve Africa's stability. The interviews cast an optimistic glow on the possibilities inherent in the young population on the continent, but a sinister, fearful undercurrent remained: How is this booming population going to feed itself? What happens if the dreams of the young go unfulfilled? He admitted that "the stability of Africa makes a huge difference to the entire world" (Toynbee 2018). In emphasizing that change required material investments—computers, seeds, tools, vaccines—Gates laid his proposed solution at the feet of the developed world. His message: provide food, education, healthcare, and infrastructure, and the youth of Africa will have a stable, prosperous future.

At first glance, Gates's approach seems to resonate with the tenets of this book—that the material means of performance are what matter; that provided with all the tools to be taken seriously, youth eventually will be people of consequence, because they will grow into their roles as adults over time and have the material support to use their talents for the good of the continent. The element of risk that so characterizes everything young people do would ostensibly be mitigated and eventually eliminated if they did not have to sacrifice and perform outrageously—and often fail—in order to be noticed. However, my own years of doing ethnographic research in Makeni, and in helping provide the young people with whom I work the material means that they desired to improve their circumstances, shed a different light on this promise. If I took my own meager contributions as a microcosm of what Gates would like to provide, the painful experiences of some of my beneficiaries proved that all the material assistance in the world does not—and cannot—matter if social personhood is still an experience of encounters where the subjective action of the agential cut is what matters to constructing boundaries. Once again it is the form of observation, interpretation, and reaction that matters in the end, not all the material means and preparations that presage the encounters. A particularly personally heartbreaking event is an excellent example of how this unfolds.

In September 2018 in Sierra Leone, my research assistant, Ibrahim, with whom I had discussed *The Beautyful Ones Are Not Yet Born*, discovered that he had failed three of eleven modules of the Sierra Leone Bar Exam, and had to retake the entire exam the following year. Ibrahim had spent the previous decade working toward the exam, having fulfilled a pact he made with me in 2005 that as long as he was enrolled in school, I would help him find a way to pay for it. This had made Ibrahim, who had come from a poor family that had been dislocated and scattered by the war, one of the lucky ones, a youth who had the opportunity to be configured as an adult by becoming a lawyer because he possessed what all young people wanted: a sponsor. I had "put my hand under him," helping him through myriad financial challenges. Ibrahim also had what so many rural young people, socially fragmented by war and finding their way in destitution in the urban areas, also lacked: a supportive, if economically bereft, social network. My contributions amounted to nothing compared to the assistance of Foday and his other friends. They sold their possessions to pay for books, went hungry to pay for photocopies, traveled from Freetown to Makeni and back to pursue work opportunities, moved into cramped quarters together, and sustained each other through thick and thin. If Ibrahim succeeded in passing the bar then they all would have succeeded, as Ibrahim would pass on his good fortune to others. However, he fell ill with three modules to go, and, despite his entreaties to postpone them, was told he had to complete them, and subsequently failed each one. A petition to the Sierra Leone Legal Society after the results were released was not heard, as illness was no excuse for failure. He would have to wait a year and try again, along with fifty-four other students who had also struggled with ill health—a common experience for people in a country with a paucity of doctors and healthcare facilities. They could retake the exam—that is, if they could afford to pay the exorbitant fee. Bill Gates would point out that better healthcare and educational facilities—such as potentially making the exam free—would have addressed this, but was the lack of clinics and schools really the problem?

Before Ibrahim took his exams, he faced numerous obstacles in completing law school at Fourah Bay College that had nothing to do with the quality of education. When we chatted in 2014 he relayed that the biggest difficulty was in "overcoming the opposition" of the law school faculty to having more lawyers in the country. First was that the faculty often made students who showed exceptional promise, according to Ibrahim, repeat a year on spurious grounds. Law school was expensive, and aside from the financial impact, he explained, "so many people got discouraged by this" and dropped out. He cited the fact that Sierra Leone, in a departure from its foundation in British law, had blended the professions of solicitor and barrister so that both required passing the bar—rather than just the barristers, who argued court cases. In Britain, solicitors prepare legal paperwork and are responsible for the bulk of property, family, tax, and other more mundane aspects of law, and do not undergo the exam that is reserved for criminal and other court proceedings. An education in law was there, ostensibly for the taking. The problem was the novel reconfigurations that were being made around the concept of "lawyer" by the legal society to deliberately and systematically exclude those who might, in joining their club, threaten their own pre-eminence, even through the seemingly banal materially mediated performances of filing paperwork. And this did not just harm Ibrahim. It harmed every young person who poured their own resources, their hope, and their dreams into his success. His bad luck echoed through his friends, spreading discouragement and negativity all around. Is it the lack of education and health that produces potential instability? Or is it adult manipulations of how young people encounter this infrastructure, and how that resonates through the social world, that really matters?

Throughout the chapters of this book, I have emphasized that the agential cut—the form of observation that generates interpretations, judgments, and reactions—is what really matters to determining the direction of encounters and the boundaries generated around individuals. The material world is fundamental to this process; it provides information and direction on processing the performance that an individual observes, but it is not coterminous with the agential cut. The cut is reflective of the stochasticity of the world: that it is both chaotic and contains patterns that are generated within its framework. Given enough data, touchstones develop; notions of the past and common tropes that inform the cut people make on encounters. Shifts in the form of interpretation also occur with seeming randomness, as there is no predicting what one or series of events precipitate them, but we certainly know them when we see them. #MeToo is an excellent example: Tarana Burke began the movement to recognize the ubiquity of sexual assault a decade before it became a mainstream trope on sexual abuse as a common and widespread phenomenon. However, it took the cacophony of voices around the dozens of sexual assaults committed by film producer Harvey Weinstein for popular opinion and action—a mass of agential cuts—to demand a light be shone on these abuses.

This is not to say that sexual assault has changed in Hollywood or anywhere else as a result. Perhaps the new agential cut that leads people to believe women rather than interpreting them as hysterical or manipulative or backstabbing is a small, temporary touchstone; perhaps it has the momentum to become something more. But unless and until it does, there is no certainty that the performances of truth-telling around assault will matter, or if they will be met with know-your-place aggression. Women can perform their truth, but the fact that their claims are still easily dismissed—as was so painfully evident when Christine Blasey Ford's testimony against Brett Kavanaugh resulted in him still being confirmed to the Supreme Court—we can see the power of boundary configurations even in repeated encounters. Performances of truth, of strength, of mattering can still come to nothing if the agential cut does not let it be so. For women, for people of color, for the young—whether it is the age of their bodies or of their ideas—their seriousness is still subject to the eye of the beholder, of those with the power to determine the contours of the social world.

Gates's Goalkeepers initiative would create infrastructure that would have allowed Ibrahim to stay in school without disruption and stay healthy for the exam, but it could do nothing to reconfigure the relationships that adults have with youth. In this way, the goalkeeper is a double entendre: Gates helping the United Nations reach their goals of reducing poverty around the world, and the Sierra Leone Legal Society—or any other configuration of adult—defending the goal, aiming at all costs to prevent Ibrahim and other aspirational lawyers from scoring. The metaphor is stark, and, I admit, generalized. This is not a situation where every adult has it in for young people. Parents want—and need—their children to succeed enough to care for them in their old age. But the game is rigged, as only certain young people can be allowed to flourish: those whose existence as adults does not, for reasons of wealth or connections or grooming, appear to threaten their elders, but instead reinforces that configuration—young people like Mohamed Bangura.

Though the situation in Sierra Leone does not translate exactly around the world, the parallels are striking. On my desk in my office is a postcard for a recent lecture at Notre Dame titled "Kids These Days: Human Capital and the Making of Millennials." In it, author Malcolm Harris muses, "Often stereotyped as lazy, narcissistic, entitled, and immature, Millennials are in fact the hardest working and most educated generation in American history." He goes on to ask, "Why are young people paying such a high price to train themselves for a system that exploits them?" (2017). I would ask this of Ibrahim, or of Foday, but Bill Gates does not consider this possibility. For some reason he is well versed in the problems of millennials, but forgets that these problems might be exactly the same in Africa, that continent for which he has both great hope and great fear: that being young in a wealthy nation does not, in fact, prevent one from being a youth.

BIBLIOGRAPHY

....

Primary Sources

African Union. 2006. African Youth Charter. https://au.int/en/treaties/
african-youth-charter

CO 267/630/6.

Keigwin, H. S. 1928. Education in the Protectorate, August 10.

Governor's Office. 1930. Education Ordinance.

CO 267/630/13.

1930. Notes on student strike at Koyeima College.

CO 267/632/12.

1931. Memo on "Bo School."

CO 267/661/14.

Nicholson, W. E. 1937. Memorandum on Bo and Koyeima Schools.

CO 267/665/8.

1938. Manifesto of the West African Youth League.

CO 267/691/3.

Bockarie, Samba. 1948. An Advance Extract on the Reorganization of the
Legislative Council.

Craig, R. J. 1938. Report, Sierra Leone Secret Dispatch. June 30, 1938. No.
C18/1932.

Fofanah, Umaru. 2012. "Fourah Bay: Sierra Leone University Closed by Students."
BBC News, August 3. https://www.bbc.com/news/world-africa-19109722.

Gates, Bill. 2018a. "Bill Gates Explains the Trends Facing the Global Population."
Now This News, last accessed September 25, 2018. https://nowthisnews.com/
videos/news/bill-gates-explains-the-challenges-facing-the-global-population.

Gates, Bill. 2018b. "The World's Youngest Continent." Gatesnotes: The Blog of
Bill Gates, last accessed September 25, 2018. https://www.gatesnotes.com/
Development/Africa-the-Youngest-Continent.

Government of Sierra Leone (GOSL). 2003. Sierra Leone National Youth Policy.
Freetown: Ministry of Youth and Sports. http://www.youthpolicy.org/national/
Sierra_Leone_2003_National_Youth_Policy.pdf.

Government of Sierra Leone (GOSL). 2007. Compendium of the Gender Laws in
Sierra Leone. Freetown: Ministry of Social Welfare.

"Maada Bio Goes Back to School." 2014. *The Patriotic Vanguard*. February 3.
http://www.thepatrioticvanguard.com/maada-bio-goes-back-to-school.

"Record Crowd as President Opens Makeni Show." 1979. *We Yone* [Sierra Leone
newspaper], January 28.

Sierra Leone National Archives. 2017. http://www.sierra-leone.org/Postcards/
SL859899.jpg.

Thomas, Aiah P. 2014. "Is PhD the Answer to Maada Bio's Problems?"
AIAHTHOMAS, June 7. https://aiahthomas.wordpress.com/2014/06/07/
is-phd-the-answer-to-maada-bios-problems/.

Toynbee, Polly. 2018. "The African Youth Boom: What's
Worrying Bill Gates." *The Guardian*, September 25. https://
www.theguardian.com/global-development/2018/sep/18/
the-african-youth-boom-whats-worrying-bill-gates.

Truth and Reconciliation Commission (TRC) of Sierra Leone. 2003.
Recommendations of the Truth and Reconciliation Commission, Vol. 2,
Ch. 3. http://www.sierraleonetrc.org/index.php/view-the-final-report/
download-table-of-contents.

Wallace-Johnson, I. T. A. 1938. Letter from the West African Youth League to
Douglas Jardine, Governor of Sierra Leone. June 16.

World Health Organization (WHO). 2012. "Cholera in Sierra Leone: The Case Study
of an Outbreak." http://www.who.int/features/2012/cholera_sierra_leone/en/.

Secondary Sources

Abdullah, Ibrahim. 2004. "Bush Path to Destruction: The Origin and Character
of the Revolutionary United Front (RUF/SL)." In *Between Democracy and
Terror: The Sierra Leone Civil War*, edited by Ibrahim Abdullah, 41–65 Dakar:
CODESRIA.

Abdullah, Ibrahim, and Ishmail Rashid. 2004. "Smallest Victims; Youngest Killers:
Juvenile Combatants in Sierra Leone's Civil War." In *Between Democracy
and Terror: The Sierra Leone Civil War*, edited by Ibrahim Abdullah, 238–53
Dakar: CODESRIA.

Alao, Abiodun. 1999. "Diamonds Are Forever . . . But So Also Are Controversies:
Diamonds and the Actors in Sierra Leone's Civil War." *Civil Wars* 2(3): 43–64.

Alie, Joe. 1990. *A New History of Sierra Leone*. London: Palgrave Macmillan.

Archibald, Steven, and Paul Richards. 2002. "Converts to Human Rights? Popular
Debate About War and Justice in Rural Central Sierra Leone." *Africa: Journal of
the International African Institute* 72(3): 339–67.

Armah, Ayi Kwesi. 1969. *The Beautyful Ones Are Not Yet Born*. London:
Heinemann.

Arnett, Jeffrey Jensen. 2000. "High Hopes in a Grim World: Emerging Adults' Views of their Future and 'Generation X.'" *Youth and Society* 31(3): 267–86.

Barad, Karen. 2003. "Posthumanist Performativity: Toward an Understanding of How Matter Comes to Matter." *Signs* 28(3): 801–31.

Barad, Karen. 2007. *Meeting the Universe Halfway: Quantum Physics and the Entanglement of Matter and Meaning*. Durham, NC: Duke University Press.

Bastian, Misty. 2005. "The Naked and the Nude: Historically Multiple Meanings of Oto (Undress) in Southeastern Nigeria." In *Dirt, Undress, and Difference: Critical Perspectives on the Body's Surface*, edited by Adeline Masquelier, 34–60. Bloomington: Indiana University Press.

Beck, Ulrich. 1999. *World Risk Society*. Cambridge: Polity Press.

Bell, Amy Helen. 2014. "Teddy Boys and Girls as Neo-Flâneurs in Post-War London." *The Literary London Journal* 11(2): 3–17.

Berman, Jillian. 2016. "Watch America's Student-Loan Debt Grow $2,726 Every Second." Market Watch, January 30. http://www.marketwatch.com/story/every-second-americans-get-buried-under-another-3055-in-student-loan-debt-2015-06-10.

Birzle, Maike. 2017. "*Ca va aller:* The Role of Hope in Burkinabe University Graduates' Navigation Toward the Future." Paper presented at the European Conference on African Studies. Basel, Switzerland, June 29.

Bledsoe, Caroline. 1990. "No Success Without Struggle: Social Mobility and Hardship for Foster Children in Sierra Leone." *Man, New Series* 25(1): 70–88.

Bledsoe, Caroline. 1992. "The Cultural Transformation of Western Education in Sierra Leone." *Africa: Journal of the International African Institute* 62(2): 182–202.

Boersch-Supan, Johanna. 2012. "The Generational Contract in Flux: Intergenerational Tensions in Post-Conflict Sierra Leone." *Journal of Modern African Studies* 50(1): 25–51.

Bolten, Catherine. 2008. *The Place Is So Backward: Durable Morality and Creative Development in Sierra Leone*. Ann Arbor: ProQuest.

Bolten, Catherine. 2009a. "The Agricultural Impasse: Creating 'Normal' Post-War Development in Sierra Leone." *Journal of Political Ecology* 16: 70–86.

Bolten, Catherine. 2009b. "Rethinking Burgeoning Political Consciousness: Student Activists, the Class of '99 and Political Intent in Sierra Leone." *Journal of Modern African Studies* 47(3): 349–69.

Bolten, Catherine. 2012a. *I Did it to Save My Life: Love and Survival in Sierra Leone*. Berkeley: University of California Press.

Bolten, Catherine. 2012b. "The Only Way to Produce Food Is to Cooperate and Reconcile? A Case Study of Failures of Cooperative Agriculture in Post-War Sierra Leone." In *Challenging Post-Conflict Environments: Sustainable Agriculture*, edited by A. Ozerdam and R. Roberts, 237–48. London: Ashgate.

Bolten, Catherine. 2012c. "'We Have Been Sensitized': Ex-combatants, Marginalization, and Youth in Post-War Sierra Leone." *American Anthropologist* 114(3): 494–506.

Bolten, Catherine. 2013. "Poisoned Patronage: Appropriating Aid and Pulling Down 'Big Men' in Northern Sierra Leone." In *Globalization, Social Movements, and Peacebuilding*, edited by J. Smith and E. Verdeja, 159–86. Syracuse: Syracuse University Press.

Bolten, Catherine. 2014a. "The Memories They Want: Autobiography in the Chaos of Sierra Leone" (Le choix de leur souveniers. Autobiographies dans le chaos de la Sierra Leone)." *Ethnologie Française* 44(3): 431–39.

Bolten, Catherine. 2014b. "*Sobel* Rumors and Tribal Truths: Narrative and Politics in Sierra Leone, 1994." *Comparative Studies in Society and History* 56(1): 187–214.

Bolten, Catherine. 2014c. "Social Networks, Resources, and the International NGO in Post-War Sierra Leone." *African Conflict and Peacebuilding Review* 4(1): 33–59.

Bolten, Catherine. 2015. "A Great Scholar is an Overeducated Person: Education and Practices of Uncertainty in Sierra Leone." *Journal of Anthropological Research* 71(1): 23–47.

Bolten, Catherine. 2016. "I Will Vote What Is in My Heart: Sierra Leone's 2012 Elections and the Pliability of 'Normative' Democracy." *Anthropological Quarterly* 89(4): 1019–48.

Bolten, Catherine. 2018. "Productive Work and Subjected Labor: Children's Pursuits and Child Rights in Northern Sierra Leone." *Journal of Human Rights* 17(2): 199–214.

Bourdieu, Pierre. 1977. *Outline of a Theory of Practice*. Cambridge: Cambridge University Press.

Bourdieu, Pierre. 1991. *Language and Symbolic Power*. Translated by Gino Raymond and Matthew Adamson. Cambridge, MA: Harvard University Press.

Bourdieu, Pierre. 1992. *The Logic of Practice*. Stanford, CA: Stanford University Press.

Bourdieu, Pierre. 1996. *The State Nobility: Elite Schools in the Field of Power*. Translated by Lauretta C. Clough. Stanford, CA: Stanford University Press.

Bourdieu, Pierre. 2010. *Distinction: A Social Critique of the Judgment of Taste*. Translated by Richard Nice. New York: Routledge.

Bowker, Geoffrey C., and Susan L. Star. 1999. *Sorting Things Out*. Cambridge, MA: MIT Press.

Buchmann, Marlis C., and Irene Kriesi. 2011. "Transition to Adulthood in Europe." *Annual Review of Sociology* 37: 481–503.

Bucholtz, Mary. 2002. "Youth and Cultural Practice." *Annual Review of Anthropology* 31: 525–52.

Bürge, Michael. 2011. "Riding the Narrow Tracks of Moral Life: Commercial Motorbike Riders in Makeni, Sierra Leone." *Africa Today* 58(2): 58–95.

Burke, Timothy. 1996. *Lifebuoy Men, Lux Women: Commodification, Consumption, and Cleanliness in Modern Zimbabwe*. Durham, NC: Duke University Press.

Butler, Judith. 2007. *Gender Trouble: Feminism and the Subversion of Identity*. New York: Routledge.

Campbell, Greg. 2002. *Blood Diamonds: Tracing the Deadly Path of the World's Most Precious Stone.* New York: Westview Press.

Carrà, Elisabetta, Margherita Lanz, and Semira Tagliabue. 2014. "Transition to Adulthood in Italy: An Intergenerational Perspective." *Journal of Comparative Family Studies* 45(2): 235–48.

Central Intelligence Agency (CIA). 2015. Sierra Leone Factbook. https://www.cia.gov/library/publications/the-world-factbook/geos/sl.html.

Chakrabarty, Dipesh. 1999. "Adda, Calcutta: Dwelling in Modernity." *Public Culture* 11(1): 109–45.

Cham, Kemo. 2013. "S. Leone opposition leader denies bigamy allegations." *The Daily Nation*, December 24. https://www.nation.co.ke/news/africa/Sierra-Leone-opposition-leader-denies-bigamy-allegation/1066-2098896-jvmjva/index.html.

Christiansen, Catrine, Mats Utas, and Henrik H. Vigh. 2006. "Introduction." In *Navigating Youth, Generating Adulthood: Social Becoming in an African Context*, edited by Catrine Christiansen, Mats Utas, and Henrik H. Vigh. 9–28. Uppsala: Nordic Africa Institute.

Cline, Elizabeth L. 2012. "The Afterlife of Cheap Clothes." *Slate*. http://www.slate.com/articles/life/fashion/2012/06/the_salvation_army_and_goodwill_inside_the_places_your_clothes_go_when_you_donate_them_.html.

Cohen, Abner. 1981. *The Politics of Elite Culture: Explorations in the Dramaturgy of Power in a Modern African Society.* Berkeley: University of California Press.

Cohen, Stanley. 1980. *Folk Devils and Moral Panics: The Creation of the Mods and Rockers.* New York: St. Martin's Press.

Cole, Ernest. 2014. *Theorizing the Disfigured Body: Mutilation, Amputation, and Disability Culture in Post-Conflict Sierra Leone.* London: African Research Institute.

Cole, Jennifer. 2005. "The Jaombilo of Tamatave (Madagascar) 1992–2004: Reflections on Youth and Globalization." *Journal of Social History* 38(4): 891–914.

Cole, Jennifer. 2008. "Fashioning Distinction: Youth and Consumerism in Urban Madagascar." In *Figuring the Future: Globalization and theTemporalities of Children and Youth*, edited by Jennifer Cole and Deborah Durham, 99–124. Santa Fe: School for Advanced Research Press.

Cole, Jennifer, and Deborah Durham. 2008. "Introduction: Globalization and the Temporality of Children and Youth." In *Figuring the Future: Globalization and the Temporalities of Children and Youth*, edited by Jennifer Cole and Deborah Durham, 3–23. Santa Fe: School for Advanced Research Press.

Coles, Kimberly. 2004. "Election Day: The Construction of Democracy Through Technique." *Cultural Anthropology* 19(4): 551–80.

Colic-Piesker, Val. 2004. "Doing Ethnography in 'One's Own Ethnic Community': The Experience of an Awkward Insider." In *Anthropologists in the Field: Cases in Participant Observation*, edited by Lynne Hume and James Mulcock, 82–94. New York: Columbia University Press.

Collins, Randall. 1979. *The Credential Society: An Historical Sociology of Education and Stratification*. New York: Academic Press.

Comaroff, Jean, and John Comaroff. 1997. "Postcolonial Politics and Discourses of Democracy in Southern Africa: An Anthropological Reflection on African Political Modernities." *Journal of Anthropological Research* 53(2): 123–46.

Cook, Joanna. 2010. "Ascetic Practice and Participant Observation, or, The Gift of Doubt in Field Experience." In *Emotions in the Field: The Psychology and Anthropology of Fieldwork Experience*, edited by James Davies and Dimitrina Spencer, 239–65. Stanford, CA: Stanford University Press.

Corby, Richard A. 1990. "Educating Africans for Inferiority Under British Rule: Bo School in Sierra Leone." *Comparative Education Review* 34(3): 314–49.

Coulter, Chris. 2005. "Reflections from the Field: A Girl's Initiation Ceremony in Northern Sierra Leone." *Anthropological Quarterly* 78(2): 431–41.

Da Costa, Peter. 1992. "The Young Guns (Sierra Leone's Coup Leaders)." *Africa Report* 37(4): 36.

De la Rica, Sara, and Amaia Iza. 2005. "Career Planning in Spain: Do Fixed-term Contracts Delay Marriage and Parenthood?" *Review of Economics of the Household* 3(1): 49–73.

DeWalt, Kathleen M., and Billie R. DeWalt. 2011. *Participant Observation: A Guide for Fieldworkers. Second Edition*. Plymouth, MA: AltaMira Press.

Diouf, Mamadou. 1996. "Urban Youth and Senegalese Politics: Dakar 1988–1994." *Public Culture* 8: 225–49.

Diouf, Mamadou. 2003. "Engaging Postcolonial Cultures: African Youth and Public Space." *African Studies Review* 46(2): 1–12.

Diouf, Mamadou. 2005. "La jeunesse africaine: entre autochtonie et cosmopolitisme." *Horizons Maghrebins* 53(1): 31–39.

Dore, Ronald. 1997. *The Diploma Disease: Education, Qualification, and Development*. London: Institute of Education.

Durham, Deborah. 2000. "Youth and the Social Imagination in Africa; Introduction to Parts 1 and 2." *Anthropological Quarterly* 73(3): 113–20.

Durham, Deborah. 2004. "Disappearing Youth: Youth as a Social Shifter in Botswana." *American Ethnologist* 31(4): 589–605.

Durham, Deborah. 2007. "Empowering Youth: Making Youth Citizens in Botswana." In *Generations and Globalization: Youth, Age, and Family in the New World Economy*, edited by Jennifer Cole and Deborah Duran, 102–31. Bloomington: Indiana University Press.

Durham, Deborah. 2008. "Apathy and Agency: The Romance of Agency and Youth in Botswana." In *Figuring the Future: Globalization and theTemporalities of Children and Youth*, edited by Jennifer Cole and Deborah Duran, 151–78. Santa Fe: School for Advanced Research Press.

Durkheim, Emile. 1982 [1895]. *The Rules of Sociological Method and Selected Texts on Sociology and Its Method*. Edited by Steven Lukes and translated by W. D. Halls. New York: Free Press.

Edwardianteddyboy.com n.d. Last accessed July 17, 2017. http://edwardianteddyboy.com/index.htm.

Ellis, Stephen. 1989. "Tuning In to Pavement Radio." *African Affairs* 88(352): 321–30.

Ellis, Stephen. 2006. *The Mask of Anarchy: The Destruction of Liberia and the Religious Dimension of an African Civil War.* New York: New York University Press.

Emerson, Robert M., Rachel I. Fretz, and Linda L. Shaw. 2011. *Writing Ethnographic Fieldnotes, Second Edition.* Chicago: University of Chicago Press

Enloe, Cynthia. 2013. *Seriously! Investigating Crashes and Crises as if Women Mattered.* Berkeley: University of California Press.

Enria, Luisa. 2015. "Love and Betrayal: The Political Economy of Youth Violence in Post-War Sierra Leone." *Journal of Modern African Studies* 53(4): 637–60.

Fanthorpe, Richard. 2005. "On the Limits of Liberal Peace: Chiefs and Democratic Decentralization in Post-War Sierra Leone." *African Affairs* 105(408): 27–49.

Farwell, Byron. 1991. *Armies of the Raj: From the Great Indian Mutiny to Independence, 1858–1947.* London: Norton.

Ferguson, James. 1999. *Expectations of Modernity: Myths and Meanings of Urban Life on the Zambian Copperbelt.* Berkeley: University of California Press.

Ferguson, James. 2013. "Declarations of Dependence: Labour, Personhood, and Welfare in Southern Africa." *Journal of the Royal Anthropological Institute* 19(2): 223–42.

Ferguson, James. 2015. *Give a Man a Fish: Reflections on the New Politics of Distribution.* Durham, NC: Duke University Press.

Ferme, Mariane. 1999. "Staging *Politisi*: The Dialogics of Publicity and Secrecy in Sierra Leone." In *Civil Society and the Political Imagination in Africa*, edited by Jean Comaroff and John Comaroff, 160–90. Chicago: University of Chicago Press.

Ferme, Mariane. 2001. *The Underneath of Things: Violence, History, and the Everyday in Sierra Leone.* Berkeley: University of California Press.

Fioratta, Susanna. 2015. "Beyond Remittance: Evading Uselessness and Seeking Personhood in Fouta Djallon, Guinea." *American Ethnologist* 42(2): 295–308.

Gable, Eric. 2000. "The Culture Development Club: Youth, Neo-Tradition, and the Construction of Society in Guinea-Bissau." *Anthropological Quarterly* 73(4): 195–203.

Gberie, Lansana. 2004. "The May 25th Coup d'Etat in Sierra Leone: A Lumpen Revolt?" In *Between Democracy and Terror: The Sierra Leone Civil War*, edited by Ibrahim Abdullah, 144–63. Dakar: CODESRIA.

Gberie, Lansana. 2005. *A Dirty War in West Africa: The RUF and the Destruction of Sierra Leone.* Bloomington: Indiana University Press.

Geertz, Clifford. 1973. *The Interpretation of Cultures.* New York: Basic Books.

Geertz, Clifford. 1998. "Deep Hanging Out." *New York Review of Books.* October 22. http://www.nybooks.com.proxy.library.nd.edu/articles/1998/10/22/deep-hanging-out/.

Gibson, Jane Whitney, Regina A. Greenwood, and Edward F. Murphy Jr. 2009. "Generational Differences in the Workplace: Personal Values, Behaviors, and Popular Beliefs." *Journal of Diversity Management* 4(3): 1–7.

Gilmore, David. 1990. *Manhood in the Making: Cultural Conceptions of Masculinity*. New Haven, CT: Yale University Press.

Goffman, Erving. 1959. *The Presentation of Self in Everyday Life*. New York: Anchor Books.

Gondola, Ch. Didier. 1999. "Dream and Drama: The Search for Elegance Among Congolese Youth." *African Studies Review* 42(1): 23–48.

Goppert, Mirco. 2013. "Bureaucratic Aesthetics: Report Writing in the Nigerien Gendarmerie." *American Ethnologist* 40(2): 324–34.

Greenberg, Jessica. 2014. *After the Revolution: Youth, Democracy, and the Politics of Disappointment in Serbia*. Stanford, CA: Stanford University Press.

Gupta, Akhil. 2012. *Red Tape: Bureaucracy, Structural Violence, and Poverty in India*. Durham, NC: Duke University Press.

Guyer, Jane I., and Kabiru K. Salami. 2013. "Life Courses of Indebtedness in Rural Nigeria." In *Transitions and Transformations: Cultural Perspectives on Aging and the Life Course*, edited by C. Lynch and J. Danely, 206–17. New York: Berghahn Books.

Hanlon, Joseph. 2005. "Is the International Community Helping to Recreate the Preconditions for War in Sierra Leone?" *The Round Table* 94(381): 459–72.

Haraway, Donna. 1992. "The Promise of Monsters: A Regenerative Politics for Inappropriate/d Others" In *Cultural Studies*, edited by L. Grossbery, C. Nelson, and P.A. Treichler. 295-337. New York: Routledge

Harris, Malcolm. 2017. *Kids These Days: Human Capital and the Making of Millenials*. New York: Little, Brown.

Hashemi, Manata. 2015. "Waithood and Face: Morality and Mobility Among Lower-Class Youth in Iran." *Qualitative Sociology* 38: 261–83.

Hautzinger, Sarah. 2007. *Violence in the City of Women: Police and Batterers in Bahia, Brazil*. Berkeley: University of California Press.

Heimer, Carol A. 2006. "Conceiving Children: How Documents Support Case versus Biographical Analysis." In *Documents: Artifacts of Modern Knowledge*, edited by Annelise Riles, 95–126. Ann Arbor: University of Michigan Press.

Hoffman, Danny. 2003. "Like Beasts in the Bush: Synonyms of Childhood and Youth in Sierra Leone." *Postcolonial Studies* 6(3): 295–308.

Hoffman, Danny. 2007. "The City as Barracks: Freetown, Monrovia, and the Organization of Violence in Postcolonial African Cities." *Cultural Anthropology* 22(3): 400–28.

Hoffman, Danny. 2011a. "Violence, Just in Time: War and Work in Contemporary West Africa." *Cultural Anthropology* 26(1): 34–57.

Hoffman, Danny. 2011b. *The War Machines: Young Men and Violence in Sierra Leone and Liberia*. Durham, NC: Duke University Press.

Hoffman, Danny. 2017. *Monrovia Modern: Urban Form and Political Imagination in Liberia*. Durham, NC: Duke University Press.

Hollander, Jocelyn A. 2004. "The Social Context of Focus Groups." *Journal of Contemporary Ethnography* 33(5): 602–37.

Honwana, Alcinda. 2012. *The Time of Youth: Work, Social change, and Politics in Africa*. Hartford, CT: Kumarian Press.

Howes, David. 1996. "Introduction: Commodities and Cultural Borders." In *Cross Cultural Consumption: Global Markets, Local Realities*, edited by David Howes, 1–18. New York: Routledge.

Hull, Matthew. 2012. *Government of Paper: The Materiality of Bureaucracy in Urban Pakistan*. Berkeley: University of California Press.

Humphries, Dave, Franc Roddam, Martin Stellman, and Pete Townshend. 1979. *Quadrophenia*. Produced by Bill Curbishley and Roy Baird. Universal Pictures.

Jeffrey, Craig. 2010. *Timepass: Youth, Class, and the Politics of Waiting in India*. Stanford, CA: Stanford University Press.

Jeffrey, Craig, Patricia Jeffery, and Roger Jeffery. 2008. *Degrees Without Freedom? Education, Masculinities, and Unemployment in North India*. Stanford, CA: Stanford University Press.

Jensen, Steffen. 2009. *Gangs, Politics, and Dignity in Cape Town*. Chicago: University of Chicago Press.

Jusionyte, Ieva. 2015. *Savage Frontier: Making News and Security on the Argentine Border*. Berkeley: University of California Press.

Kandeh, Jimmy. 1996. "What Does the 'Militariat' Do When It Rules? Military Regimes: The Gambia, Sierra Leone, and Liberia." *Review of African Political Economy* 23(69): 387–404.

Kanu, K. 2013. "A Tale of Two SLPPs." Cocorioko. November 13. http://cocorioko.net/a-tale-of-two-slpps/.

Kaplan, Robert D. 2000. *The Coming Anarchy: Shattering the Dreams of the Post Cold War*. New York: Random House.

Kleinman, Adam. 2012. "Intra-Actions." *Mousse* 34(6): 76–81

Kotcheff, Ted. 1982. *Rambo: First Blood*. Orion Pictures.

Kpundeh, Sahr. 2004. "Corruption and Political Insurgency in Sierra Leone." In *Between Democracy and Terror: The Sierra Leone Civil War*, edited by Ibrahim Abdullah, 90–103. Dakar: CODESRIA.

Labaree, David F. 1997. *How To Succeed in School Without Really Learning: The Credentials Race in American Education*. New Haven, CT: Yale University Press.

Lahai, John Idriss. 2012. "Youth Agency and Survival Strategies in Sierra Leone's Postwar Informal Economy." In *African Childhoods: Education, Development, Peacebuilding, and the Youngest Continent*, edited by M. Ensor, 47–60. New York: Palgrave Macmillan.

Lave, Jean. 2011. *Apprenticeship in Critical Ethnographic Practice*. Chicago: University of Chicago Press.

Levi-Strauss, Claude. 1966. *The Savage Mind*. Chicago: University of Chicago Press.

Liu, Shao-hua. 2011. *Passage to Manhood: Youth Migration, Heroin, and AIDS in Southwest China*. Stanford, CA: Stanford University Press.

Luvaas, Brent. 2010. "Designer Vandalism: Indonesian Indie Fashion and the Cultural Practice of Cut 'n' Paste." *Visual Anthropology Review* 26(1): 1–16.

Mains, Daniel. 2012. *Hope Is Cut: Youth, Unemployment, and the Future in Urban Ethiopia*. Philadelphia: Temple University Press.

Mark, Monica. 2016. "My Bloody Valentine." Buzzfeed News. https://www.buzzfeed.com/monicamark/what-do-you-do-with-your-life-after-youve-already-been-the-w?utm_term=.yd2ONKNVoa#.vdM7qvq1g3.

Marx, Karl. 1906. *Capital: A Critique of Political Economy*. Translated by Samuel Moore and Edward Aveling. New York: Modern Library.

Mbembe, Achille. 2001. *On the Postcolony*. Berkeley: University of California Press.

Miers, Suzanne, and Igor Kopytoff. 1977. "Introduction." In *Slavery in Africa: Historical and Anthropological Perspectives*, edited by Suzanne Miers and Igor Kopytoff, 3–84 Madison: University of Wisconsin Press.

Millar, Gearoid. 2015. "Investing in Peace: Foreign Direct Investment as Economic Restoration in Sierra Leone?" *Third World Quarterly* 36(9): 1700–16.

Miller, Daniel, and Sophie Woodward. 2012. *Blue Jeans: The Art of the Ordinary* Berkeley: University of California Press.

Mitchell, Koritha. 2013. "Love in Action: Noting Similarities between Lynching Then and Anti-LGBT Violence Now." *Callaloo* 36(3): 688–717.

Mitchell, Koritha. 2015. "Keep Claiming Space!" *CLA Journal* 58(4): 229–44.

Mitchell, Timothy. 2000. "The Stage of Modernity." In *Questions of Modernity*, edited by Timothy Mitchell, 1–34. Minneapolis: University of Minnesota Press.

Mitton, Kieran. 2013. "Where Is the War? Explaining Peace in Sierra Leone." *International Peacekeeping* 20(3): 321–37.

Moniuszko, Sara M. 2018. "Dwayne Johnson Shares Sweet Hug with His Daughters Before 'Daddy's Arms Are the Last Place They Want to Be.'" *USA Today*, December 28. https://www.usatoday.com/story/life/entertainthis/2018/12/28/dwayne-johnson-shares-sweet-hug-daughters/2430170002/.

Moran, Mary. 2006. *Liberia: The Violence of Democracy*. Philadelphia: University of Pennsylvania Press.

Moreno Mínguez, Almudena. 2003. "The Late Emancipation of Spanish Youth: Keys for Understanding." *Electronic Journal of Sociology*. https://www.sociology.org/content/vol7.1/minguez.html.

Murphy, William P. 1980. "Secret Knowledge as Property and Power in Kpelle Society: Elders Versus Youth." *Africa: Journal of the International African Institute* 50(2): 193–207

Murphy, John. 2011. "Protest or Riot?: Interpreting Collective Action in Contemporary France." *Anthropological Quarterly* 84(4): 977–1009.

Newell, Sasha. 2012. *The Modernity Bluff: Crime, Consumption, and Citizenship in Cote d'Ivoire*. Chicago: University of Chicago Press.

Nordstrom, Carolyn. 1997. *A Different Kind of War Story* Philadelphia: University of Pennsylvania Press.

Niewenhuys, Olga. 2001. "By the Sweat of Their Brows? 'Street Children,' NGOs, and Children's Rights in Addis Ababa." *Africa: Journal of the International Africa Institute* 71(4): 539–57.

Nuttall, Sarah. 2004. "Stylizing the Self: The Y Generation in Rosebank, Johannesburg." *Public Culture* 16(3): 430–52.

Nyberg, Daniel. 2009. "Computers, Customer Service Operatives, and Cyborgs: Intra-actions in Call Centers." *Organization Studies* 30(11): 1181–99

Nyerges, A. Endre. 1992. "The Ecology of Wealth-in-People: Agriculture, Settlement, and Society on the Perpetual Frontier." *American Anthropologist* 94(4): 860–81.

Ocobock, Paul. 2017. *An Uncertain Age: The Politics of Manhood in Kenya.* Athens: Ohio University Press.

Opala, Joe. 1994. "Ecstatic Renovation! Street Art Celebrating Sierra Leone's 1992 Revolution." *African Affairs* 93(371): 195–218.

Paley, Julia. 2002. "Toward an Anthropology of Democracy." *Annual Review of Anthropology* 31: 469–96.

Penketh, Anne. 2013. "Charles Taylor: Liberia's Former President Finally Faces Punishment for His Horrific War Crimes." *The Independent*. http://www.independent.co.uk/news/people/profiles/charles-taylor-liberia-s-former-president-finally-faces-punishment-for-his-horrific-war-crimes-8845092.html.

Peters, Krijn. 2011. *War and the Crisis of Youth in Sierra Leone.* Cambridge: Cambridge University Press.

Peters, Krijn, and Paul Richards. 1998. "Why We Fight: Voices of Youth Combatants in Sierra Leone." *Africa: Journal of the International African Institute* 68(2): 183–210.

Pope-Chappell, Maya. 2016. "Millenials Are Delaying Adulthood Because of Crushing Student Loan Debt." LinkedIn, June 15. https://www.linkedin.com/pulse/millennials-delaying-adulthood-because-crushing-loan-pope-chappell.

Population Pyramid. 2017. https://www.populationpyramid.net/western-europe/2017/.

Rashid, Ismail. 2004. "Student Radicals, Lumpen Youth, and the Origins of Revolutionary Groups in Sierra Leone, 1977–1996." In *Between Democracy and Terror: The Sierra Leone Civil War*, edited by Ibrahim Abdullah, 66–89 Dakar: CODESRIA.

Rasmussen, Susan. 2000. "Between Several Worlds: Images of Youth and Age in Tuareg Popular Performances." *Anthropological Quarterly* 73(3): 133–44.

Reed, Adam. 2006. "Documents Unfolding." In *Documents: Artifacts of Modern Knowledge*, edited by Annelise Riles, 158–77. Ann Arbor: University of Michigan Press.

Reeves, Madeleine. 2013. "Clean Fake: Authenticating Documents and Persons in Migrant Moscow." *American Ethnologist* 40(3): 508–24.

Reich, Adam. 2010. *Hidden Truth: Young Men Navigating Lives in and Out of Juvenile Prison.* Berkeley: University of California Press.

Reno, William. 2008. *Corruption and State Politics in Sierra Leone.* Cambridge: Cambridge University Press.

Richards, Paul. 1996. *Fighting for the Rain Forest: War, Youth and Resources in Sierra Leone.* Oxford: James Currey.

Richards, Paul. 2001. "Are Forest Wars in Africa "Resource" Conflicts? The Case of Sierra Leone." In *Violent Environments*, edited by Nancy Lee Peluso and Michael Watts, 65–82. Ithaca, NY: Cornell University Press.

Riles, Annelise. 2006a. "Introduction: In Response." In *Documents: Artifacts of Modern Knowledge*, edited by Annelise Riles, 1–38. Ann Arbor: University of Michigan Press.

Riles, Annelise. 2006b. "[Deadlines]: Removing the Brackets on Politics in Bureaucratic and Anthropological Analysis." In *Documents: Artifacts of Modern Knowledge*, edited by Annelise Riles, 71–92. Ann Arbor: University of Michigan Press.

Roche, Sophie. 2016. *Domesticating Youth: Youth Bulges and Their Socio-Political Implications in Tajikistan* New York: Berghahn Books.

Rosen, David M. 2007. "Child Soldiers, International Humanitarian Law, and the Globalization of Childhood." *American Anthropologist* 109(2): 296–306.

"Shaki Opens Makeni Show: Emphasis on Production." 1980. *Daily Mail* [Sierra Leone newspaper], February 2.

Shankar, Shalini, and Jillian R. Cavanaugh. 2012. "Language and Materiality in Global Capitalism." *Annual Review of Anthropology* 41: 355–69.

Sharp, Lesley. 1995. "Playboy Princely Spirits of Madagascar: Possession as Youthful Commentary and Social Critique." *Anthropological Quarterly* 68(2): 75–88.

Shaw, Rosalind. 2000. "'*Tok Af, Lef Af*': A Political Economy of Temne Techniques of Secrecy and Self." In *African Philosophy as Cultural Inquiry*, edited by I. Karp and D. A. Masolo, 25–49. Bloomington: Indiana University Press.

Shaw, Rosalind. 2002. *Memories of the Slave Trade: Ritual and the Historical Imagination in Sierra Leone*. Chicago: University of Chicago Press.

Shaw, Rosalind. 2010. "Linking Justice With Reintegration? Ex-Combatants and the Sierra Leone Experiment." In *Localizing Transitional Justice: Interventions and Priorities After Mass Violence*, edited by R. Shaw and Lars Waldorf, 111–34. Stanford, CA: Stanford University Press.

Shepler, Susan. 2005. "The Rites of the Child: Global Discourses of Youth and Reintegrating Child Soldiers in Sierra Leone." *Journal of Human Rights* 4: 197–211.

Shepler, Susan. 2014. *Childhood Deployed: Remaking Child Soldiers in Sierra Leone*. New York: New York University Press.

Simone, Abdou Maliq. 2004. "People as Infrastructure: Intersecting Fragments in Johannesburg." *Public Culture* 16(3): 407–29.

Simone, Abdou Maliq. 2008. "Some Reflections on Making Popular Culture in Urban Africa." *African Studies Review* 51(3): 75–89.

Simone, Abdou Maliq. 2011. "The Ineligible Majority: Urbanizing the Postcolony in Africa and Southeast Asia." *Geoforum* 42: 266–170.

Sinfield, Alan. 1989. *Literature, Politics, and Culture in Postwar Britain*. Berkeley: University of California Press.

Singerman, Diane. 2013. "Youth, Gender, and Dignity in the Egyptian Uprising." *Journal of Middle East Women's Studies* 9(3): 1–27.

Sommers, Marc. 2012. *Stuck: Rwandan Youth and the Struggle for Adulthood*. Athens: University of Georgia Press.

Sommers, Marc. 2015. *The Outcast Majority: War, Development, and Youth in Africa*. Athens: University of Georgia Press.

Spitzer, Leo, and LeRay Denzer. 1973. "I. T. A. Wallace-Johnson and the West African Youth League. Part II: The Sierra Leone Period, 1938–1945." *International Journal of African Historical Studies* 6(4): 565–601.

Starecheski, Laura. 2015. "'Visibly Pregnant' Girls are Banned from School in Sierra Leone." National Public Radio, April 6. http://www.npr.org/sections/goatsandsoda/2015/04/06/397272538/visibly-pregnant-girls-are-banned-from-school-in-sierra-leone.

Strutner, Suzy. 2016. "Here's What Goodwill Actually Does with Your Donated Clothes." *Huffington Post*. http://www.huffingtonpost.com/entry/what-does-goodwill-do-with-your-clothes_us_57e06b96e4b0071a6e092352.

Sultana, Farhana. 2007. "Reflexivity, Positionality, and Participatory Ethics: Negotiating Fieldwork Dilemmas in International Research." *ACME: An International Journal for Critical Geographies* 6(3): 374–85.

Taylor, Louise. 2003. "'We'll Kill You If You Cry': Sexual Violence in the Sierra Leone Conflict." New York: Human Rights Watch.

Tom, Patrick. 2014. "Youth-Traditional Authorities' Relations in Post-War Sierra Leone." *Children's Geographies*: 1–12. DOI: 10.1080/14733285.2014.922679

Tulgan, Bruce. 2016. *Not Everyone Gets a Trophy: How to Manage the Millenials*. Hoboken, NJ: Wiley.

Turner, Terence S. 2012. "The Social Skin." *HAU: Journal of Ethnographic Theory* 2(2): 486–504.

Turner, Victor. 1987. *The Anthropology of Performance*. New York: PAJ Publications.

Twenge, Jean. 2014. *Generation Me: Why Today's Young Americans are More Confident, Assertive, and Entitled, and More Miserable Than Ever Before*. New York: Atria Books.

Urdal, Henrik. 2006. "A Clash of Generations? Youth Bulges and Political Violence." *International Studies Quarterly* 50: 607–29.

Utas, Mats. 2003. "Sweet Battlefields: Youth and the Liberian Civil War." PhD diss., Uppsala University.

Utas, Mats. 2005. "Agency of Victims: Young Women in the Liberian Civil War." In *Makers and Breakers: Children and Youth in Postcolonial Africa*, edited by A. Honwana and Filip de Boeck, 53–80. Oxford: James Currey.

Utas, Mats. 2012. "Introduction: Bigmanity and Network Governance in African Conflicts." In *African Conflicts and Informal Power: Big Men and Networks*, edited by M. Utas, 1–31. London: Zed Books.

Van 'T Wout, Merel. 2016. "'We Don't Need Them Anymore': Creating Belonging and Performing Work Among 'Game Boys' of Tamale, Ghana." Paper presented at the European Conference on African Studies, Basel, Switzerland, June 29.

Vigh, Henrik. 2006. *Navigating Terrains of War: Youth and Soldiering in Guinea-Bissau*. New York: Berghahn Books.

Weiss, Brad. 2009. *Street Dreams and Hip Hop Barbershops: Global Fantasy in Urban Tanzania*. Bloomington: Indiana University Press.

West, Kanye. 2005. *Diamonds from Sierra Leone*. Rock a Fella/Def Jam Records.

Whyte, Chrsitine H. 2008. "School's Out: Strategies of Resistance in Colonial Sierra Leone." In *The Resistance Studies Reader*, edited by C. Kullenberg and J. Lehne, 96–103 Gothenberg: Resistance Studies Network.

Willis, Paul. 1977. *Learning to Labor: How Working Class Kids Get Working Class Jobs*. New York: Columbia University Press.

Woronov, T. E. 2016. *Class Work: Vocational Schools and China's Urban Youth*. Stanford, CA: Stanford University Press

Zack-Williams, A. B., and S. Riley. 1993. "Sierra Leone: The Coup and Its Consequences." *Review of African Political Economy* 56(1): 91–98.

Zelizer, Viviana. 2017. *The Social Meaning of Money: Pin Money, Paychecks, Poor Relief, and Other Currencies*. Princeton, NJ: Princeton University Press.

Zwick, Edward. 2006. *Blood Diamond*. Warner Bros. for Bedford Falls Production.

INDEX

....